THE
RUSSIAN
REFUGEES

A Family's First Century in Canada

MICHAEL ANDRUFF

Copyright © 2022 Michael Andruff
Foreword copyright © 2022 Laurie Cooper

All rights reserved. No part of this publication may be reproduced, stored in a retrieval system, or transmitted in any form or by any means—electronic, mechanical, audio recording, or otherwise—without the written permission of the publisher or a licence from Access Copyright, Toronto, Canada.

Heritage House Publishing Company Ltd.
heritagehouse.ca

Cataloguing information available from Library and Archives Canada
978-1-77203-419-6 (paperback)
978-1-77203-420-2 (e-book)

Edited by Karla Decker
Proofread by Lesley Cameron
Cover design by Setareh Ashrafologhalai
Interior design by Nayeli Jimenez
Cover photograph: The Andreeff family, circa 1931: From left, Akim, Nikifor, Philip, Zinayeda, Valentina, Anesya (smallest), Elena, and Constantine. ANDRUFF FAMILY ALBUM
Maps by Eric Leinberger

The interior of this book was produced on FSC®-certified, acid-free paper, processed chlorine free, and printed with vegetable-based inks.

Heritage House gratefully acknowledges that the land on which we live and work is within the traditional territories of the Lkwungen (Esquimalt and Songhees), Malahat, Pacheedaht, Scia'new, T'Sou-ke, and W̱SÁNEĆ (Pauquachin, Tsartlip, Tsawout, Tseycum) Peoples.

We acknowledge the financial support of the Government of Canada through the Canada Book Fund (CBF) and the Canada Council for the Arts, and the Province of British Columbia through the British Columbia Arts Council and the Book Publishing Tax Credit.

  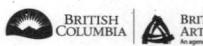 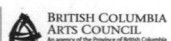

26 25 24 23 22   1 2 3 4 5
Printed in Canada

To Claire, the love of my life, my inspiration

and

*to the millions of refugees in the world,
may you find your path to freedom.*

TABLE OF CONTENTS

Maps   vi
The Andriev, Andreeff, Andruff Family Tree   x
Foreword   1
Preface   4

PART ONE

Chapter 1   The Beginning   11
Chapter 2   Homeglen, the First Years: 1924–29   24
Chapter 3   The Luck of the Russian Refugees: 1930–55   40
Chapter 4   The Port Alberni Years: 1956–67   74
Chapter 5   The ACKA Years: 1968–75   95
Chapter 6   The Later Years: Hospitality, Service, and Solitude   105

PART TWO

Chapter 7   New Canadians and the Baby Boom Era   123
Chapter 8   Leaving the Valley   143
Chapter 9   The University of British Columbia   149
Chapter 10   Joining the Working World   160
Chapter 11   The Golden Era of Family Life   166
Chapter 12   New Horizons in the 1990s   175
Chapter 13   This Beautiful Life   181
Chapter 14   Reviewing the Boomer Era   185

Chapter 15   Here Comes Generation X   *190*
Chapter 16   Mind the Gap   *197*
Chapter 17   In Pursuit of Critical Thinking   *201*
Chapter 18   Circling Back to the Refugees   *210*
Chapter 19   Conclusion: A Call to Pay It Forward   *212*

PART THREE
Chapter 20   Today's Refugees   *217*
Chapter 21   The Catalytic Converters of Private Sponsorship   *224*

Appendix A   How to Privately Sponsor a Refugee   *229*
Appendix B   The Canadian Naming Game of the 1920s   *232*

Acknowledgements   235
Notes   236
Bibliography   251
Index   254

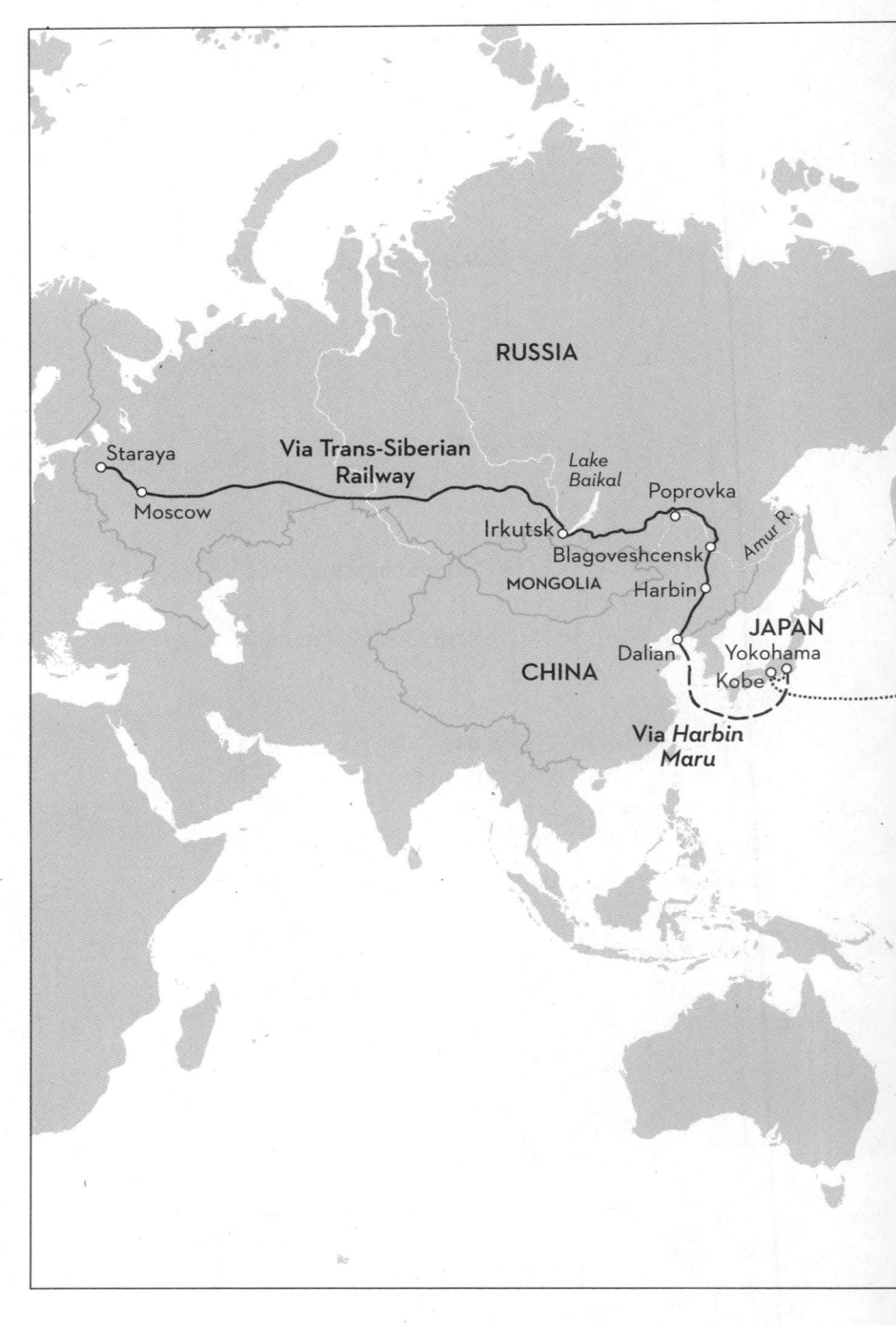

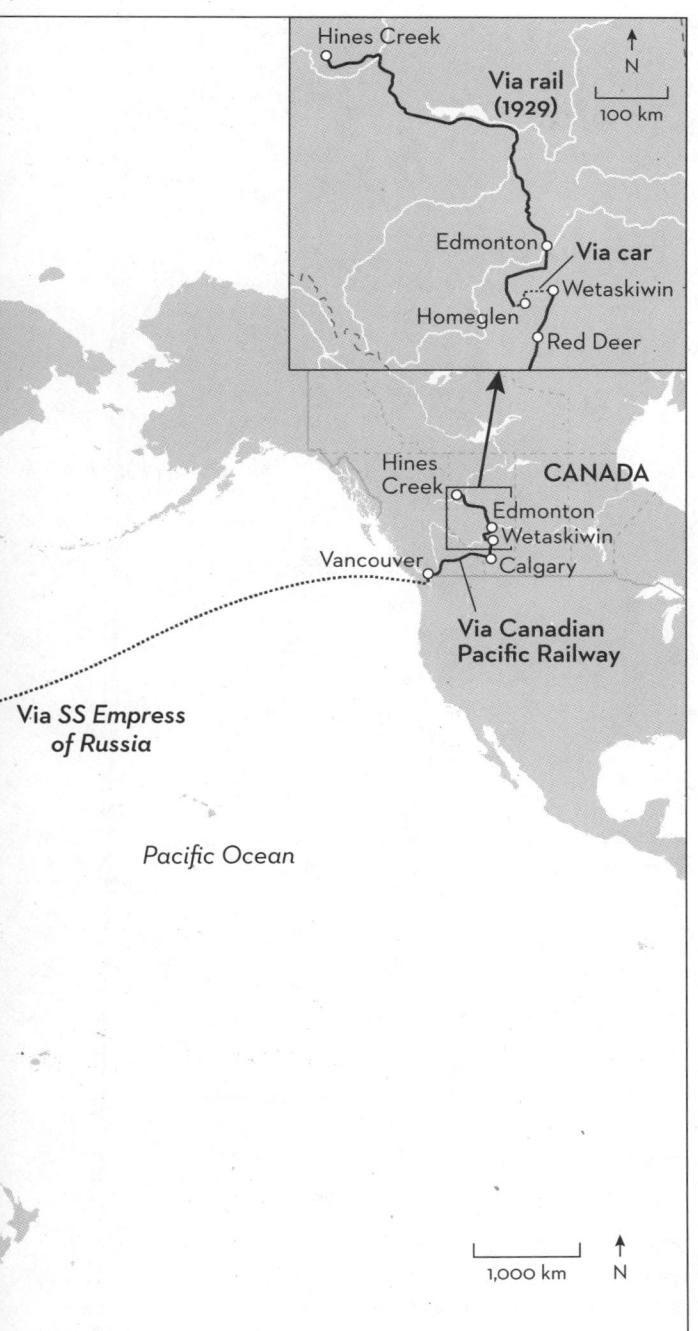

The journey taken by the Russian refugees, across the world from Russia to Canada.

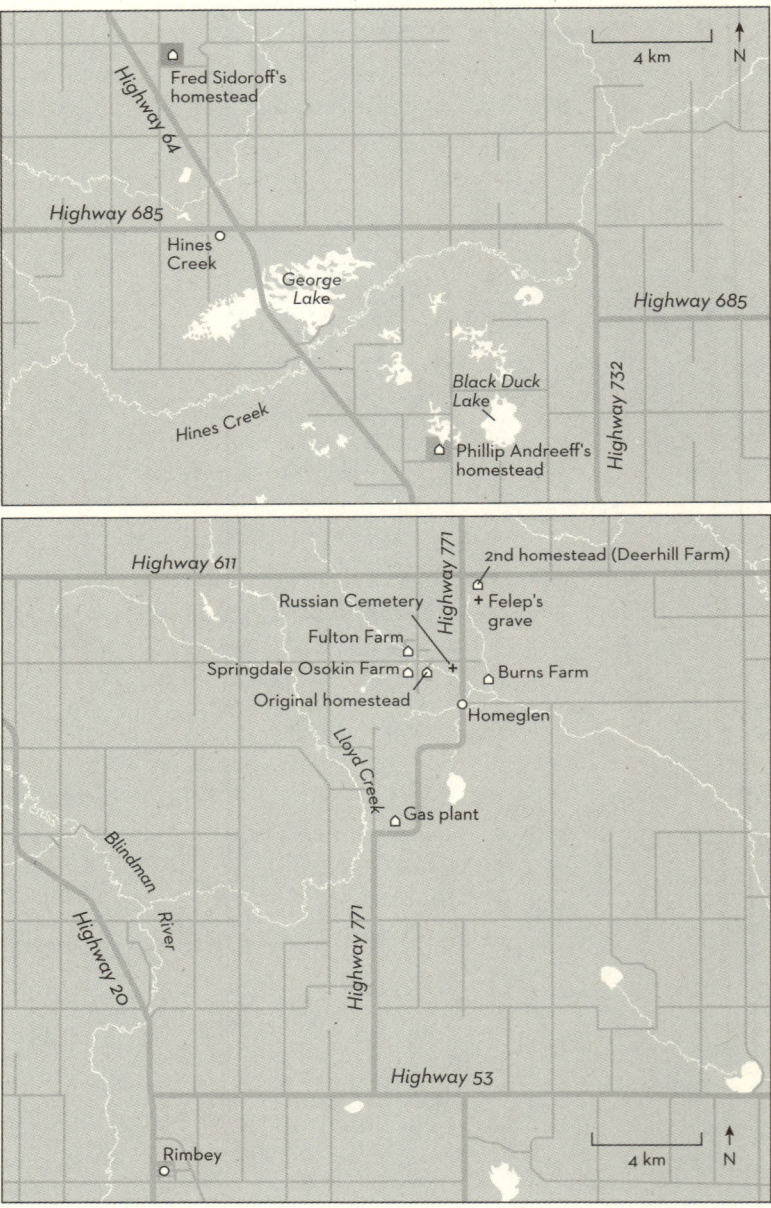

TOP: The proximity of the Sidoroff homestead to the Andreeffs' made it easier for Phillip Andreeff to set his son Mike up with his future wife, Natalie.
BOTTOM: The original CPR colony of Homeglen. Eleven families of the Old Believers would eventually move north from here to Hines Creek in 1929.

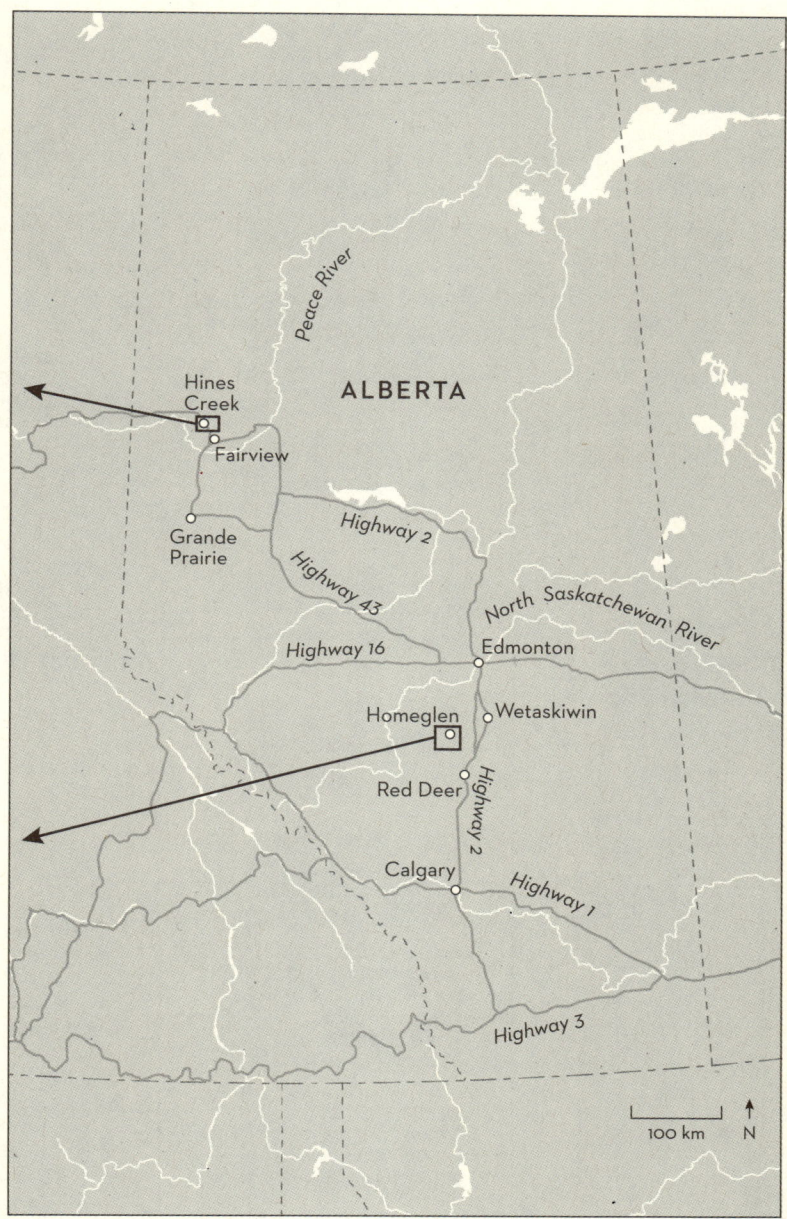

The Russian refugees first settled in the community of Homeglen and later moved further north to Hines Creek.

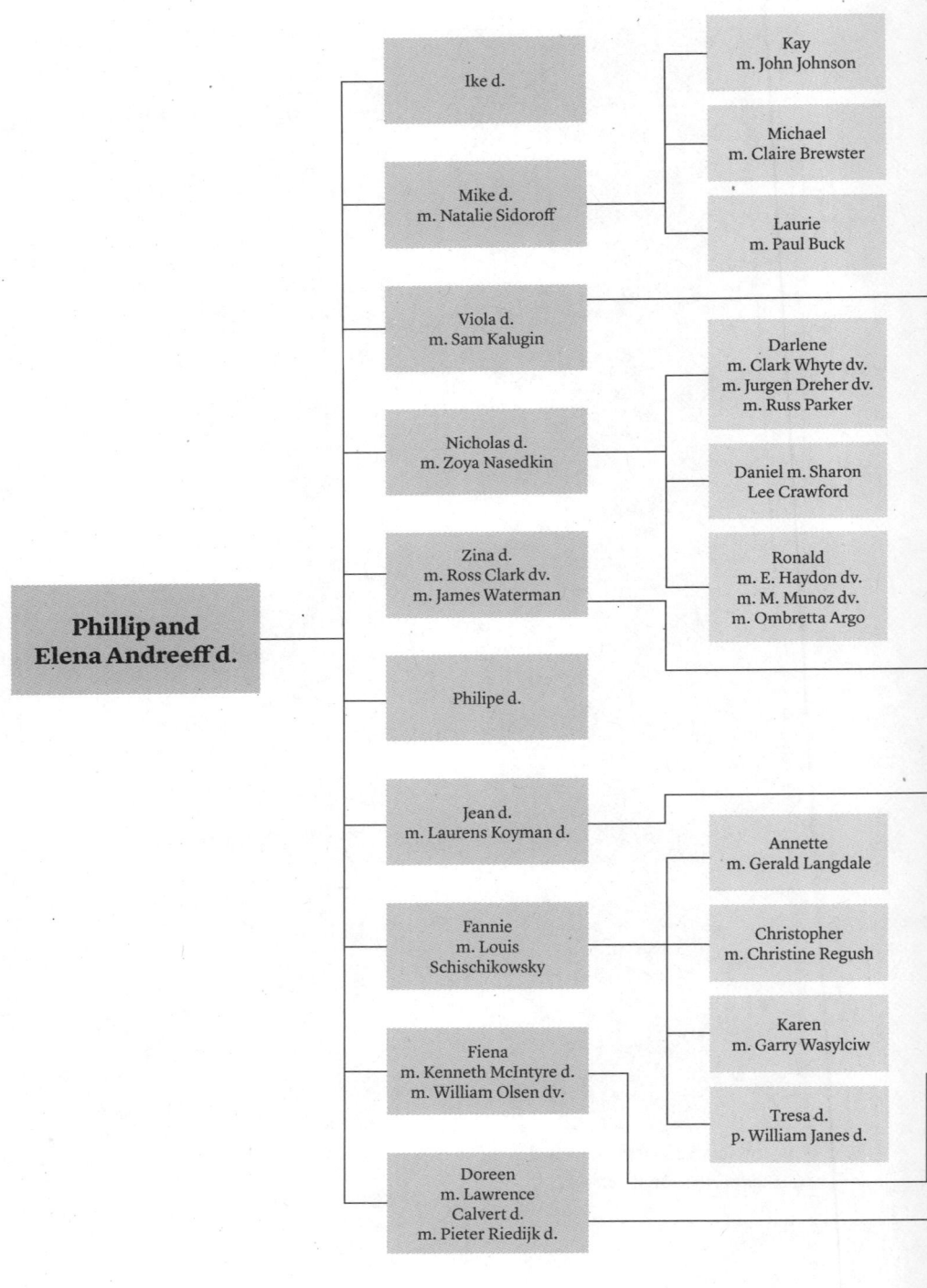

THE ANDRIEV, ANDREEFF, ANDRUFF FAMILY TREE

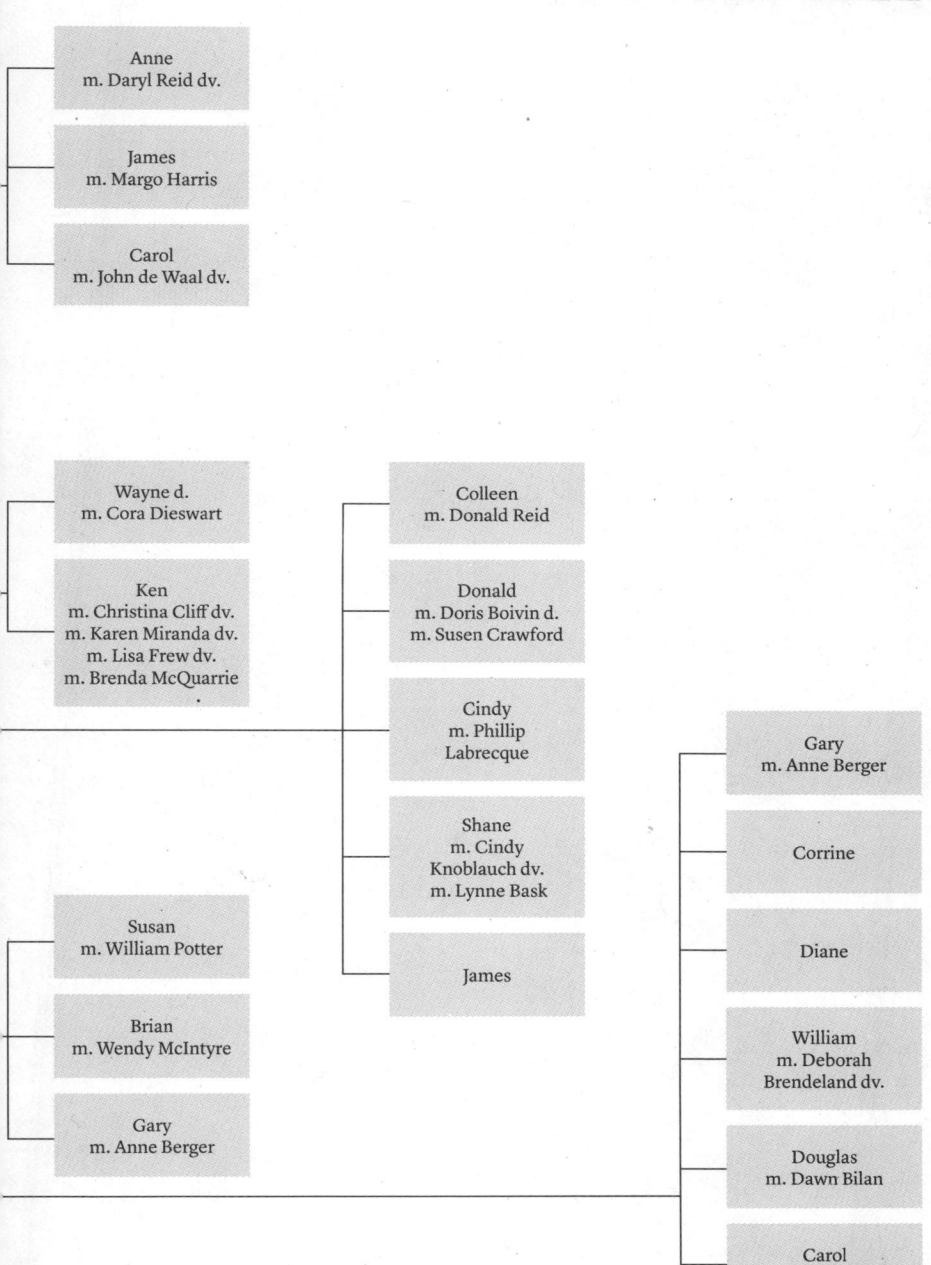

FOREWORD

Humans have always been on the move—looking for new resources, more territory, running away from warring neighbours—so, in a sense, there have always been refugees. The United Nations High Commission for Refugees defines refugees as "people who have fled war, violence, conflict, or persecution and have crossed an international border to find safety in another country."

There are currently more people who have been forcibly displaced than ever before in human history. As of June 2022, the UNHCR recognizes 89.3 million people as having to leave their homes to escape persecution, conflict, human rights violations, and events seriously disturbing public order. Over a third are children under the age of eighteen.

Many of these people have been displaced from their homes but stayed within their country; over 27 million have been officially recognized by UNHCR as refugees, having left their country of origin. Ninety per cent of these refugees have not only been forced to flee from conflict and violence but also come from countries on the front lines of the climate emergency. Environmental refugees are quickly becoming an urgent issue.

Canada is renowned for its record of welcoming refugees, and it is currently the only country in the world that has a private sponsorship program allowing individual citizens to come together in small groups to identify refugees they would like to assist and bring them to safety in Canada. As of 2016, the Global Refugee Sponsorship Initiative is developing similar programs in other countries, including Argentina, Ireland, New Zealand, United Kingdom, Spain, and Germany.

Canada's Private Sponsorship of Refugees Program officially began in 1978 after Canadian citizens lobbied the federal government to allow them to help refugees fleeing the Vietnam War. Between 1979 and 1980, more than 60,000 Vietnamese people found refuge in Canada and over half of those were supported by private sponsorship groups. Since 1979, a total of 327,000 refugees have been welcomed and supported by private sponsors.

My experience with private sponsorship began seven years ago. In the fall of 2015, I saw the photograph of the young Syrian boy, Alan Kurdi, who had died as his family tried to make their way to safety in Europe. Like millions of other people, my heart broke and I felt the need to do something. Within two months of seeing that photo, I found myself on the beaches of Lesbos, Greece, greeting families like Alan's who had made the perilous crossing from Turkey to seek refuge in the European Union.

That first trip was followed by three more to work with refugees overseas. During those trips, I met people of all ages and backgrounds who had made the difficult decision to leave their country. The uncertainty and danger of their flight was less terrifying than living in the midst of cruel and devastating war. Most of the people were travelling in family groups, including the elderly, newborn babies, and people with disabilities. Their one desire was a safe place to live.

On returning to Canada after my second trip, I started to explore the possibility of undertaking private sponsorships. It seemed like an intimidating process at first and I have a strong aversion to paperwork and bureaucracy, but I worked my way through the many forms and, in 2018, the first of our sponsored refugees started to arrive.

Since 2016, I have personally been involved in the sponsorship of eighteen people, and I have supported the sponsorship of over 250 more individuals and families through a number of initiatives including a partnership with Fairmont Hotels and Resorts and the creation

FOREWORD

of Operation #NotForgotten, a project to bring hundreds of refugees who had been detained for years by the Australian government.

I was fifty-five years old when I went to Greece the first time. I took a huge leap out of my comfort zone and it changed my life. It opened my eyes and allowed me to see the world completely differently. Instead of seeing the differences between people, I started to see the similarities. I recognized the love of family, the desire for peace, and the deep humanity in all the refugees I have had the privilege to work with and assist.

We are privileged in Canada to have the opportunity as private citizens to offer refuge to people who deserve the opportunity to live in safety and build a life for themselves and their families. If you can find it in your heart to get involved in refugee sponsorship, I can guarantee it will change you. It will open your heart, expand your world, and you may be saving someone's life.

LAURIE COOPER
Founder, Canada Caring Society
July 2022

PREFACE

WERE IT NOT for one individual approving further financial support for 116 Russian refugees, my life and those of others might not have occurred. In 1924, the immigration department of the Government of Canada required all immigrants and refugees to have their own landing money. These refugees were well short of the $25,000 required upon arrival. An American organization of expatriate philanthropists provided the necessary top-up funds to appease the immigration department, thus allowing the refugees to land in Vancouver, BC.

All refugees have a story. This one looks at how one of the 116 refugees lived in his new land and then how his descendants improved their lives based on his sacrifices and those of his parents. It covers almost a century of Canadian living and was planned as a family centennial project. However, while writing this story, it became evident that private sponsorship of refugees had been critical for our family's future. Were it not for the advancement of funds demanded by the Canadian government, the fate of the refugees would have hung in the balance. (A mere ten years earlier, the passengers on the *Komagata Maru* arrived in Vancouver and were rejected for entry by immigration officials. Without the private sponsor, a similar fate was within the realm of possibilities for the 116 Russian refugees.) The benevolence of this humanitarian organization also helped define the importance of private sponsorship for refugees. The story continues

PREFACE

by examining a contemporary refugee's experience. It illustrates the difference between landing money and private sponsorship. The comparison of these two refugee stories reinforces the theme that private sponsorship is critical to helping refugees enter Canada and that refugees make important contributions to our society.

Part One of this story is about a Russian refugee named Nikifor. His story resembles the stories of millions of other refugees who have shared a vision and a hope for what Canada could offer them and their families. His life experience was bittersweet. He was raised on a farm in his family's traditional Russian Orthodox faith. Those of his father's generation were called Old Believers (some have used the term Old Brothers). Initially full of promise, his earning ability was devastated by fate. He and his family moved to the Vancouver Island community of Alberni. Their lives were sadly filled with financial hardship and dysfunctionality. They eventually moved to BC's Lower Mainland, where they reinvented their employability several times. After full working lives, they settled peacefully in their retirement years. Canadian social benefits and their family provided for all their needs. They lived just long enough to see their first great-grandchild arrive.

Most of this story is based on facts. From time to time, characters are portrayed in fictional accounts to create relatable accounts of the times.

Part Two first describes the baby boomer and Gen X generations. The three children of the Russian refugee proudly grew up as first-generation Canadians. The story continues through my eyes; I am Nikifor's son. My parents struggled to survive financially. My mother wrestled with her demons, which led to family upheaval. I was nurtured by proxy through my community's church, schools, youth programs, and sports. Hockey was my passion. The sport became my passport to a better life. I wouldn't admit it, but I also fell under the spell of my junior-high-school sweetheart. When my family moved to New Westminster, BC, I pursued my hockey career. Fortuitously, my sweetheart had also moved to Vancouver. Her positive influence led me to join her at university, where I studied and continued to play hockey. We married. While we were at university, we also managed to travel widely. After graduating, we started a family, and I joined the corporate world. Halfway through my working life, I opted for self-employment. Our lives were happy and positive. Lessons I learned from my father led me into the real estate business, and I made a good living from it by applying myself with drive and initiative.

It was in this later stage of my life that I realized that I and some of my fellow baby boomer generation had prospered at the expense of our grandchildren. Both government debt and environmental devastation are poor legacies for the next generation. I believe that the Indigenous Peoples are right: the betterment of humankind lies not in the conquest and transformation of nature, but in learning to live with it in harmony.

Part Two next examines the life of the paternal second-generation Canadian through our eldest child, Thea. She belongs to the cohort described as Generation X. This part portrays the line of succession from a female perspective. Her story includes experiences in sports, travel, education, working life, motherhood, and the challenges of dealing with an uncertain future. Like most parents before her, she was prepared to sacrifice her immediate needs and desires for a happy and productive life for her three daughters.

This story reflects how the lives of Russian refugees changed from being destitute and stateless to being humble and productive citizens of Canada. Within several generations, their families' well-being advanced as Canada, a humane and caring nation, also advanced in its social policies. This story gives hope to new refugees to Canada that their futures will also improve. But there is a message. This cannot happen without a deep and abiding respect for an invisible but crucial ideal called freedom. It cannot be taken for granted by future generations.

Part Three of the story transitions from a refugee story of almost one hundred years ago to the current experience of refugees. How have things changed? What has stayed the same?

At the conclusion of the story, the focus turns to the current worldwide plight of refugees. Canada continues to open its doors

PREFACE

to refugees, who are but a subset of all immigrant intake annually. The need to do more is always dependent on financial resources. An appendix lays out the steps to privately sponsor refugees.

Families of refugees who have settled in this country and have had good lives as Canadians are encouraged to consider paying these good lives forward through private sponsorship of refugees. With the large number of descendants who followed the original settlers, opportunities to help change the lives of others are many and ever-present.

Also noteworthy is the assistance and support of Mosaic BC. They are a leading British Columbia immigrant support organization and a federal government approved Sponsorship Agreement Holder. They have offered a landing page on their website to collect sponsorship donations for the descendants and friends of the Homeglen Legacy Fund. The fund is aimed at paying forward donations in recognition of the support our forefathers received from people they did not even know.

MICHAEL ANDRUFF
Spring 2022

PART ONE

CHAPTER 1

THE BEGINNING

THREE-YEAR-OLD NIKIFOR ANDRIEV stood on Canadian soil. He was overwhelmed by all the activity around him. The big steam engine of the train was still huffing and puffing. He could smell the dust that the recent rainfall had raised. People were shouting in English. At least he was beside his brother and, nearby, the rest of his family. His mother, Elena, was holding his one-year-old sister, Valentina. She was crying, perhaps because her diaper needed changing or because she was hungry. His father, Phillip, was holding the shoulder of Akim, Nikifor's older brother. His grandpa, Gregori, was standing with Nikifor's aunt and uncles, Lucaria, Vasili, and Ivan, and their families. The Andriev and Sidorov families and the other Russians were posing for a picture in front of the Canadian Pacific Railway (CPR) passenger car that had transported them from Vancouver.

Nikifor, like the other children present, had few thoughts in mind aside from the thought that his winter coat was making him uncomfortable in the muggy, rainy June afternoon.[1] He was hungry, and he was also upset at being jostled for the picture. The rest of the group, also in winter apparel, stood rather grim-faced. Perhaps it was their weariness from travel, or maybe they had thoughts of the past or, more likely, their future. In any case, smiles were few, and frowns born of anxiety were plentiful.

THE RUSSIAN REFUGEES

THEIR JOURNEY HAD begun several weeks earlier in Harbin, China. A CPR agent and former officer in the Imperial Russian Army, Colonel Orest Dournovo, had organized this first group of 116 Russian refugees to go to Canada. First, they had travelled by rail from Harbin to the coastal city of Dalian, China. There, they boarded the ship *Harbin Maru*, which was bound for Yokohama, Japan.[2] Yokohama had just experienced a devastating earthquake. They had little time to survey the damage, because the Canadian Pacific Royal Mail steamship *Empress of Russia* was ready for boarding. It still had to put into Kobe for one last stop before crossing the Pacific Ocean. They crossed the Pacific in steerage class, which confined men to one side of the ship and women on the other, separated by a canvas wall.

Upon arrival in Vancouver on June 16, 1924, they were subject to review by Canadian Immigration and medical officials over the next two days. Another CPR agent, Mr. Sewell, acted as their intermediary, given their limited knowledge of the English language. He expedited their immigration reviews, arranged for medicals, and organized their transfer from the ship to the train.[3] When the train drew into Wetaskiwin, Alberta, the Ladies Auxiliary of the Kiwanis Club offered the group a welcome luncheon, a photo to mark the significance of their landing in Canada, and transportation to their new homesteads in Homeglen.[4]

Gregori's mind was likely racing, with thoughts of the past haunting him. He thought to himself, "Everything and everyone is so different here. Can I trust these officials? Have Luka and I made the right choice for our families? We have committed our family to Canada. My dear God, we place our futures in your loving hands." He was sixty-eight years old. His life had begun in Staraya, Russa, approximately six hundred kilometres northwest of Moscow. His father, Andrei, was probably an indentured serf during his lifetime. While Gregori's upbringing was harsh, his life improved as the years went by. Serfdom ended in 1861. He married a woman named Irena, and they had five children before her untimely passing in 1903.

In 1905, Luka Sidorov, Gregori's lifelong friend, had returned home to Novgorod (north of Staraya) from the Russo-Japanese war.

Luka spoke of the fine soil he saw when in the Amur Valley in Siberia on his way back from the war. The Andriev and Sidorov families weighed the pros and cons of moving to the east. It was decided that Gregori, Luka, and Luka's brother Afanasi would be part of an advance party to travel across the country to survey the potential for moving the families to the east.[5] They returned triumphantly, extolling the virtues of a move to eastern Russia. Gregori recalled telling his family, "Luka, Afanasi, and I want a better life for our families. Let us leave our old lives in Novgorod and start a new life in the east."

In a coincidental turn of serendipitous events, Tsar Nicholas II was anxious to turn the tide of negative public opinion after losing the war to the Japanese. Pyotr Stolypin, prime minster of the Russian Empire under the tsar from 1906 to 1911, implemented a policy to open the country's vast resources and ease densities in the urban centres. Each family who agreed to move to farmland in the Amur Valley would receive on average sixteen and one-half hectares of land, a small subsidy, exemption from some taxes, and farming advice from state agencies.[6] Gregori took this opportunity to move his family east on the Trans-Siberian Railway. Word-of-mouth accounts indicated that Gregori and his sons, Phillip, Vasili, Ivan, and Larivon, were each allocated land in the Amur Valley. "Along with the land, they were exempt from paying taxes for five years, were given one cow, one horse and one hundred rubles for start-up costs."[7]

From serf to landowner! Life had improved for some who chose to move with the times. In his early fifties, Gregori had his family around him, his farm established, and a new life. Unexpectedly, after approximately seven good years of farming, the First World War began.

Gregori's eldest son, Phillip, and his son-in-law, Prokofi Sidorov, were conscripted into the Imperial Russian Army. They fought on the German Eastern Front in 1914. Three years later, the Bolsheviks came along and aggressively vied for their farmland. The forthcoming changes to the country meant, among other things, no more monarchy. Instead, Russia became a state-controlled governance suppressing land ownership and religion.

Gregori had all he wanted in life, but now he had a sense that he was at risk of losing more than just land. He had to get his family out of Russia. "We've had such a good life in this fertile valley. My son even fought for this country and now this! Survive we must, but not with the Bolsheviks," thought Gregori. The Republic of China was the best solution that he could see under their circumstances.

He had luck on his side this time, because he was able to escape the Russian Revolution (1917 to 1923) and enter China just before it closed its borders to Russians. Good luck or good graft, it is unclear how the planets aligned for their risky but safe passage to their new country.

Now residents of Harbin, China, the family toiled at a variety of jobs and enterprises as they planned their next strategy for freedom. Several years later, upon meeting Colonel Dournovo, it was evident to Gregori that his family had a second chance at freedom and land ownership in Canada. It was a new country keen on developing its vast prairie lands. To Gregori's disappointment, his son Larivon and his family chose to emigrate to Australia.

Standing for the picture in front of their railcar with his large family, Gregori wrestled with the question of whether his good fortune could return, as it had in the past. "Will my family live in peace? Can we follow our faith? Will some force reveal itself to snatch our future away from us again? The people here seem helpful and friendly, but they are different than us. Can they be trusted?"

His son Phillip, now thirty-six years old, was happy to have another chance at farming. He knew his work ethic and ability to cope with challenges would carry him forward. Phillip remembered the good life back in Russia, before civil war forced them to flee their land. Together with his brothers and father, they had worked and prospered together. They were good at farming. Phillip admired his father for his vision to seek new opportunities and for his desire to improve his family's life. Now, with his loving wife, Elena, he sought to do the same for his young family. Phillip thought, "With my good and faithful friend Prokofi and our families, we will make a fresh start here. We will farm like no others. We are Russian farmers!"

THE BEGINNING

No one knew about post-traumatic stress disorder (PTSD) in the 1920s. Phillip and his lifelong friend Prokofi were affected by the trauma of war. They had no outward signs of distress, but below the surface were anguished remembrances of terror.

Twelve million Russian soldiers had been dispatched to the Eastern Front in the First World War. Russia sustained 9,150,000 casualties of war (in contrast, Canada sent 424,000 military personnel overseas and had 235,000 casualties).[8] Two of those casualties were Phillip and Prokofi. It is said that Phillip was "wounded in action while trying to carry his commanding officer to safety." For his valour in combat, Phillip was awarded the Cross of Saint George.[9] Prokofi was taken as a prisoner of war and kept imprisoned for three years. Phillip, now a decorated war veteran, stood on that railroad siding hoping Canada would allow him to return to the good life they had known previously, while leaving the past behind him.

Quiet Lucaria, Phillip's only sister, was also lost in her thoughts. She bound the Andriev and Sidorov families together with her marriage to Prokofi. She knew her dear Prokofi had suffered terrible conditions during the war years. In his absence, she had struggled with her own loneliness, depression, and loss. Lucaria had lost four children in Russia, either in childbirth or by drowning.[10] She carried her own burdens well as she cared for others. She was known for her caring nature and her ever-present smile. Her hope was to settle in Canada so her family would grow, be safe, and prosper. "My dear husband will provide for us. He is a strong man with courage, and he takes the Lord as his Saviour. Our family is together again and I will do everything I can to keep it that way," pledged Lucaria to herself that day.

For this group of refugees, there was no looking back. The life they had known had been irreversibly altered. They had been pushed out of their own country and lived in a foreign one, China. Their religious beliefs and opinions would cause certain persecution or death at the hands of the Bolsheviks if they returned to Russia. In any event, it was time for Nikifor, who would later become my father, and his broad extended family to move forward in their new home, Canada.

Canadian immigration

In the 1920s, Canadian immigration officials were selective and often prejudicial in gatekeeping the flow of migrants entering Canada. In fairness, they followed the dictates of prescribed and ever-changing policies. Refugees alone were but a small portion of the entire immigration process.

Canadian immigration policy typically changed with the government of the day. Initially, it was favourably inclined toward British and American immigrants, due to their ease of assimilation. These groups were preferred, while most other nationalities were not.

The following are several examples of restrictive Canadian immigration policies. In 1923, just prior to Nikifor's arrival, Prime Minister William Lyon Mackenzie King and his Liberal government had passed the *Chinese Immigration Act*. This act essentially banned ethnic Chinese people from Canada.

In 1914, Prime Minister Robert Borden's Conservative government committed a disgraceful act when they ordered the *Komagata Maru*, a ship carrying 376 hopeful immigrants back to India (more on this later). It was denied landing under a 1908 order-in-council, a simple law to deal with an emergency circumstance by decree. This order specified a continuous-journey regulation, which was relied upon to deny the Indians entry into Canada.

Another illustration of prejudicial intervention was in 1911 by the government of Sir Wilfrid Laurier, again by way of an order-in-council. It blocked Black Americans escaping segregation in the American South from entering Canada. This order died with a change in government.

These incidents show that a great deal of luck and good timing was required to steer through the myriad whims of the Canadian immigration system over the years.

Back in Harbin, as Gregori was making his case for emigration to the CPR agent, he was relying more on skill than luck. He was, no doubt, touting the farming skills honed by his family while in the fertile Amur Valley. He was also a man of means. He had more than four hundred dollars as a required condition of immigration. He would have mentioned he was Orthodox when asked about his religious affiliation. To the agent, busy filling his quota for the first shipment of immigrants, this Orthodoxy matter was not as important as Gregori's status as an exemplary farmer. Canadian immigration officials at a later time would deny the applications of Orthodox immigrants; their Chinese passports were deemed inadmissible because they did not meet the requirements of Canadian regulations.

Gregori's Orthodox religion, although not initially viewed as an impediment to Canadian immigration, in subsequent times proved to be a disqualifying factor. Russian "Old Believers," like Gregori and his family, had historical ties to the traditional Greek Orthodox Church in Constantinople. They lived a life of communal sectarianism. Marriage was within Russian-speaking members of the same religious group. Women were expected to be subordinate to men in all matters of importance. Consumption of tobacco and commercially produced alcohol was banned. Assimilation outside the Orthodox group was discouraged. Exposure to education was limited to learning the rudimentary lessons of reading and writing. Their religious connection also became the basis of an insular commercial network.[11] Notable in their appearance was a long beard for men and a babushka (a head scarf tied either under the chin or behind the neck) worn by women. Because of these characteristics, and the Gouzenko Affair, which took place in Ottawa in 1945 (more on this later), Canadian immigration officials tended to view groups of Russian immigrants as "non-preferred," even though they would turn out to be successful prairie farmers.

The White Russians (defined as ethnic Russians from the area between Russia and Poland) who inhabited Harbin viewed it as Russia's eastern outpost in pre-revolutionary days, and they enjoyed their culture freely, having eluded the Bolsheviks' harassments. This area, known as Manchuria in China, was growing in numbers with expatriate Russians. By July 1923, the Russian Red Cross had received over ten thousand applications for admission to the new country of Canada.[12] In addition, there were 170,000 Russian refugees based in Constantinople. The Canadian immigration department was at somewhat of a loss to determine the right course of action to take.

In early 1923, domiciled in the Russian enclave of Harbin, the families of Gregori Andriev and Luka Sidorov had no idea it would take over a year for four major players to reach a meeting of the minds before they would arrive in Canada. These decision makers would be the Russian Red Cross, the Russian Refugee Relief Society of America Inc. (RRRSA), the Government of Canada, and the Canadian Pacific Railway (CPR).

The Russian Red Cross, led by Prince Alexander V. Golitzin, was a humanitarian organization and aimed at solving the growing refugee problem in China. Anytime there is strife in a war-torn country, refugees will flee. Aside from the 170,000 refugees already in Constantinople, by January 1924, Russia's strife had led to 16,000 more amassed in Harbin. The Russian Red Cross had taken applications from refugees in Harbin who wished to emigrate.[13] These applications identified two major groups of refugees. The first group were those with the skills and means to help them transition to a new life. The second were classed as the "helper" variety who relied on others to support them.[14] Golitzin knew his organization needed the help of others to move this needy population. To this end, he relied on the media, both locally and internationally, and the RRRSA.

R.P. McGrath was the face of the RRRSA. He represented philanthropists sympathetic to the plight of the Russian refugee. It was their intention to support the refugees financially when the help was needed. In countries like Canada, this help would be necessary.

W.J. Egan was deputy minister of immigration for the Government of Canada. His policy guidelines expected immigrants to arrive in Canada prepared to work and build the country. Most importantly, they should come with the means to support themselves until they became independent. Canada at that time had no social services. Egan had surveyed the plight of the refugees of Constantinople and Harbin and had decided in favour of the Harbin refugees, based on reports received from his friends at the Canadian Pacific Railway.[15] He additionally cared more for the group of emigrants filtered by the

Red Cross as skilled with means. His initial threshold was that each immigrant should come to Canada with $400 (over $6,000 in 2021 dollars, adjusted for inflation). Of the thousands of refugees, Canada set its initial intake at four hundred families. Overtures were being made to the RRRSA for indemnification of the refugees.[16] They were asked to provide a long-term surety bond of $100,000 and take responsibility for any refugees who arrived with mental or physical deficits. This was a big ask, and the RRRSA considered it too open-ended to offer their agreement.

The government's partner in this undertaking was the CPR. They had been tasked with opening the prairies with economic immigrants who could develop the prairie farmland. Now they were asked to facilitate refugee immigrants for both humanitarian and economic reasons.

Chief Commissioner of the CPR Department of Colonization and Development Col. J.S. Dennis had vast resources at his disposal. He employed a Russian agent in Vancouver, Col. Vladimir Dmohovsky (who was also an agent for the RRRSA), and Col. Orest Dournovo in Harbin. Dennis knew he had to do this right. He wanted refugees with integrity. If they said they would farm, he needed them to be true to their word. If refugees came over and then rushed to the cities, Dennis viewed the exercise as wasted. Dennis suggested to Egan that they start the process by bringing small groups over, rather than one large group.[17] He wanted to organize them into colonies. They could settle on CPR land for four years, with free use of the land, and if they did well, they could move on to buy their own land. Then a new group of immigrants could be delivered to repeat the process at the pre-established settlement. The CPR would provide their passage from Dalian, China, to Vancouver for one hundred dollars per family.[18]

Egan wanted assurances they were getting bona fide immigrants. He asked McGrath to indicate how he could attain a level of confidence in the type of people coming. McGrath called for a list of the first group of thirty families that included their names, ages, occupations, and the amount of capital they possessed.[19] This was a very rudimentary immigrant application process. It really came down to trusting the immigrant selection methods of one man: Dournovo.

The prominence of the Andriev and Sidorov families in the refugee community was evident, because they were included in the first thirty families listed. Through media reports and word of mouth, they had managed to connect with the key organizer for the CPR, Col. Dournovo. They had won his trust through their stories and their enthusiasm. They were successful farmers, war veterans, and the type of peaceful people any country would be glad to have as citizens. The list was advanced to the key decision makers for their review.

This process for moving only a select group of refugees was handled by slow-moving correspondence over many months. It required a considerable amount of patience for all concerned.

Finally, on May 6, 1924, the British consul general in Harbin was advised by the Government of Canada to issue visas to the thirty families for entry into Canada.[20] With this approval, Dournovo planned to move his group of refugees by rail from Harbin to Dalian to access a trans-Pacific departure that would leave Kobe, Japan, on May 15, 1924, on the *Empress of Asia*. It had been decided earlier that each group would pay for their own passage and collectively would be in possession of $25,000 (over $375,000 in 2021 dollars, adjusted for inflation). Since his earlier communications, Dournovo's final list had shrunk to only twenty-one families ready to move, and they only had $15,200 among them. He had some problems and needed solutions.

Of the original thirty families selected, nine were unable to travel. They did not possess their required passage money, nor did they have the required capital. Their late escape from the Bolsheviks in Russia meant, unlike the Andriev and Sidorov families, they did not have enough time to raise the money they needed. They would have to step out of the queue and stay in Harbin to earn their passage. Should they be replaced with others at this late date? The decision was made to proceed with the reduced group.

Just prior to the intended departure time, yet a bigger surprise was revealed to the group. Dournovo confessed he did not have enough passage money for his family's transit.[21] He knew that Col. Dmohovsky had connections with the RRRSA. Could they be tapped for relief? Would his smaller group, with its smaller capital base, still be accepted?

For Dournovo's part, it is unclear how he promptly collected passage money, because the Dournovos did join the other families. It is likely those travelling together took up a collection for them. For example, on the original list of emigrants, Gregori reported the capital he possessed as $700, but on his Declaration of Passenger to Canada, he reported having $500 upon arrival, suggesting perhaps he contributed $200 to help Dournovo.

Again, perhaps through delayed communications or visa procurements, the departure date was pushed back. It was now scheduled to be June 5, 1924, on the *Empress of Russia* from Kobe.[22] They boarded that ship in Yokohama on June 4, 1924.

Having to house and feed thirty-two mouths with so much waiting time and uncertainty every day must have been very difficult for the Andriev and Sidorov families. Big players were making decisions, but the emigrants were dealing with raw emotions, not to mention dwindling cash reserves. And some were pregnant, which meant even more stress caused by elevated hormone levels.

At long last, the twenty-one families were on the ship, bounding over the Pacific. Meanwhile in Canada, Egan was coming to terms with his position on the $15,200. He confided to division commissioner of the Department of Immigration and Colonization, Percy Reid, in Vancouver, that he could live with that amount rather than the earlier amount required of $25,000.[23]

As the *Empress of Russia* was passing Victoria, the Canadian government learned the organizer, Dournovo, had collected only $7,200 from the refugees.[24] A flurry of correspondence and telegrams ensued between the CPR and the government about the refugees' admissibility. Upon the ship's arrival in Vancouver on June 16, 1924, Dournovo was among the busiest people organizing his charges. He arranged medical examinations for all and then completed the paperwork for immigration processing. It fell to the Vancouver-based CPR agent, Col. Dmohovsky, to cable the Russian Refugee Relief Society in New York to say that his group of refugees was in financial need. He explained that the Canadian government had expected them to have $25,000 altogether. Initially, he would have only needed to request $10,000 from them, because they had started out with $15,000. However, between Harbin and Vancouver, they had unexpected expenses, leaving them with just $7,200. Ultimately, $17,500 was guaranteed by the RRRSA president, Serge Ughet, to the Commerce Bank in Vancouver.[25] As this drama was unfolding on dry land, Ughet was on a ship in the Atlantic Ocean; he likely cabled his approval. In addition to the guarantee he provided, Ughet further produced a deposit of $5,000 at the Canadian Imperial Bank of Commerce in Calgary, Alberta. Most of the funds in the accounts were controlled by Dournovo, who was still on the ship with the refugees. But when the group arrived in Dalian, the capital they collectively gave to the CPR's representative came from an account given by Maria von Rosenbach, Dournovo's daughter. In her book, *Family Kaleidoscope: From Russia to Canada*, she explained that this was how the CPR was aware of the group's cash shortfall.

With their trust in the RRRSA, and having passed all the required medicals and processed all documents, the Russian refugees were finally approved for entry into Canada after Deputy Minister Egan cabled Division Commissioner Percy Reid in Vancouver on June 18, 1924.[26]

These were panic-stricken times for all parties. Egan was responsible for protecting his country from immigrants not able to provide for themselves and for populating the prairies with productive farmers. Dennis had already bought animals and tents to accommodate the group, and arranged their welcome in Wetaskiwin, Alberta. Dournovo's lot would have been hopeless without the expected support of the RRRSA. The refugees did not want to be returned to China.

What if fate had intervened before the advice was sent to the British consul general in Harbin back on May 6, 1924, permitting their entry visas? Say a terrorist bombing had occurred just prior, and both Canada and Australia closed their doors to all Russian refugees. Imagine what the Andriev and Sidorov families would do for their next move. They were in transition and stateless. Would they have been returned to the then-Soviet Union? Would they have been returned to Harbin and become Chinese citizens? Good fortune smiled upon them this time.

This was a victory for all the players, most of all the Russian refugees who were now permitted to be on Canadian soil.

A happy ending to be sure, but looking back, one can see that these refugees surmounted staggering odds to even be selected for immigration. Canada was highly discriminatory when it came to immigrants and even more so for refugees. The government did not appear to be overly supportive of helping these refugees, as compared to modern times. Moreover, the government expected the refugees to immediately support themselves once they arrived in Canada. They were required to have their own "landing money." If they couldn't support themselves, the government expected guarantees from philanthropic organizations. The barriers to enter Canada as a Russian refugee were substantial. And yet, little Nikifor and his family had arrived.

It had taken a worldwide partnership of favourably inclined decision makers to make Gregori and Luka's plan a reality.

"I often wonder," Gregori told his old friend Luka on their train ride from Vancouver, "like having a nightmare, what the chances were of us being sent back to Japan without the help of the RRRSA?" One other element of their good fortune was related to the RRRSA. The Canadian government may have known, but surely the Russian refugees would not have known, that RRRSA funding for refugees was switching back to American immigrants in July of that year because American immigration quotas were being renewed that summer.

"Gregori," said Luka, "this country needs us to help open up their prairies as much as we need them. But God bless the RRRSA. Its anonymous financial support showed us there is still compassion in this hostile world."

CHAPTER 2

HOMEGLEN, THE FIRST YEARS: 1924–29

PHILLIP CARRIED YOUNG Nikifor on his shoulders as he walked toward the camp with the others. The Andreeff (formerly Andriev) and Sidoroff (formerly Siderov) families were newly landed and possibly unaware their names had been anglicized by Canadian immigration officials as they walked into the camp together, approaching the tents lined up in a military fashion. "I have lived in tents before," Phillip thought to himself. He remembered the smell of wet canvas and how it becomes unbearably warm in the direct sunshine. This would become their colony settlement in Homeglen, Alberta. "I promise you, young Nikifor," said Phillip, "we will do better than this."

He was uneasy with the notion of being a refugee and living in a colony. Even though he had been travelling with this group for several weeks, he did not know most of them.

When Col. Dournovo was organizing the group in Harbin, his principle had been "First come, first served, and our family."[1] Of course, he didn't want the CPR or the Canadian government to know his refugee screening application process was not following the Russian Red

Cross classifications. His representation to them was always that he had personally vetted these great farmers from the Amur Valley. This, he knew, was consistent with the CPR's and the Canadian government's ideal candidates. He was really talking about a small group of religious people called the Old Believers. Of the 116 Russians present (85 adults, 18 children, 12 infants, and 1 priest), no more than 40 were Old Believers (OB).[2] (Talking with descendants today, they would say the use of the term "Old Believers" was more like "Old Brothers" in the Russian translation. It was not common for them to describe themselves as Old Believers.) Of the balance of the group, designated as "Others," Dournovo's daughter Maria had the opinion right from the beginning of the trip that the conduct of the Others was no better than the Bolsheviks'.[3] This may have concerned the immigration officials, had they used better screening methods. Said Maria, "From the very beginning of our journey, there were the nice people, I heard they were a religious group called the Old Believers, and then there were the Others. The Others were just like the rest of them. They were always concerned about receiving rather than giving. They were not nice to be with. They caused problems for Father."

The CPR's notion of the perfect settlement was to have all colony members work their fields collectively and live a communal life. They had supplied a big tent, four stoves, and wooden tables and benches for communal dining.[4] Colony managers had plans for a more permanent solution.

Dournovo remained the "go to" person from the railway's point of view. His sidekick, Col. Dmohovsky, was also now living in Homeglen. Dournovo at various times described himself as the head, the organizer, or the president of "his organization." The CPR was counting on them both to bring more Russian settlers to Canada. While their combined expertise had successfully delivered a self-funding group of refugees to Canada,[5] perhaps the CPR was beginning to stretch the organization's management capabilities too widely. For example, the CPR suggested Dournovo launch a start-up project to provide a meeting hall for the group and help strengthen community ties. He was designated to be project manager for a big building that would be a residence, town hall, and store. The colony members affectionately called it the "Bolshoi Dome" project.[6] Commissioner Dennis reckoned it could be used by future groups arriving; for the present, it would serve as an infrastructure project. As described earlier, Dournovo and Dmohovsky had received some $17,500 from the Russian Refugee Relief Society of America. With plans supplied by the government, these funds were used to pay workers for their time in the construction of the 140-by-24-foot wooden log structure. The work began in July.[7] Dournovo paid workers, most of them of the OB variety, a good wage to help them get on their feet.[8] The "Others" for the most part were just trying to get by with limited involvement.

It was most likely a shortage of funds that caused the work to cease on the Bolshoi Dome, leaving the structure substantially built except for a roof. Another reason for the abrupt end to the work was the refugees' need to provide for their own families. The summer was on the wane, and the approaching fall and winter motivated the men to build secure wooden shelters for their families instead of just living in tents.

Phillip wanted three things: to live in peace and harmony with his extended family, to pray, and to farm.

He was a master craftsman with an axe. During the summer, neighbours from the surrounding area would drop by to witness the intricate quality of the OB's work. Says Maria Rosenbach, "Never could I imagine to work (*sic*) so fast and so well with just an axe as did those Old Believers."[9]

After completing his own log cabin, Phillip and the other OBs also built a *banya*, a communal steam bathhouse. He analyzed their work with a critical eye. He took pride in the work he did for his community. One more structure they built was a temporary church.[10] He and the others knew that God would hear their prayers in this structure, but they would have to do better in time to show their proper respect for their Lord by building a proper church in time.

It is clear there were two distinct groups forming in the colony. The Others moved along day to day, farming the colony land as directed, whereas the OB group continued to be somewhat independent and strategic in their work. Luka said to Gregori, "Our boys are working hard and making some good earnings. Let's encourage them to buy our own land. Working for the colony offers us very little in return. With our own land we can benefit from our own labours." Within a year, they owned their own quarter sections of farmland acquired via property tax recovery sales.

Young Nikifor had run barefoot all summer. During the day, he would follow his mother to get milk from a neighbouring farmer, and then he helped her work in their garden. His mother liked to use the nickname "Mikifor" when they were together.

Nikifor loved his older brother. He would ask his mother, "When is Akim coming home?" When Akim (Ike) got home from school, Nikifor would follow him around as best he could. Akim was good to Nikifor. He would teach him new English words, helping his little brother learn to speak.

During the second half of 1924, two blessed events occurred in the OB camp. Phillip's sister Lucaria (Prokofi's, or Peter's, wife) had a son they named Boris (Syd) on July 31. Then, Phillip and his wife, Elena, had a daughter they named Zinayeda (Zina) on October 11. These two women, thirty-two and thirty years of age respectively, delivered their babies in their own little cabins with limited outside help. Their hardships were epic, and their courage was remarkable under the circumstances. Another reflection on their nature was Maria Rosenbach's comment in her recollections of the journey on the boat: "Best of all were the Old Believer's (*sic*) women. They were quiet, modest, believing completely in father, and behaved with a great respect towards mother."[11]

Dournovo and Dmohovsky were urging Dennis and Egan to bring out another forty families. Col. Dennis had visited the colony in June, and he was encouraged by what he saw. However, his assessment of the crops in Alberta influenced his opinion. He and Egan decided that the next tranche of refugees from Russia should wait until the spring.[12]

In the fall, twenty of the older children attended the Lonesome Pine School. Their mission was to learn English. However, the teacher had her hands full because the English-speaking students relished the opportunity to learn the Russian language. It took a stern individual to remind the students who was the teacher.

For the men, earning a wage to provide for their families was tricky. They had arrived too late in the year to farm. They made good money working on the Bolshoi Dome, but other opportunities existed outside of the colony, where speaking English was helpful. Prokofi Sidoroff worked laying track west of Calgary for the CPR. Phillip got work in a winter logging camp.

The first winter was tough on all the families. They were "blessed" to have their two-room log shelter, but a grandfather, parents, children, and newborn lived in very close quarters.

Homeglen had forty inches of snow the first winter.[13] The colony members were used to cold weather. Where they had lived in Siberia, there were few trees and the wind blew harshly, adding to the coldness. Cons (Constantine) Mishukoff recounted his grandmother describing coldness in Siberia. She said, "When one spit and the saliva froze before it hit the ground, then it was considered to be very cold."[14]

When it was cold, Grandpa Gregori loved to work his trapline. Beaver, fox, weasels, and rabbits offered nice pelts that earned a few pennies from the traders. Besides, with his son Phillip away working at the logging camp, Gregori was the head of the household. Gregori also had time to play *peshki* with his granddaughter Valentina (Viola).[15] When he found a moment or two for himself, he corresponded with his son Larivon in Australia. He wanted all his sons together. Life was good in Canada, please come!

Landowners again!

The year 1925 was a fresh new start for the OBs and the Others. They could sow the land for themselves or the CPR and harvest it. They were farming at last, and the Andreeffs already owned four quarter sections purchased from property tax sales. In less than a year after landing in Vancouver, they owned land again.[16]

Many men continued to find work in neighbouring farms or on their colony land. In those days, spring farm labour paid forty to fifty dollars per month, while in harvest season it paid three to four dollars a day.[17] The colony was settling into a routine. The men were working the fields, the women were tending to their young families, and the children were attending school. On the weekends, the OBs were practising their faith. Life was simple, or at least it should have been.

Some of the Others had formed a cabal of sorts to undercut Col. Dournovo. It had started in Harbin. These were people of a "lack-of-abundance" mentality. They continuously questioned the manner in which finances were handled by Dournovo. Why did they start their journey with $15,200 in Harbin and arrive in Vancouver with only $7,200? They were told that extra expenses were unexpected and foreign exchange considerations were a surprise. Some may have heard that Col. Dmohovsky used $3,000 for the settlement of a divorce in Vancouver.[18]

In Maria Rosenbach's accounts of these early days, she writes that Dmohovsky was always at Dournovo for money. He chided Dournovo for giving the builders of the Bolshoi Dome a premium wage. It was clear to the CPR management, based on complaint letters they received, that Dournovo was being challenged on his ability to manage and lead the colony effectively.[19] The CPR sent an emissary, Nicolai Vassilievich, to talk to people other than the individuals who lodged the complaints. They seemed content with Col. Dournovo's management style, particularly the OBs, who gave him a ringing endorsement.[20] But the die was cast. Dournovo lost his ability to keep this group focused on farming the CPR land. In November 1925, the CPR brass made their decision. They did not give up on Col. Dournovo's ability to draw immigrants. Instead, they moved him and his family to Calgary to continue his work. He used his organization, such as it was, to continue to draw hundreds of Russian refugees to Alberta. Of the thousands in Harbin seeking refuge in Canada, fewer than a thousand eventually landed.

There were happier times in 1925, particularly for the Andreeffs. Phillip's brother Larivon (Lawrence), his wife, Palagaya (Polly), and daughter, Marusa (Mary), emigrated from Australia on September 19, 1925.[21] Grandpa Gregori could not have been happier. Next, less than a week later, Elena had her fifth child, Constantine (Nick), on September 25, 1925—another brother for Akim, Nikifor, Valentina, and Zinayeda.

The Sidoroffs were also joyful as Lucaria had her eighth delivery, a daughter named Jessie, on October 16, 1926.

Earlier in the year, the Kalugins and two other families joined the colony at Homeglen, arriving from Japan and contributing to the growth of the colony.[22]

Nikifor looked forward to attending Lonesome Pine School with his brother Akim, but he was only five years old in 1926, so he had to wait another year.

Sadly, the year 1926 would not end well. On November 27, Elena gave birth to a son, Philipe, who did not survive. The death of an infant is extremely painful for a family, and it was no less for the Andreeffs. Young Nikifor would remember the pain of losing his baby brother Philipe for the rest of his life. He later reminisced, "My little brother was a beautiful little baby. His skin was so soft and wrinkly. I loved being with him, but sadly he was only with us for a short time."

Colony business

Days, months, and years passed. The colony was ready for the next group of settlers, although, for a variety of reasons, their settlement seemed to occur in other communities.

The planned immigration model of colonization conceived earlier by J.S. Dennis of the CPR was showing signs of faltering. On January 12, 1926, there was an interdepartmental correspondence, a "Memorandum. Regarding Russian Immigration." N. Van der Vliet, of the CPR in Calgary wrote, "The failure of organizing agricultural communities is due not so much to their unwillingness to settle on the land, as their strongly individualistic tendencies and opposition to all co-operation where their interests would be inter-woven and responsibility shared by all."[23] He further suggested that Col. Dournovo indiscriminately used funds, from Serge Ughet of the RRRSA, which had appeared to dry up. If he had instead considered a business model like a co-op, the colony may have had greater success with retaining farmers.

As the colony began to split up, a local farmer recognized the potential of the Bolshoi Dome if it had a roof. He made an offer to the CPR to lease it for three years, in return for installing the roof. Sadly, nothing came of it. The CPR didn't own it, and the further settlement of immigrants had not occurred as planned.[24] The future of the Homeglen colony now appeared uncertain.

Homeglen had another problem for the settlers: its soil. Back in Siberia, the soil was outstanding. These Russian farmers knew good soil. Ilarion (Lorne) Sidoroff wrote, "One will never find soil like that anywhere, like we had in Siberia—exceptional soil! Maybe there is some like it here around Red Deer. Fields were absolutely stone free..."[25] Brother Prokofi (Peter) described the soil in Homeglen as "sandy hills and muskegs."[26]

The Sidoroff and Andreeff families were of an individualistic mind in their farming practices. Homeglen had been their home for four years, but now they wished to move on. The desire for better land and the opportunity to settle by themselves as a group was being discussed among the OBS. Gregori and Luka discussed their next move. "Well," said Gregori, "our crops have not been as productive as we had hoped." "I agree," said Luka, "and while we likely can't sell our land profitably, we should take our families north where land is available and make our own community." He further suggested, "Like our family did in Russia, let's send our boys off to find us more productive farmland."

Rules of the game

Having rules for any game makes it fair for all the players. However, in those early days of building Canada through immigration, the rules appeared to apply to some but not others.

The Russians enjoyed their freedom and new lives in Canada. They often asked the CPR people around them and wrote letters to the railway to see if the government would allow more Russians to immigrate to Canada. They also asked if the CPR might consider helping more of their Russian compatriots to emigrate from Harbin. In 1926, Ilarion (Lorne) Sidoroff wrote a letter to Boris Pical, the deputy head of the colonization department. He questioned why the CPR was helping Mennonites and Germans with travel credits, but not Old Believers.[27] Ilarion was simply told that Russian Old Believers were not entitled to assistance.[28] This may have appeared unfair at the time, but the CPR had intended assistance given to the Mennonites to be repaid. The scheme fell apart due to administration difficulties, and it also put an end to the travel credits program.

This theme of inequity pertaining to immigration and travel arrangements as mentioned above is discussed at length by the Canadian scholar David Scheffel. Canadian immigration officials like Frederic C. Blair and W.J. Egan were discriminating gatekeepers. Blair's perspective was that "people should be kept out of Canada instead of being let in." The CPR recruiting strategy had created a temporary success in Homeglen, but officials like Blair and Egan would continue to strongly affect further immigration with more bureaucratic shuffling. This came in the form of stringent passport requirements, which further reduced the emigration of hundreds of remaining Russian refugees from Harbin.[29] Between 1924 and 1928, of the 17,000 Russian refugees in Harbin, just over 600 made it to Canada.[30]

In 1927, Larivon (Lawrence) and Palagaya (Polly) Andreeff welcomed Klavdia (Gladys) into the world. Family gatherings, prayer, and farming continued through that year and the next. The men continued to discover more about their new land. They had experienced better land for grain farming in the Amur Valley in Russia.

The women were running their simple households with a focus on their families. Owning their own cows made their lives more convenient because they didn't have to walk to the neighbours' place for milk any longer.

This group of Old Believers continued living as an insular community. They were not widely known in the colony, because they kept to themselves, as their faith required. Nikifor and his brother were learning a new language and meeting new people, unlike their parents. A peek at the Canadian way of life was greeting them daily with each new lesson at Lonesome Pine School.

The year 1928 marked the families' fourth year in Canada. Earlier, the CPR had requested they stay a minimum of four years, and that milestone arrived midway through the year.[31] The OBs had been talking about seeking better soil, and they wanted to have a more isolated and autonomous community. They sent out scouts to learn what else Alberta had to offer. For the Andreeff family, it was Lawrence who was asked to explore for all the family members. He was likely selected because he was more fluent in speaking and writing English than the others, a necessity for making applications for land acquisition.

During this time, the rules of the immigration game always favoured British subjects and northern Europeans. The others were considered "non-preferred" by immigration officials because they lacked either a skill or any degree of proficiency in English.

Land history in northern Alberta

The twenty-eight-year-old Lawrence understood little of the history of the new land he was about to procure, other than that the soil conditions needed to be better than at Homeglen. A mere twenty-eight years earlier, the Canadian government was implementing its plan for nation building as it opened up the Canadian prairies for economic development and immigration for families like the Andreeffs.

Federal Minister of the Interior Sir Clifford Sifton was known for removing barriers to populating the prairies—barriers such as large companies like the railroads, the Hudson Bay Company, who controlled significant portions of the land, and the First Nations who actually owned it.[32] With the companies brought into line, he next organized the First Nations' lands by way of treaties. (More will be said later of Treaty 8, which covered northern Alberta and some of northern British Columbia.)

In the late 1800s, Canada had initiated a uniform land survey of the three Prairie provinces. This system of land identification gave the

Canadian prairies the uniquely checkerboard characteristic you see today when you look down while flying over them. The intention of these surveys was to accurately describe and locate land before any letters patent could be issued to homesteaders. (Letters patent were used to grant or confirm title to a portion of the land. They served as proof that the land no longer belonged to the Crown.)[33]

The basic units of the surveys were thirty-six-square-mile townships. They were numbered from south to north, starting at the US border. They were organized between seven north-south meridians, which were used as baselines for surveying and numbering townships. Ranges were numbered east to west, starting from each meridian.[34]

This system covers 200 million acres and is the world's largest survey grid laid down in a single integrated system. It led to the creation of more than 1.25 million homesteads, and Lawrence was on his way to claim his.

Mike Mihailoff was a good friend of Lawrence's. He had just returned from the north and was able to advise Lawrence to use rail to get as far north as Falher, and then continue trekking north using the Fort St. John trail. There were no roads. Lawrence managed to trek to just north of the present-day town of Fairview. At the time, it was the Beaver Indian Reserve No. 152. In 1929, it was surrendered to settlers seeking more farmland.

Lawrence filed applications for land for his father, his three brothers, and himself. With each application, he was required to pay ten dollars for a quarter section (160 acres). As a homesteader he was then required to live six months in each year on his land and in a habitable house for three years.[35] The quarter section of land Lawrence picked for his brother Phillip on November 6, 1928, was legally described as Township 83, Range 4, South East section (one quarter) of the 12th section, West of the Sixth Meridian.[36] (The family still owns the property.) With his job done, Lawrence returned to Homeglen.

Lawrence was perhaps not aware that around the time he filed his land applications, the Beaver Indian Reserve lands, located just a half mile south of his claims, would be surrendered on September 21, 1928. Future neighbouring farmers could acquire this land because the reserve was relocated.[37] This marked the second time these Indigenous people were forced to bargain away their ancestral land for others to farm.

Most of northern Alberta was acquired from Indigenous Peoples by the Dominion of Canada in 1899 under an agreement called Treaty 8. In exchange for reserve lands, hunting and fishing rights, and an annual stipend and education for Indigenous children, the Canadian government was ceded almost 850,000 square kilometres of land. By any measure, if this deal had been proposed with qualified legal counsel advising the First Nations, it would likely have had a far different outcome. When Sir Clifford Sifton approved Treaty 8,[38] he wanted European farmers landing on the prairies. He had little interest in the Indigenous inhabitants of this area.

In his governmental affairs, Sifton supported budget cuts to the Department of Indian Affairs and to Indigenous education. The education proposed in the agreement became the government's insidious tool to assimilate Indigenous youth in residential schools, hence forcing, as the Truth and Reconciliation Commission of Canada states, "a cultural genocide" of Indigenous Peoples.[39] Ultimately this led to a formal apology from Prime Minister Stephen Harper for the past Canadian governments' attempts to eradicate the identity and culture of Indigenous Peoples.[40]

These actions by the government would have been important to know at the time, because these Russian immigrants, too, were downtrodden in their former country, and the broad brush of new Canadians swept these events under the carpet, so new immigrants were none the wiser. Still, the Russian immigrants would likely have done little if the facts were known to them because, as with so many instances in life, "When in Rome, do as the Romans do."

The events of 1928 are not quite complete without mentioning the arrival of newborn Polly Sidoroff on October 28—a happy day for her family.

The last item of note during this year was the completion of the railroad extension to Fairview on November 2, 1928. This meant relocating to the new farms in the north would be easier.

Exodus

In early 1929, eleven families were focused on how to move livestock, farming machinery, and their established households from Homeglen to their new land near Gage, Alberta. Nikifor's dad, Phillip "prefabricated a house in Homeglen and moved it in pieces, by train to Gage, Alberta."[41] "My dad was really smart," said young Nikifor, "he built our house before we left our beloved Homeglen. I look forward to another train ride."

The CPR was again helpful to immigrants, giving them a freight discount to ship all their effects north.[42] Back then, each of these moves was a logistical nightmare. Livestock needed feed and water for the three-day train ride. Manure had to be dealt with inside a crowded boxcar. At the other end of the journey, the livestock had to be moved from the train siding to the new farm many miles away.

This exodus from Homeglen started in February 1929. Children were bundled in jackets; babies were transported in boxes full of blankets; and animals needed to be sheltered overnight because of snow. Nikifor reflected on this family event: "I didn't know why we had to move in the middle of my school year. It was cold. Everyone had to help. It was hard work." It was not an easy transition. Fortunately, they worked as a community of families, and they did their absolute best to help each other despite the harsh conditions. The account of Peter Sidoroff being helped by his brother-in-law, Lawrence, is typical of those moving to their new homesteads: "Your sister Lucaria and I are deeply indebted to you and Palagaya for being so hospitable and kind to us. We cannot thank you enough." And from his wife, Lucaria, "Give our regards to Palagaya and our *bolshoi spaseeba* (a big thank you). We will not forget what you have done for us."[43]

UNBEKNOWNST TO THE farmers, toward the end of 1929, the grinding gears of the engines of commerce were getting louder as the stock market worked itself into a frenzy and crashed on October 24, 1929.

HOMEGLEN, THE FIRST YEARS: 1924-29

This event was hardly noticed by them. None of them owned a stock portfolio. Not so, however, for one of their greatest benefactors of 1924, Prince Felix Youssoupoff.

How did this Russian, Prince Felix, become a benefactor to Nikifor's Russian refugee family? He used his celebrity to raise funds in the high echelons of New York society. He directed these funds to the RRRSA to support the Russian refugees. Prince Felix had been a lifelong friend, more like a brother, to the Romanoff tsar Nicholas II, who was murdered on July 17, 1918. The Youssoupoff family still had great wealth in the 1920s. Felix Youssoupoff was a member of the Executive and Finance Committee of the RRRSA, based in New York. He was financially crushed in the stock-market crash. This was also the case for the other board members of the RRRSA, and the organization ceased to exist.[44] This is important to know because it spelled the end of this group's private sponsorships to refugees.

To connect the dots to the RRRSA, here is some history. Russia was mostly impoverished, a backwards, undeveloped country with an enormous starving peasantry and many poor industrial workers, downtrodden under the aristocratic royal Romanoff rule. Beginning in 1917, the country was separating into two factions. The Red Russians were the revolutionary Bolshevik army supporting communism, which was led by Lenin and Trotsky; they wore red stars on their apparel to symbolize their cause. Their enemies were the White Russians, who were the loyal monarchists and aristocrats.

Although not yet a part of my father's history, my maternal grandfather was a White Russian: religious, supporting the tsar, and against the Bolsheviks. When I was a child, my mother Natalie would tell us that he was a gold worker for the tsar in the Old Country before farming and changing countries.

Prince Felix Youssoupoff was a son of the wealthiest Russian aristocratic family in the Russian Empire. Prior to the downfall of the Russian monarchy in the Russian Revolution (1917 to 1923), the Youssoupoffs had many beautiful palaces (and today, one of their restored palaces is a big tourist attraction in St. Petersburg).

Due to being the largest landowners in the Russian Empire, the Youssoupoffs were wealthier than the Romanoff tsars. This is huge wealth, because the Romanoffs were the wealthiest of all the European royal families at the time.

Nicholas II rewarded his friend Youssoupoff for his counsel, support, and loyalty with the honorary title of "prince." Prince Felix was famous for many reasons, including his wealth, his many beautiful Russian palaces, and his marriage to Nicholas II's niece, but most notably, he arranged the murder of Grigori Rasputin in 1916.

Rasputin was a tough religious fanatic, and Prince Felix, with cohorts, conspired to murder him. But it took a long time to kill him. First Rasputin drank wine that was secretly poisoned by Prince Felix while they were in Rasputin's personal garden-level suite. Prince Felix watched him drink it; then came a beating outside in the garden, followed by a gunshot. Finally, he drowned after he was thrown in the river. Prince Felix and his cohorts expected the murder of Rasputin to help with the optics for the newly granted Russian legislature and the Romanoff family. It didn't.

The reign of tsars in Russia began in 1547. Over time, this tsardom caused a significant and growing split of haves and have-nots within the population. In 1917, there was the February Revolution and then the October Revolution, which were followed by a civil war. These combined events became known as the Russian Revolution. This ended when the Bolsheviks established the Soviet Union between 1922 and 1923. The Bolsheviks and the Red Army were led by the leftist revolutionary Vladimir Lenin, whose army seized power, abolished the monarchy, and murdered all the ruling Romanoff family. The Bolsheviks later became known as the Communist Party of the USSR, which ruled until 1991, when the USSR broke up. The Russian Federation, commonly known as Russia, has been in place since 1991 and is an autocracy ruled by Vladimir Putin.

Prince Felix escaped from the Red Russians and the Bolshevik Revolution, taking his wealth. He moved from Russia to southern France and frequently visited New York City, where he became a board member of the RRRSA.

HOMEGLEN, THE FIRST YEARS: 1924–29

In Alberta, 1929 held one last joyous event for Phillip and Elena. On Christmas Day, Anesya (Jean) was born in their new little home on their new homestead.

Phillip was a happy man: He had a wonderful family; he had managed a move to their new land; and now he owned his own farm. He couldn't wait to see what the 1930s had to offer.

CHAPTER 3

THE LUCK OF THE RUSSIAN REFUGEES: 1930–55

THESE RUSSIAN REFUGEES had the fortune to be permitted into Canada.

As a nine-year-old kid in 1930, Nikifor had no sense that he and his family were dirt-poor subsistence farmers. He had lived in a one-room wooden cabin with seven others, aged one to seventy-four. They had no electricity, running water, plumbing, or refrigeration. They had to walk to the creek to get water in buckets for their daily needs. They ate whatever they produced off the land and they traded with the local Indigenous hunters for moose meat. They kept honeybees. Their food in the non-growing season was baked, canned, or salted. Evenings were brightened with coal oil or kerosene lamps. Walking to the outhouse by moonlight in almost –30°C (–20°F) temperatures was common in the winter months.

The immigrant children had less trouble assimilating in their new land than their parents. Nikifor was speaking English now, having completed three grades at school in Homeglen and preparing for his fourth year as soon as his dad, Phillip, finished building the new school, to be named Ranger. Nikifor was now called Mike at school.

THE LUCK OF THE RUSSIAN REFUGEES: 1930–55

Although he was registered as Nikifor in his Declaration of Passenger to Canada, family members say they used a nickname and called him Mikifor at home. It is likely that Mikifor's name was shortened to Mike by his schoolteacher. Elena liked to use "Michael" when talking to her son. The beautiful and unique Russian names of most of the refugees were sadly subjected to anglicization. Maybe because he was now being called Mike at school, some in the family still playfully teased him by saying his Russian name as Mikifor-Mikiforvitch.

His jobs were to milk the cows, feed the animals, clean the barn and chicken coops, split wood for the stove, and help his dad clear land. He loved working with his big brother Akim, particularly at harvest time. There was lots of work to do on the farm. Praying, going to school, and doing chores left precious little time in the day for much else.

Luck had to be on Lawrence's side when he selected their Gage farmland, near Fairview. Had he known its latitude was the same as Moscow's, he might have considered it too cold to farm. But this land was an extension of the Canadian prairies. It was not what many assumed, a part of the Canadian northlands. The two factors that made this farmland so productive were the long hours of summer sunshine and the number of frost-free days. January temperatures had a mean of –17°C (1.4°F) and July a mean of 16°C (60°F), like those of Edmonton and Calgary.[1] The wind was not as strong as in Saskatchewan or Manitoba, where people had experienced the dust bowls. And they had an abundance of trees in northern Alberta. The trees made clearing land tedious, but they were useful as a source of fuel for heating homes in the winter, as a windbreak, and for building materials. Fires had never threatened farmers' homes or outer buildings. Lastly, due to this collection of favourable attributes of the north, the farmers never had to deal with crop failures.

The main crops were wheat, yielding on average thirty bushels per acre; barley, yielding forty bushels per acre; and oats, yielding sixty bushels per acre. They planted their crops in May and harvested them in September.[2]

Phillip took his crop of grain by horse and wagon to the local elevator after the 1930 harvest. Unlike past years, as in 1928, when he got $1.70 per bushel for wheat, that year the elevator agent told him, grim-faced, they were buying wheat for 21 cents per bushel.[3] Phillip had only thirty-eight acres of crops in 1930.[4] With a yield of thirty bushels per acre, his wheat sale for 1930 would amount to no more than $240. Such were the times. A farmer's joke was that he just kept on farming until he ran out of money. After December of 1930, the Hines Creek community, just north of Fairview, and the surrounding farmers would see the arrival of the railway to service the grain elevators.

No one had any money in those days. Phillip would take his wagon to town loaded with cords of wood. The best price he could get was two dollars a cord, but it usually went for between $1 and $1.50 per cord.[5]

Gregori and his grandkids cleared ten to twenty acres of land per year, year in and year out. Each of the kids who could swing an axe would cut down trees, rain or shine. They made piles of picked roots and cut trees and then burned them. Next, the land was plowed. Lastly, the crop for the season was planted. Gregori would exclaim, "Everyone join in, we need to work together to make this land productive!"

All this work needed much deserved nourishment. The Andriev (anglicized to Andreeff, then Andruff) family were fortunate. As good subsistence farmers, they grew a large garden. They had beef cattle, cows, pigs, and sheep. Phillip's faith guided him even in the toughest times. He reflected often on scripture, "My God shall supply all my needs."[6] It was Elena who supplied the tasty and nourishing food. Typical meals included mushrooms in cream; fish pies (white fish was ordered from eastern Canada); *blini* (pancakes); *pelmeni* (like wonton); *kielbasa* (sausage) with hot mustard; and last but not least, her fried bread (like doughnuts but better!). In the fall she would shred cabbage into a wooden barrel to make sauerkraut and process cucumbers to make pickles.[7]

Home building again

In 1931, Phillip set about building a bigger home for his growing family. The new house was a much larger structure and served them well. Thirty-foot-long Jack pine logs were hand-hewed to be the same size from one end to the other. This work was done with a double-handled plane that Phillip forged himself. Nikifor (Mike) gave an account of his father's handiwork: "There is a science to building a house the way Dad did it. The corners were dovetailed. The top log was hollowed and fit together with the one below it with precision. There wasn't an eighth of an inch of space throughout the length of the log."[8] This was the same precision some neighbouring farmers had witnessed in Homeglen several years earlier.

Elena was expecting again. On the happy day of March 27, 1931, Feodosia (Fannie) arrived. Economic times may have been hard, but an event like Fannie's arrival perked up everyone.

It was another busy year indeed, as Phillip put the final touches on the local Ranger school for the neighbouring children and his own four school-aged kids. His final contribution to this community school was building the desks.

The Mother's Day tragedy of 1931

Mother's Day is a day of recognition for mothers throughout the world. It started in the United Sates around 1911 and was quickly recognized by other countries, including Canada, as an appropriate day to celebrate mothers. In Canada, it is celebrated on the second Sunday in May. While the Russian immigrants may not have been up on local customs, they did recognize this tradition in later years.

Mike's only aunt, Lucaria Sidoroff, who was married to Peter, was the binding soul of the Andreeff and Sidoroff families. She had a zest for learning English and cherished Canada's democratic way of life.[9] She herself was full of life.

One beautiful Sunday morning in early May 1931, she and Peter were inspired to plant their spring garden. Most gardeners typically wait for Queen Victoria's birthday on May 24 before they start planting, but the soil had warmed up enough by then for seeds to sprout. That year, there seemed a particular urgency for Lucaria, because she was soon to deliver for the tenth time.

Giving birth without complications in these times could not be taken for granted. Lucaria was a silent pillar of strength in this family. She ran a happy household so that Peter could focus on working the farm. Since their early days in Russia, they had been through a great many travails together. They relied on each other to get past the dark times. Sadly, fate was about to intervene in their lives.

On Friday, May 8, Lucaria suffered a miscarriage. Very soon after the miscarriage, she started to feel worse. Through Saturday and Sunday, she suffered in her bed. Typically, on Mother's Day, children happily celebrate their mother by giving her thoughtful little gifts. The Sidoroff children were not happy but anxious because of their mother's condition. By Monday morning, this thirty-seven-year-old mother of five was comatose, and in the afternoon she died. A medical evaluation of her condition in today's terms is that she likely died of a stroke, explaining the paralysis of her left side. The stroke was brought on by eclampsia, seizures triggered by high blood pressure during pregnancy.

Peter was devastated. His five young children gathered around him, trying to make sense of what had just happened to their mother. They wondered who would look after them now. Peter would try to fill in, but a farmer's life is in the field. He experienced boundless grief. She was gone.

When someone dies in the Orthodox faith, the extent of the grief can only be matched by the extent of the praying. The body lies in a homemade coffin beneath *icona* (images, idols), and the men of the community take turns reading pre-burial scriptures. Phillip was no doubt involved in such prayer for his sister. Prayer and scripture readings continue day and night until the third day; in this case, it was four days because relatives from out of town needed travel time to attend the funeral. Following this, everyone goes to the burial site for another service before the interment. After the burial, funeral attendees gather at the home of the deceased for a big communal dinner. A collection is taken for the priest, because he is obliged to buy candles and continue praying for the soul of the departed. This whole process left everyone drained emotionally, particularly the children.[10]

Life goes on

Fortunately, the Sidoroff extended family became the support Peter needed to get back on his feet after grieving. Cousins and aunts came forward to clean, cook, garden, and care for his family. What was a family tragedy became a sort of comfort as family bonds strengthened among the relatives. Within a year, Peter married Paraskavaya (Pearl) Reznick, and his household regained its balance.

As the year moved on and into the next, Mike attended school during the day. He liked school and the friends he made there. It was a stimulating break from the work of the farm. He enjoyed the opportunity to learn and play sports. His second language, English, was now mastered. Henceforth, our young Mike was no longer recognized by his Russian name, Nikifor. Most every immigrant yearns for such assimilation. To his parents, this had to feel like their heritage was fraying in front of their eyes. However, they, too, were resigned to accepting the ways of their new country.

After school, Mike would run the two miles home and join in the afternoon chores. He remembered being affected by one particular aspect of farm life. The milk from the cows was both a food for the family and a commodity for trade. A separator, located in the kitchen next to the stove, received the milk from the cows, where it was separated into skimmed milk and cream by a hand-cranking device. The cream was collected, stored, taken to town, and sold to a creamery. If the separator was not cleaned properly, the smell of the sour milk on the bottom of the separator became quite repugnant. Cheese making added to the odour. The smell of these activities in the farm kitchen made Mike sick to his stomach, and, as a result, he avoided eating any type of cheese for the rest of his life.

His farming abilities were now improving. Phillip and the eldest son, Ike (Akim), could handle the main tasks, but when called upon, Mike offered a worthy contribution to their work.

As the school year for 1933 ended, Mike had completed Grade 6. He was now a strapping twelve-year-old. He could not wait for the fall; he really enjoyed school. Unfortunately, during the summer an event happened that erased any further possibilities of Mike attending school.

Ike had a ruptured appendix in August. When this happens, medical attention is necessary immediately, or the rupture will cause infection to spread throughout the abdomen. Septicemia (bacteria in the blood) will lead to death. Ike was eighteen years old when he died. Another farming family was grieving. While grieving for the loss of his beloved big brother, Mike also felt the regrettable loss of his school friends and any chance for furthering his education.

For this harvest season, Mike let farming become his institution of higher learning. He had watched his father work from a distance before, but now they worked side by side. Mike was now a twelve-year-old farmer.

The old Russian Orthodox church of Saint Pokrovsky

The Old Believers (or Greek/Russian Orthodox Christians, depending on one's point of view) had set out from Harbin, China, fully intending to take their cherished faith and their priest with them to Canada. Father Artemy Solovieff was among the 116 landed Russian refugees.

During their time in Homeglen, they practised their faith in a house that Vasili (Bill) Andreeff had built and made available for the congregation.

In 1934, on a quarter section of Sidoroff land near Hines Creek, the Sidoroff and Doumnoff families committed to building a church large enough to hold their congregation. (A second, smaller church was started in Gage on some land donated by Gregori Andreeff, but it lacked a priest and congregation to support it.) It took several years to complete, but this group of devoutly religious Russians could now do something in Canada that was no longer allowed in their former country: praying with their fellow congregants. It was maybe a small thing for Canadians to be tolerant of other religions, but it was big for these good, honest, hard-working farmers from a foreign land.

Polly Elder (daughter of Peter and Lucaria Sidoroff) offered these reflections on religious practices of the time:

> I was always in awe at how sincere and committed my dad was as he stood in front of those icons during his prayers, truly and reverently into his prayer as he went through scriptures in the New Testament. [All their prayers were scripture-based. Their Bible was the New Testament, known as *Ivangilla*. I have one.] Then he would cross himself, genuflect three times and go off to bed. This was not expected of us. Our simple prayer time was just crossing ourselves and bowing three times; before bed we would add the Lord's Prayer to our evening prayer, standing with folded arms, genuflecting once, crossing ourselves three times. Always prayers were in front of the icons. Our prayer time seemed to be just a ritual, but my dad's was so real. When he told us the story of Good Friday & Easter, he wept... a true and devoted believer![11]

Fi (Fiena) Andreeff McIntyre-Olsen commented on how her family practised their rituals and religion:

> Prayer was always a very important part of our lives. Every occasion demanded a prayer. We prayed at the beginning of each school year, before seeding and harvest. Mom and Dad would cross themselves and say a prayer upon entering someone's home. Praying in the Greek/Russian Orthodox Church on special holidays (and there were many) was a marathon. Evening prayer started right after supper and continued into the wee hours of the morning. I think the only thing that kept us kids going was looking forward to spending the rest of the night and the next day with our cousins, the Pete Sidoroffs. We loved them and still do. The men stood on the right side of the church and the women on the left. The only seats were the

benches at the back and the sides of the church and were used only for rest periods. Sitting was not permitted during singing or during the reading of Jesus' words.[12]

The service was spoken in Old Church Slavonic, the liturgical language of the Russian Orthodox Church. For the younger congregants, who now knew as much English as Russian, this added linguistic complexity and left them unable to understand the recitation of scriptures. To them it was a long service: a long time to stand and a long time without sleep. The elders were satisfied with the way things were done. This is what they had dreamed of for so long. However, things were amiss for the next generation. For any congregation to grow, they need to have context in relation to the teaching of the scriptures. The clergy of Saint Pokrovsky were traditional. This was how they were trained in Russia, but these new Canadians needed something else in their homilies. Over time, as they had their own families, they moved from the traditional Russian religion to the more linguistically understandable faiths.

Despite the best efforts of Peter Sidoroff and others, the congregation dwindled. The beautiful and lovingly built church is uniquely Russian Orthodox. It is now owned by an organization in Oregon. The grounds are maintained by Peter's son, Tom Sideroff. Unfortunately, it is no longer used for services.

Contagion

In epidemiology, the branch of medical science that studies the incidence, distribution, and control of infectious diseases, there is a value called $R0$ (pronounced *R zero* or *R naught*). This represents the number of infections expected to be generated from one case in a population where all individuals are susceptible to infection. A virus like COVID-19, for example, has an $R0$ value of 3.8 to 8.9.[13]

In the Hungry Thirties on the prairies, there were known diseases with an even higher infection rate. Mike's sister, Fannie, lamented about the quarantine periods of ten to fourteen days that she and others were subjected to in her childhood.[14] She could not go anywhere or have anyone over.

Unlike COVID-19, most of these diseases typically affected children. Often passed around at school, they had devastatingly high RO values of between 10 and 18. Fortunately, over time, vaccines were developed for chicken pox and measles, two of the most prolific viruses. Before the vaccines however, these diseases were a terrible menace to vulnerable schoolchildren.

Disease and inadequate public health practices took their toll in these early days of Canada. Both Lucaria and Ike would likely have survived with current medical intervention. The scourge of a disease like polio was a continual threat to the young into the 1950s, when a long-awaited immunization program was developed. Medical advances continue every day to the betterment of mankind, but not in these earlier days.

The British subjects are coming

Immigrating to Canada was one thing, but the chances of staying in Canada were another matter. Canadian immigration in the 1930s experienced a significant reduction from the 1920s due to economic hardship and more restrictive entry requirements. On average, a mere 16,000 immigrants arrived each year, compared to 126,000 per year in the 1920s. Canada, under the Conservative government of Prime Minister R.B. Bennett, deported over 28,000 people from 1930 to 1935. In 1933, one immigrant was deported for every three who entered. As relief rolls swelled from the pressure of unemployment, the government felt compelled to rid the country of the indigent.[15]

Phillip Andreeff and the OBs had established a "reputation throughout the prairies, for reliability, fortitude, and performance of good work."[16] They were the type of immigrants building this young nation one farm at a time, as Sir Clifford Sifton had envisioned.

Phillip could see there were advantages to being a Canadian—most importantly, having the ability to vote. He had dedicated ten years of hard work to his family and community in Canada. Why not have a say in who forms the government? To this end, on March 14, 1934, he applied to become a naturalized citizen. His Declaration of Passenger to Canada, which he presented to immigration officials upon landing in Vancouver in 1924, must have served as his official government record because it also carried this naturalization date.[17]

A person did not acquire legal status as a Canadian once they became naturalized. Instead, they became a British subject. British subjects in Canada did not become Canadian citizens until January 1, 1947, under the *Canadian Citizenship Act*.[18]

On February 27, 1935, Phillip Gregory Andreeff, under the *Naturalization Act* of the Dominion of Canada, was granted his Certificate of Naturalization Where the Names of Children are Included. Here is the elegant language on the certificate:

> I, the undersigned, Secretary of State of Canada, do hereby certify and declare that Phillip Gregory Andreeff whose particulars are endorsed hereon, is hereby naturalized as a British subject, that is entitled to all political and other rights, powers, and privileges, and subject to all obligations, duties, and liabilities to which a natural born British subject is entitled or subject, and that he has to all intents and purposes the status of a natural born British subject. Application having been made therefore, the minor children of the said Phillip Gregory Andreeff born before the date of this certificate, whose names are endorsed herein, are included in this certificate.

This is how Michael Andreeff (born June 15, 1921, as Nikifor Andriev in Svobodnyy, Russia) and Viola Andreeff (born March 6, 1923, as Valentina Andriev, in Svobodnyy, Russia) became British subjects. It is also interesting to note that on the back of this certificate under "Name of Wife" is a notation: "Not Hereby Naturalized." Having been married in Russia, before Phillip's naturalization, Elena would not be granted a similar status under Canadian law at the time, meaning she could not vote.

Also, again, names are changed. On his entry to Canada, he was known as Philip Andriev; with his naturalization, he became known as Phillip Gregory Andreeff.

Lastly, on April 6, 1935, the *Canadian Gazette* listed Phillip, Michael, and Viola Andreeff as "listed Aliens to whom certificates of naturalization under the Naturalization Act were granted by the Secretary of State of Canada, during the month of February 1935."[19]

These events are typically capped by a celebration worthy of a toast. However, there are no stories of a celebration. Phillip and the kids headed back to the farm.

Back on the farm

Who was this young former Russian refugee, now a British subject of the Dominion of Canada called Michael Andreeff? Look to his father, Phillip, for answers. Every good apprentice needs a good mentor.

Phillip was a battle-hardened war veteran who loved his independence and living off the land. He had fought for his native country; he fought for his family to get away from oppression; he endured poor farming for four years in colony conditions in Homeglen; and he tirelessly maintained his faith. He had extraordinarily little money, a few simple assets, and very poor English.

What he did have, which in some instances was priceless and in others regrettable, he imparted to his now eldest son. He gave Mike a work ethic. From early in the morning until late at night, there was always work. His moral compass was pointed straight to his heart. Being a good person and an honest neighbour who always did the right thing were important to an Andreeff. Phillip showed Mike what hospitality meant. Thinking of your guests before yourself and making them feel cherished and important was the Andreeff way. Never be loud or draw attention to yourself. And most of all, love your family and follow your faith.

These were standards that stayed with Mike his whole life. But life could be full of secrets. Unseen or unmentioned publicly in the

Andreeffs' family life, the absolute authority was the paternal head of the household. In fact, behind the scenes, although Phillip never struck his wife, she was effectively his chattel, expected to cope in quiet servitude. This is not to be cruel or unkind, as much as it is to do with the nature of the times. Mike would also come to understand and take this with him into his own secret world. It was not uncommon among some farmers in those times to use this authority to force their physical domination upon their spouse in a physically abusive manner.

In 1936, things were looking up on both the local front and the economic front. On March 11, 1936, Phillip was granted title to his land, having successfully homesteaded for the previous seven years.[20] Wheat crops now sold at $1.25 per bushel.[21] For his now 80 to 110 acres of cropped land for wheat, Phillip could now realize roughly $3,000 to $4,000 per harvest.[22] At this point in the Andreeffs' farming experience, profit was not a word they had ever used. But things were beginning to improve. The Andreeff girls knew when things were good. Their father would buy a box of Okanagan apples for the winter (one only got half an apple in their lunch box), and would place a one-hundred-dollar order from the "farmer's bible," the T. Eaton catalogue. The order typically was a bolt of fabric for dressmaking and a pair of shoes for the child wearing the most worn-out hand-me-down shoes. (Daughter Zina was the master dressmaker of the family. After she left the farm, she continued her passion for dressmaking as a profession, ultimately in Victoria at the Sussex Dress Shop. She later managed McMaster's Fine Clothing.)

The Andreeff farm was still using a team of four horses in the fields.[23] The young kids and their grandfather were still chopping trees and clearing land. There were more animals to tend, but each of the children had their assigned duties to care for them. Mike's brother Constantine (Nick) was now twelve and beginning to contribute more to the farm work.

Mike's mother, Elena, was carrying her tenth and last baby. She was forty-three years old. On March 29, 1937, Darya (Doreen) arrived. Elena was sixty years old when Doreen finished high school.

THE LUCK OF THE RUSSIAN REFUGEES: 1930-55

Doreen shares these memories in her account of the year she was born: "Hit songs were 'Whistle While You Work'; 'The Lady is a Tramp'; 'My Funny Valentine'; and 'Thanks for the Memory'. Top stars were Shirley Temple, Clark Gable, Gary Cooper, Robert Taylor, Fred Astaire, and Ginger Rogers. The best-selling books were *Gone with the Wind* and *How to Win Friends and Influence People*."[24]

The farming cycle was a five-month period from May to September. The other seven months of the year were spent working outside the farm for extra cash, working on construction, or repairing farm buildings and equipment. Phillip always had a forge in the barn, and Mike was becoming a master craftsman like his father. He made tools, sharpened axes, and repaired plowshares. He was competent at any task that required working with metal and was becoming a Phillip clone (except that he did not have a traditional beard like Phillip's and the Old Believers'). Like farming, metalwork was dirty work. But at the end of the week, it was time to clean up. Mike put on his glad rags and went to town.

At seventeen years old, Mike was becoming enamoured with the fairer sex. He attended parties and local dances with his buddies, and his head was being turned by Lucy Slyshack, a pretty young woman. Throughout 1939, he started to see her on a regular basis, and it was clear that he had feelings for this English-speaking, Catholic woman.[25] Phillip recognized this as well.

At fifty years old, Phillip had concerns about how he would keep his farm producing after he reached retirement age. Additionally, the orthodoxy of the Old Believers had strict conditions about marriage. According to tradition, if Phillip's sons were to marry, it must be to Russian-speaking, Orthodox-practising women. Phillip decided his oldest living son, Mike, and his relationships needed sorting out, so he nixed the current one with Lucy and arranged a more viable alternative.

Phillip was a convincing type. By harvest season, a more appropriate and extremely attractive Dolly (Natalie) Sidoroff was coming over to help Elena prepare meals for the men in the field. Elena could stay at home with her youngest toddler. Dolly, who had left home at the age of eighteen, worked at a café in Fairview. Her employer provided her with a one-room accommodation above the café. At Phillip's request, she started turning up more frequently at the farm.[26]

Dolly's father, Fred Sidoroff, had secured passage for his family three years after the Homeglen group, in 1927. They initially lived in Shouldice, Alberta. After a time, they, too, moved to farm in the area near Hines Creek. Before leaving home, Dolly had completed Grade 8. A teacher at her school anglicized her name from Natalie to Dolly. She was born Natalie Sidorova in Vladivostok, Russia, on September 8, 1921. Like Mike, Dolly became a naturalized British subject in April 1940. And she was no stranger to Mike, as they had known each other from church and Andreeff/Sidoroff family functions.

The Second World War years

The call to enlist went out through the communities of northern Alberta in 1939. Mike was eager to join up.[27] There are two prevailing stories of his experience. The first was that he was declined for medical reasons. Could he have had flat feet? Maybe he was colour blind? There is no evidence to support these claims. The second story was that he was declined for a common reason: he was needed for "helping on the farm." The farmers had to keep producing food for the troops.

There is possibly a third scenario. If Mike wanted to join up, it is unlikely he would have mentioned the farm. Phillip had exhibited his influence on girlfriends, and over the young Mike's life generally, the year before. Vexed that another war was threatening to take his family, it is plausible Phillip appeared at the recruiting barracks, Cross of Saint George medal festooned on his chest, to plead his family had given to the cause of freedom before, and Mike could be far more helpful in the war effort by supplying grain. Certainly, a hard-working young farmer could be spared. Send another young chap to the front! Otherwise, his father's farm might cease operations due to lack of help. The result? Mike stayed home from the war and the farm continued producing grain.

Had this been the case, who could fault Phillip? He was doing his utmost to build a future for the Andreeff family. Mike was the key to the succession of his farm. Phillip did have his younger son, Nick, to rely upon, but in the patriarchal fashion of the day, the eldest son was the designated successor.

Perhaps spending some money might improve their lot. And it did! In 1940, Phillip bought a Massey-Harris Model 101 rubber-tired tractor. This would make life much easier, and it would also allow for some contract work to bring in a little more cash.[28] Phillip had paid approximately $895 for his new farming technology.[29] Clearly, he had been saving his money, year in and year out.

Family finances were always handled by the patriarch of the Andriev family. No one ever knew how much money they had, or what they could afford. If you talked with the youngest family member, she would always say they arrived in Canada with ten cents in their pockets. A frugal father knew better. This fiscal dominance would follow Mike into his new relationship and marriage with Dolly. It would not be until the next generation of Mike and Dolly's grown children, Kay, Michael Jr. (me), and Laurie, that in matters like family finances, egalitarianism would become the norm.

Until this time, none of the Andreeff progeny had married. Phillip and Elena's eldest daughter, Viola, married Sam Kalugin in October.

The last significant event in 1940 involved Mike's grandfather, Gregori. Now eighty-four years old, he had travelled across two continents, seeing more than most. He had been a driving force in his family's quest for peaceful living in Canada. He and his good friend, Luka Sidoroff, had supplied the brains and finances behind the scenes. He had spent a large portion of his adult life widowed without a partner. He involved himself with his grandchildren. When not playing with the children, he was trapping. When not reading his Bible, he was reading books about the end of time, which made the young ones laugh. He was a dear, sweet man, often alone in his thoughts, or in his bedroom upstairs. One freezing December morning, he left to check his trapline and never returned. Perhaps there was no more fitting way to go for this grand Russian man. When he didn't return, his grandson Nick searched for him and brought his body home. Said Nick, "They sent me out to look for granddad because I knew his trapline. There he was, face down in the snow. I hadn't expected that. I went back for help, but before I did, I said a prayer for my granddad." He was buried in the Holy Trinity Graveyard on land he had donated to the Gage community. (Like Homeglen, Gage no longer exists as a community.)

The world was at war. From a distance on the vast prairie landscape was the silhouette of a man on a tractor. In the still silence of the waning evening light, as he made his way home, only the clatter of the engine was audible. A light wind created a plume of dust behind the tractor like an expanding vapour trail against the evening sky. It was a picture of solitude and peace. But at that very tranquil moment, halfway around the world, the fury of munitions exploding on the landscape like rolling thunder and its fire lighting the sky was in stark contrast: it was the reality of the war in Europe.

Germany's leader, Adolf Hitler, incited the German population by telling lies to stir anger and hatred toward Jewish people. He forced segregation of the disabled and various ethnicities, but especially Jews. Hitler began a campaign of world domination. In his social philosophy, he embraced eugenics.

Eugenics (/juːˈdʒɛnɪks/; from Greek εὐ- "good" and γενής "come into being, growing") is a set of beliefs and practices that aim to improve the genetic quality of a human population, typically by exterminating people and groups judged to be inferior and promoting those judged to be superior.[30]

Eugenics became popular thinking in Britain in the early part of the twentieth century and soon spread to North America. Civil liberties could be impaired if the political process engaged this line of thinking. It soon became clear to most that it must be challenged on moral grounds. If the political process of advancing eugenics remained unchecked, as it did under Germany's Adolf Hitler in the late 1930s, and the country's military complex could enforce it, then genocide and expansionism would follow. Germany's advances through Poland, Belgium, Holland, and France, drew the United

Kingdom into war, and therefore the Commonwealth of Nations, including Canada and Australia, and the US.

Germany was intent on ruling the world as a master race, sometimes described as Aryan. It sought to exterminate ethnic Jewish people. This campaign became a tragedy of colossal proportions—the Holocaust—over the course of the war, costing 85 million lives in total, including 6 million Jewish people.[31] This was the horror of war, and it reminded Phillip of the type of insanity he had experienced in Russia. His motivation to help his son avoid war was well placed.

Back on Phillip's farm, the chickens kept laying eggs, the cows kept supplying milk, and Mike and Dolly continued their romance. In the summer of 1942, at the age of twenty-one, Mike asked Dolly to marry him. She said yes.

The Hines Creek Russian Orthodox church no longer had a priest. For Mike, it had to be a Russian Orthodox wedding, so they took a train to the closest alternative. On July 15, 1942, they were married in the Russian Orthodox Church of St. Vladimir, in Edmonton.[32]

It was a simple ceremony, but when they returned to the farm, they celebrated joyously. There was an abundance of Russian foods, including the traditional drink of homemade *braga*, and lots of it. No doubt, there was singing and dancing to their traditional songs—maybe an accordion and the *balalaika* knocking off a favoured rendition of "Kalinka." This was how the Russians celebrated into the wee hours of the morning.

Dolly and Mike were provided with their own house on the farm that they had helped build. It still had no running water, no refrigeration, and no electricity. There was no honeymoon to Niagara Falls. Life quickly became farm-focused again. No immediate plans were made for starting a family. It was rumoured that Elena and Dolly had their differences. Dolly was a new Canadian woman. She wore her hair short, which was not Elena's way. It was known that Dolly liked to party, and she also liked to drink beer. These characteristics carried less weight for Phillip when he was choosing Dolly for Mike. Besides, he had reckoned, she was to be Mike's subservient wife in the Russian tradition.

THE RUSSIAN REFUGEES

The tractor mechanized the farm, reducing the amount of manpower required. They had increased their ability to clear land and Mike adapted all the equipment to the tractor. While horses still provided a means of transportation, reliance on them for farming tasks was significantly reduced and soon eliminated completely. In 1943, Phillip bought a 1937 Ford.[33] Getting around was now a whole lot easier.

Some of Mike and Dolly's friends were starting to migrate off the farm. Two of the Sidoroff boys had departed: one to enlist in the army and one to ride the rails, looking for work. Farming was hard, low-paying, and demanding. Radio reports of the war, world events, and news of the improving economy were common in their household. Mike and Dolly were contemplating their future direction.

CANADIAN FARM LIFE was at its zenith. In the early 1940s, there were over 700,000 farms in Canada.[34] The CPR had done its job of populating the prairie farmland. The specialized colonization department, which had brought the Russian refugees and so many others, had now wound down its efforts and was not bringing in any more immigrant farmers. Canada was now looking for immigrants with more varied skills and seeking to populate urban centres. At this time, the Department of Labour was increasingly influential in immigration policy, forcing a change in the type of immigrants selected. Coupled with this new direction, after 1945, Canada was developing new policies for welfare and social programs.

Communications in those days were by word of mouth and written correspondence. Mike Sidoroff managed to get word back to the farm about good-paying jobs available at Sinclair Mills, a sawmilling town located on a rail line in British Columbia.

Population movement in Canada was driven by changing economic conditions. It was estimated that between 1946 and 1958, 39,000 farm workers annually left the farm.[35]

Recognizing that the winds of change were blowing, Mike and Dolly were getting their big announcement ready. The next chapter of farm life for Phillip's family was soon to be written.

"How ya gonna keep 'em down on the farm, Once they've been down to the farm?"

Mike and Dolly were young lovers at this stage of their lives. They would have been absorbed with each other. What next? Would it be the farm life and starting their own family, or would they fly the coop, seeking adventure, like many in their generation?

There was glorious news. The war had ended in Europe in early May of 1945. The couple thought it was opportune to announce to their respective families that they were moving to Sinclair Mills in British Columbia.

The news was probably received with mixed emotions. How could Phillip be happy when his oldest son, so very helpful and important to him, had decided to quit farming and walk out the door? Was there a backup plan for Phillip? He came from a long line of family farmers in which the eldest son inherited the farm. Would Nick, the next brother down the line, therefore be his successor? Phillip likely did not give any thought to the idea of his daughter Jean running the farm. It was a day when Phillip probably went for a long walk, maybe into a fallow field, searching for answers.

It was possible Phillip took one more stab at influencing others to help keep his dream of a happy retirement. It was alleged he sent a letter to the mill manager in Sinclair Mills. In it, he suggested this fellow Mike Andreeff was an unreliable sort who should be fired and sent back to the farm.[36] Apparently, Mike continued his employment at the mill.

The Canadian wake-up call

During the first half of the 1940s, Canada was an ally to the Soviet Union. Canada, like many Western allies, was providing the USSR with aid, supplies, and relief to assist them with the defeat of Germany. It turned out, to the public's amazement, that's not all Canadians were doing.

In September 1945, a cipher clerk at the Russian embassy in Ottawa, concerned about the possibility of a "third world war," walked out of his embassy with important documents and defected to Canada.[37]

Igor Gouzenko's story was validated by the documents he had spirited from Room 12 in the Russian embassy.[38] In the three years he lived in Ottawa, while working at the embassy, he observed Canadian life. He was stunned at the abundance of food available to ordinary Canadians. He noted other freedoms that a democracy provided people: freedom of the press, freedom of movement, freedom of speech, and most importantly to Igor, freedom to elect governments.

While making these observations, he understood his government was surreptitiously turning thousands of Canadians into espionage agents to help gain an advantage over its Western allies. Some Canadians, ideologically allied with the concept of communism, were passing intelligence to Soviet authorities. Mr. Gouzenko observed in his book, *This Was My Choice,* that it was incomprehensible to him how highly intelligent Canadians, having grown up in the freedom of democracy, could be won over to such a miserable, falsified political ideology as communism.[39] He further suggested this "fifth column" really needed to find out about the difference between theoretical communism as envisioned in Canada and how communism was practised in his homeland. Communist leader Vladimir Lenin is attributed with coining the best description of these people: "useful idiots."

In Gouzenko's book, he also states that the Kremlin has no humanitarian ideals or ethics regarding the use of biological weapons. The Kremlin knew then and knows to this day that this audacity is absolutely foreign to the democratic world.[40]

Before coming to Canada, Gouzenko was told, "Canada is a vast country sparsely populated and with almost unlimited resources. In recent years, and even since the start of World War II, the Party's success there has exceeded our most optimistic expectations. But there is still formidable opposition to overcome. As a softening measure, leading to complete demoralization before military action, the Party is concentrating on gaining control of labour unions..."[41]

Some at the time called Igor Gouzenko a hero. Others were not convinced. Their skepticism was based on the few numbers of spy convictions achieved in a court of law. Regardless of how history judges Mr. Gouzenko, he was one of the catalysts of the Cold War.

To a Russian immigrant like Mike, these revelations were more than worrisome. His family had already escaped from Russia to avoid such tyranny. This incident cast a long shadow of suspicion over all of his extended family. The Royal Canadian Mounted Police were watching all of them more closely.

Since his early days in the Lonesome Pine School, Mike had identified as a new Canadian. He was grateful to his new country and proudly loved being one of its citizens. Mike always did everything he could to exemplify being a good, honest, and loyal Canadian.

The roadmap to the middle class

The era of industrialism flourished with the end of the Second World War. There was a movement from subsistence farming to well-paying jobs with weekends off. This was the aim of many a young couple. Mike and Natalie, as she was now called, were also headed in this direction.

A beautiful country with lots of land and a smaller population than the US, Canada abounded with opportunities. Canada is for the most part a classless society and possesses a democratic ideology that rejects the historical class and power structures of Europe.[42] It does, however, offer better-paying opportunities in white-collar occupations.[43]

The town of Sinclair Mills provided job opportunities. Labouring jobs were typically eight hours of work per day for five days of the week. On weekends, people were free to do as they liked. But to a farm boy like Mike, this work was too easy. Also, it was monotonous. On the farm, one would multitask throughout the day, every day. At the sawmill, work was boringly repetitive: just do your job and collect your pay.

Adapting to the new work schedule took time. They often worked in loosely formed small groups, talking together at the same time as working. A topic of interest to Mike was discussion about a new pulp mill being planned in Port Alberni, on Vancouver Island. To Mike, this meant building. He was good at fixing and creating things, particularly out of metal. He wondered how Natalie would like another move, even farther away from Alberta.

They moved to the Valley, as the twin cities of Alberni and Port Alberni were often called, in the spring of 1946. Soon after, on June 23 at 10:15 AM, Vancouver Island experienced a magnitude seven earthquake.[44] It was the most destructive quake in the history of British Columbia. Natalie recalled that all they could do was to hold on to tree trunks to stay on their feet. Fortunately, their household suffered no significant damage.

Mike was hired as a welder for construction of the mill. Word of plentiful jobs moved swiftly: Mike was joined that year by two of his sisters and their spouses, and his brother soon followed. Names of friends and family from the farms included the Schischikowskys, Kalugins, Andreeffs, and Doumnoffs. Two more weddings in the family included Mike's sister Zina (Zinayeda), to Ross Clark, and his brother Nick, to Zoya Nasedkin, in July. Mike and Natalie built their second home in Alberni because they were starting their family.[45] Their daughter Kathleen was born on November 20, 1946.

The Bloedel, Stewart, and Welch partnership had secured large tracts of forests as a fibre source for their newly constructed kraft pulp mill. They merged with BC's former chief forester, H.R. MacMillan, who had similar timber holdings, creating one of BC's greatest companies, MacMillan Bloedel (MB).[46]

By 1948, the pulp mill construction was finished. If there is one thing the young Mike Andruff (formerly Andriev, Andreeff) knew, it was that he worked better for himself than for an employer. He had the same individualistic spirit of his forefathers. Rather than take a job at the new pulp mill, Mike talked to Natalie about striking out on their own. He said to her, "Let's go back to Hines Creek. Our families are there. We can build a business and live and work with the people we know. We can raise our family there with the help and support of our families."

He had just developed proficiency as a welder; Phillip had taught him how to use a forge. He proposed setting up a machine-shop business. He knew he had a ready market with northern Alberta farmers. If they moved back to Hines Creek, they could begin the next chapter of their lives with friends and family, in familiar surroundings. With the capital earned from the sale of their house in Alberni, and the savings collected from his well-paying job, Mike decided to start his own business. Prior to leaving the Alberni Valley, they received word that Mike's sister Fannie had married Louis Schischikowsky.

In spring 1949, Mike and Natalie returned to Alberta. They bought property in Hines Creek and constructed a machine shop with an adjacent small house.[47]

Andruff Iron Works

In 1949, Mike was a twenty-eight-year-old family man, a former refugee, farmer, naturalized Canadian, labourer, and welder. He was now planning to combine his skills to become a businessman, operating a machine shop in northern Alberta. His visionary business plan and figuring things out was crafted by the "seat of his pants" business-planning model. This risky approach to launching a business illustrated a can-do attitude that prevailed among many Albertans.

A major oil well, Leduc No. 1, was established in 1947 near the village of Leduc, after many failed attempts.[48] Its discovery put Alberta on the map as a major petroleum-producing world player. This unleashed a terrific economic boom, with companies searching for oil and natural gas in the Peace River country. When more discoveries occurred, the economy surged with oil company investments. Services for the oil and gas fields also drove local economies. Welding was key among them, and Mike found himself perfectly positioned to prosper in this new economy.[49]

Phillip Andreeff and his cohorts must have been confounded at the news of significant natural gas reserves existing below their farms. There was a certain irony, because they had heated their homes by arduously collecting wood for all those decades, unaware they were sitting on top of a better but untapped home heating alternative: natural gas.[50]

In his new business, Mike also repaired farm machinery. Tom Sideroff recalls, "Mike ran a super good business repairing machinery for farmers. The sign on his shop read Andruff Iron Works."[51]

A young cousin of Natalie's, Vic Sideroff, worked for Mike briefly. He recalls that Mike designed and built an automated root puller to clear land.[52] With his experience and insight into the needs of the farmer, he created efficient farm equipment.

Mike and Natalie were well liked in Hines Creek. Mike served his community on town council for several years. They both curled in the winter and played ball in the summer; Mike was a pitcher on the local ball team. In 1952, a second child was born. Their son, Michael Jr. (me!), arrived on March 5.

As the business grew more profitable, and with his family growing as well, Mike decided to build a proper house in town. In later years, Natalie was proudly heard to declare how she loved this beautiful house! It was the first home in the area to have hot and cold running water, an inside toilet, and a bathtub. If this was middle-class living, Mike and Natalie had certainly arrived.

Another change took place in 1952, one that signalled a widening of Canada's social safety net. The country's first universal old-age pension, Old Age Security, for people aged over seventy years, was implemented in January.[53] It paid four dollars a month (about forty dollars in 2022).

The only certainty in life

For many years, a newspaper called *Novoye Slovo* (meaning "New Word"—it contained Russian propaganda) was published in Berlin. The Old Brothers occasionally subscribed to it so they could read current stories about life in Russia. Reading about how things were back in Russia by comparison to their new home was a revelation. Validation of their choices always left them feeling good. However, this newspaper may have been scrutinized by local authorities as questionable reading material, given the Gouzenko findings.

Of course, the imperial Russia they had once known had been transformed into the Union of Soviet Socialist Republics (USSR). Social reforms under communism seemed bleak. The dictator Joseph Stalin was legendary for his controlling power over the masses. The Old Brothers were glad to be away from the USSR, wanting nothing to do with Stalin. Russian immigrants thanked their God every day that they were now Canadians.

By coincidence, my first birthday, March 5, 1953, was the day Joseph Stalin died. It was the end of a brutal era.

In 1953, another concerning event was unfolding. Phillip had cancer, and treatment necessitated leaving the farm. But any farm with animals needs attention daily, so Mike's sister Vi (Viola) came back from Port Alberni to help. Unlike in previous years, when medical services were unavailable, Phillip was being treated in Edmonton with the best medical practices available at the time. Ultimately, his illness progressed later in the year, and they made him as comfortable as possible at the Fairview Hospital. On Friday, October 2, 1953, Phillip succumbed to his illness.

He was a titan among the original Russian refugees. He had many life experiences: served a country in the First World War, farmed his whole life, strictly raised a God-fearing family, lived with lack and loss, and always excelled at leading an exemplary Christian life. And yet, his death was untimely at the age of sixty-five, leaving a big hole in his family. The family was grateful to have the Reverend Solovieff conduct his interment service.[54] They had come over together on the *Empress of Russia*, and Phillip valued their Russian Orthodox traditions and time together over the years. The extended family would have prayed over Phillip all weekend. His interment took place at the Holy Trinity Cemetery—the Gage cemetery his father had created. Now both Mike's grandfather and his father were gone.

It's commonly noted that the only certainties in life are death and taxes, but change is another notable certainty of life. As Nick had left the farm in 1950, no more sons were living on the farm to run it, so Phillip's wife, Elena, was left with the legacy of his estate. She received the whole estate, valued at $14,135 (roughly $140,000 in today's dollars). This included two quarter sections of land with appropriate structures, two horses, fifteen horned cattle, and twenty pigs.[55] She relied on her daughter Jean to keep the farm going.

Jean and Laurens Koyman married in 1954, had a family of five, and, with Elena, continued to live in the house built by Phillip on their farm so many years ago.

Jean worked the farm and Laurens took a job in town. As Jean mentioned in her account of how they managed their household, "Laurens worked outside the farm for almost thirty years just to keep the farm afloat."[56] But credit should also go to Jean. Through thick and thin, she kept the original homestead in the family and running.

In October of 1954, Fiena Andreeff was married to Ken McIntyre in a very impressive wedding. Her mother, Elena, and eldest brother, Mike, gave her away. The popular couple gathered 150 of their friends and family at Elena's home for a gala reception.[57] Unlike Fiena's brother Mike, who had an Orthodox wedding, Fiena and Ken chose St. Paul's United Church. This departure from the past was a continuing trend for these young first-generation Canadians.

The Andruff (Andriev, Andreeff) farming family had changed dramatically in thirty years. By 1954, all of Phillip and Elena's offspring were either married and/or had moved away from the farm. This was the evolution of not just the Andreeff (Andriev, Andreeff) family, but of many other farming families in a young Canadian nation.

MCMLV

The year 1955 was a pivotal year for Mike. His business was established. He had built a comfortable home, his fourth. He enjoyed being with his many relatives at family get-togethers. He still had his sisters Jean, Doreen, Fannie, and Fim living close by. He could visit his mom on the farm whenever he had free time. He could even pitch in at harvest time, if necessary.

On April 30, Mike and Natalie had their third child, daughter Laurie. They were now a family of five. Child-minding was Natalie's job in the family. She had not worked outside the home since they had married. With a newborn, plus myself, aged three, and Kathleen now a nine-year-old, she had her hands full.

Natalie did have help. Her niece, Vera Sidoroff (daughter of her brother Sam), was fourteen years old. Vera had been living with the Andruffs so she could go to school more easily than by commuting from her parents' farm. She was a helpful babysitter on weekdays, and on weekends, Natalie drove her to the farm to stay with her family. Vera and Natalie had a very caring relationship. Life in the Sidoroff household could occasionally get heavy-handed. Natalie knew Vera's best interests were served by living in a safer family setting. It was Vera who nicknamed me Muka-shoe. Vera said I always seemed to be without one of my shoes when she cared for me, and I am told I pronounced my name as Muka, hence Muka-shoe.

A happy event was the high school graduation of Mike's sister Doreen. Few Andreeffs had finished high school. Sister Fiena was the first in 1952, and Doreen was the last of the family to accomplish this feat.

Family superstitions

In farm life, everything had to be explained. Due to the lack of science at the time, the Bible and fear were two typical foundations for superstitions, untrue explanations for certain events that have happened or will happen. Someone in heaven is sending a message, and because fear of death is common, it will likely be a bad message.

Vera had learned from my grandmother Elena that on the morning of August 4, a black bird flew into a window on the farm.[58] Could this be a message from Phillip or Gregori? Was it a bad omen? What should one make of this message? One should tread very lightly this day.

August 4, 1955

That Thursday was planned as a sleep-in day. Later the same day, Mike and Natalie had also planned family time and were going to the Sports Day Fair at the Waterhole Oldtimers' fairgrounds south of Fairview. Farmers typically had their country fairs in August because September was harvesting season. Mike, being a baseball player himself, looked forward to watching a local ball tournament. At thirty-four years old, and with the demands of running his business and raising a family, his playing time had diminished to mostly watching now.

Vera could handle baby Laurie until she was taken to Baba Palagaya (her maternal grandmother) for child-minding. The other kids, and Mike and Natalie, could enjoy a leisurely start to the day. After breakfast, Mike put on his "going to a party" black-and-pink shirt and then decided to head to the shop to see if his employee had everything under control.

Just before noon, Mike, Natalie, Kathleen, Vera, and I settled into Mike's 1952 black Pontiac and headed to the fair. Before going to the fairgrounds, Mike and Natalie stopped at the local beer parlour. Vera and Katheen took me to the restaurant for treats. We kids were all looking forward to pony rides, a Ferris wheel, concessions, horse races, and the baseball games.

After having some rides, we went to an area inside the racetrack to watch baseball. We had watched two games when Natalie suggested we go back into Fairview for a break. It was common for Mike and Natalie to socialize at the local beer parlour. Again, they left the kids in the restaurant.

They returned to the midway at the fairgrounds about 5:30 PM. They decided Mike and I would go to the baseball field to get an update on the games, and the girls would wait for us at the midway. Once we returned, Natalie would take everyone home, and Mike would stay to watch more of the tournament.

When we returned, Mike asked where Natalie had gone. Vera thought she had gone to the restroom. He asked Vera and Kathleen to watch me until Natalie returned and went off to watch more baseball.[59]

A horse race had begun.

I was a three-year-old boy, similar in age to Nikifor standing for his picture in Wetaskiwin those thirty-odd years earlier. Like Nikifor, I had few thoughts about my day. I no doubt knew one thing, though: I wanted to be with my dad at that moment.

In an instant, I was trailing behind, following Mike, who was almost across the racetrack.

"Get that kid off the track!" the race announcer exclaimed.

Of the thousands in attendance, no one had time to move a muscle.

Life sometimes finds a person at the intersection of destiny and fate. One can choose a direction, but each choice determines the price paid. Such was the case for Mike on this afternoon.

Everything he saw around him went into slow motion. He stopped in his tracks while glancing over his shoulder. His senses took over. He could feel the vibration of the four thundering stallions streaking forward—pound, pound, pound, pound, pound. He could smell the sweat from the horses as they closed in. Turning back, he saw his little son, directly in their path!

Adrenaline shot through his body. Every muscle and sinew heaved Mike toward his son to save him from certain death.

Vic Sideroff recounted, "I was at the Waterhole that day. I didn't see the accident, but I heard what sounded like an explosion."[60] Vera Sidoroff explained she had not seen the accident either, but she heard a collective and emotional gasp from the stands. Kathleen recalls that while looking through the aperture of the fence, she saw a black-and-pink shirt spinning, as if in the spin cycle of the washing machine.[61]

A pall descended on the crowd. Two bodies lay irregularly in silence on the racetrack, like rag dolls. Witnesses to the accident were frozen in silence. I am told that after a long pause, I started screaming. Someone from the crowd approached to comfort me. People started murmuring.

"We need a doctor!"

"We need an ambulance!"

"Someone, help them!"

Mike's heroic choice had been to save his son's life. He could have done nothing, but he instinctively chose his son's life over his own. The cost of his choice became his fate.

The event managers didn't foresee the need for emergency support at the outset of the fair. What could possibly go wrong? Unlike current times, it was not common practice to have a first-aid post or medical officers standing by for the people attending the fair, the fair's invitees. It took some time to organize the emergency care needed for the critical injuries sustained.

At approximately 7 PM that evening, my dad and I were wheeled into the Fairview Hospital. The attending physician, Dr. Letts, suddenly had his hands full. My ankle was broken.

As he triaged his cases, Dr. Letts had immediate concerns for Mike. He said, "Nurse, put this man in the operating room, stat!" Mike was comatose and unresponsive. In fact, his heart stopped on the examination table. He was technically dead. At this point it was clear that if Mike was to survive, something needed to be done. One of the nurses had just trained in cardiopulmonary resuscitation (CPR). She resuscitated Mike. Mike was a strong man at this stage of his life, and he responded with a revived heartbeat.

By Saturday, Dr. Letts decided Mike needed more advanced treatment, and Mike, along with Natalie, was flown in a chartered plane to Edmonton and the University Hospital. Mike's sister Fannie said she remembered going to the Grand Prairie airport to see her brother before he flew to Edmonton.[62] Fannie said, "I didn't know if this might be the last time I saw my brother Mike alive."

The August 11, 1955, edition of the *Fairview Post* reported Mike was "under the care of a brain specialist; and reports are he is suffering from fractured ribs and head injuries, along with paralysis of his right arm and leg. Definite seriousness of injuries is not known, but doctors say he will live."[63]

The Tuesday bus

The report of Mike Andruff's grievous injuries shocked and saddened the community. Natalie's cousin Tom Sideroff wrote, "In 1955, our community was shocked with the sad news that Mike Andruff was seriously hurt by racing horses at a rodeo. A tragedy to a nice person saddened everyone. People living in small towns care about each other, a lot."[64]

Vicki Lomax (Natalie's cousin, formerly Vera Sidoroff) wrote, "Your Dad's (Mike's) tragic accident. It's like yesterday for me. I can remember the heartache, we all suffered."[65]

Grief-stricken, emotionally exhausted, and physically drained, Natalie returned home four days later. She wanted to collect her family, hug them, and hold them. I sported a cast on my ankle and I needed plucking up by my mother. She struggled to explain what happened to Dad. These times were exceedingly difficult for the young Andruff family.

Natalie, at thirty-four years old, found her life existed somewhere between despair and hopelessness. She hadn't slept for days. The shock of the accident still weighed heavily on her. Mike had always been there for her. He was her golden boy. Her reality now frightened her. She was a mother to three young children, didn't have an income to support them, and had a disabled husband soon to return home from the hospital.

She was alone. Was she reaping what she had sown in her past relationships with friends and family? She received many well wishes and kind thoughts, but no one was there for her. Women of lesser character, faced with Natalie's prospects, may have thrown up their hands and left town, leaving it all behind her. To Natalie's credit, she accepted her plight. She decided to deal with her challenges head on, one day at a time.

The *Fairview Post* revealed several days later that Natalie had returned "to transact the selling of his [Mike's] business establishment in Hines Creek, the Andruff Iron Works." Given the serious extent of Mike's injuries, their lifestyle as they knew it ended.

The road of helplessness

After six weeks in University Hospital in Edmonton, Mike returned home to Hines Creek. He was a pitiful sight. He wore a steel leg brace on his right leg. His right arm was in a sling. He needed a wheelchair to get around. He also needed a great deal of care and attention. For those who knew Mike in his prime, this was an unfathomable circumstance.

MIKE'S LOT WAS akin to that of a war-damaged refugee. If he wanted to apply for immigration under these circumstances, he would have been denied entry to Canada. It was not until 2018 that Canada recognized a more inclusive policy for persons with disabilities.

His therapists said he needed movement to get better. He needed to learn to stand. He had to move his paralyzed arm.

A workout room was fashioned in their living room. It consisted of parallel bars to use for standing and walking, and ropes and pulleys to aid movement for his arm.

People who came by the house to help didn't realize Mike had become addicted to morphine. "I need my morphine!" he would shout to Natalie in the early morning hours. Pain relief on a protracted basis can cause reliance on medication. In this case, the morphine was administered by a local nurse. Mike had up and down moments during the day, but his shouting, pleading, and screaming through the night had everyone on edge. "I need my morphine!" Natalie did what she could to help him deal with his pain. This intense time in their family life took a toll on all of them, particularly Natalie.

Universal health care did not arrive in Alberta until 1957.[66] It cost Mike $1,356 in medical expenses to aid his recovery.[67] This represented over three months of wages he did not have. The life insurance policy Mike had earlier possessed had sadly lapsed in June. By his own inattention to the small detail of renewing his policy, he was not insurable for his injury.

With winter approaching, Mike and Natalie discussed the notion of living where the climate was warmer. Mike said, "Natalie, you know

I can barely stand with this brace on my leg. A little bit of slick ice and I'll be down like a rock. Unlike you, I don't have two arms to break my fall." The ice and snow would be much too hazardous for Mike's physical mobility. They remembered their experience with the milder Port Alberni weather. It did rain a lot, but at least they wouldn't have to shovel it. There were also more opportunities and better-paying jobs, and Mike had family there. They decided to sell their house in Hines Creek and move to Port Alberni. Elmer Low, a local, purchased the shop.[68]

To save on moving costs, an auction of all household effects took place. In keeping with their current spate of bad luck, all their possessions went for a song or were simply abandoned. Additionally, Mike did a lot of his work for farmers on credit, with payment promised at harvest time. Sadly, making collections was not possible, given the circumstances.

Their finances were in a shambles.

The little choices made in life can be so trivial—sitting for another beer, going to watch a baseball game, or just taking a minute more for some little distraction. But fate can use little choices to make big differences in life's outcomes. Mike had lived a good life; he didn't deserve to be handcuffed by fate. And yet, fortunate to still be alive, new challenges in life awaited him in Port Alberni.

As the Pontiac pulled out of Hines Creek, tears were shed by all connected with their misfortune.

CHAPTER 4

THE PORT ALBERNI YEARS: 1956-67

IT WAS LIKE moving to another country, from Alberta's flat prairie land to the trees and mountains covering British Columbia in all directions. The mountain passes and the Fraser Valley segment of the Trans-Canada Highway were downright scary to some prairie people. Mike and Natalie didn't need their passports, but British Columbia was a completely different kettle of fish compared to Alberta. It was the mountains versus the wheat fields.

Travelling up the Island Highway, the Pontiac had just crested the giant Beaufort Mountain Range, the spine of Vancouver Island. Although their map did not show it, they were driving toward the lands of the Tseshaht and Hupačasath First Nations, now known as the Alberni Valley. As the Pontiac motored down into the valley, they could see some of the large Sproat Lake off in the distance, a sign that they were nearing the town of Port Alberni. The "smell of money" assaulted visitors' noses on arrival in the town in the form of gaseous sulfur compounds. The horrible smell was caused by stinky emissions, much like rotten eggs, pumped into the atmosphere from the local pulp mill.

At the time of Mike and Natalie's arrival, two towns existed in the Valley, Alberni and Port Alberni. They were recognized as twin cities.

History of the land

The Tseshaht and Hupačasath Nations have owned the land in the Valley for thousands of years.[1]

Since the Royal Proclamation of 1763, the British Crown had recognized Indigenous title to land in the Dominion of Canada. The Crown's policy was to allow only the Crown to acquire land from Indigenous Peoples, and only by treaty. The land east of the Rocky Mountains had been acquired by treaties.

Up until 1854, James Douglas, who at the time was working for the Hudson Bay Company, was directed to purchase, under treaties, small portions of Indigenous lands, primarily around Victoria, on the southern end of Vancouver Island. Later, when he was governor of British Columbia before it joined Confederation, he did not have sufficient funds and his British overseers were not committing British taxpayers' money to continuing the treaty purchases. Douglas decided individual Indigenous people could participate in the affairs of the new colony in a fashion equal to that of the settlers. This decision, while serving as a makeshift solution, gave colonists tacit approval to use unceded land, but it was untenable for the Indigenous people, who were often displaced from their land by the colonists. Perhaps a fuller consultation with First Nations may have yielded a better result. Instead, First Nations' title and the inherent rights of Indigenous people were ignored by the pioneer settlers.[2]

The colonization of Vancouver Island led to the Island's Indigenous Peoples losing their rights to their land. Colonists shared the view that "the betterment of humankind lay not in harmony with nature but in its conquest and transformation."[3]

After Douglas's retirement as governor of Vancouver Island and British Columbia in 1864, there was a stark change in policy to reflect the conviction that "the Indians have no right to the lands they claim..."[4]

BC's Chief Commissioner of Lands and Works Joseph Trutch represented the new view of the settlers. Through his efforts, when British Columbia entered Confederation in 1871, BC negotiated a deal for the Dominion Government Indian agents to manage Indigenous interests. Reserves, the forced removal of Indigenous children from their families and placement into residential schools, and complete indifference to Indigenous rights, culture, needs, and land entitlement in BC became the order of the day.

For decades, this injustice has been without remedy. Unlike the rest of Canada which allows the federal government to represent the Crown, the British Columbian government represents the Crown's interest. It determines the use of the land, rights to minerals, and use of the water. However, the dawn of a new era is forthcoming. First Nations *have never ceded their land to the Crown*. It is now recognized that the relationship between the Crown and First Nations has been inappropriate in British Columbia. Most governmental meetings in BC these days start with an acknowledgement of gathering on the traditional, ancestral, and unceded territory of the First Nation (usually stating the name of the Nation) appropriate to the location in question). Social justice for Indigenous Peoples is slow in coming; however, errors in previous decades are being recognized.

Indigenous people have a unique place in Canada. Their customs and traditions must be respected and valued, as with any other nation. The reconciliation of Indigenous interests with the interests of contemporary British Columbians is a vital process and over time will correct the injustices of the past. It is a process all parties are required to engage in for successful and peaceful outcomes. Through the report of the British Columbia Claims Task Force, all parties have committed to a six-stage process for the negotiation of modern-day treaties. It will take time, but the past wrongs will be addressed.[5]

Some may question why I have included this discussion as part of this story. It should be clear that people being displaced from their land and being directed to a place they don't want to be is akin to the plight of the refugee. The colonists acted no differently than self-aggrandized autocrats. Acknowledging this will be difficult for some, but the fact remains that the British Columbian colonists were wrong in their actions.

The history of the twin towns of Alberni and Port Alberni goes back to the 1860s, when British pioneers began to settle here. Captain Edward Stamp, representing James Thomson and Company from England, negotiated a land deal with Governor James Douglas to provide for a settlement and timber rights in the Alberni Valley. In return, the Anderson sawmill was built.[6]

Later, in 1905, a successor company, the Anderson Land Company, moved forward to develop its holdings in the valley. For settlers in most of Canada, land was offered in quarter-section sizes of 160 acres per lot, as in the Prairie provinces. The means of purchasing this land was quite different in BC, however. The land was bought at $1 per acre, or $160 down. In addition, improvements had to be made, and additional payment at $2.50 per acre, or $400, was payable over a five-year period.[7] This was a far cry from the $10 Phillip and the other immigrants paid for their quarter sections in Alberta.

The settlement also included a townsite. Street grids were laid out in both Alberni and Port Alberni. Lot sizes were substantially reduced to city-sized lots, for a home and a yard.

Port Alberni was touted as the closest Canadian shipping port to the Panama Canal. The city's board of trade of the day hoped to build grain elevators in Port Alberni to receive grain from the prairies, like the shipments of grain sent east to the Great Lakes. Regrettably, in 1914, the federal government decided in favour of Vancouver as the site for the grain elevators.[8]

Also in 1914, the ill-fated *Komagata Maru* had a brush with a potential docking in the Alberni Inlet. Two Sikh gentlemen passed through the valley trying to contact the ship by wireless from Bamfield before it entered Canadian waters. They thought that if Victoria and Vancouver denied disembarkation, maybe Port Alberni could be used instead. In the end, the captain of the boat was unaware that Port Alberni was a viable port of entry to Canada, and he continued on to Vancouver where, as anticipated, they were denied entry.[9]

The last major notable event in Port Alberni in 1914, the year the First World War broke out, was the daring feat of one Baron Alvo von Alvensleben. He and his syndicate of German investors had their eyes on the property and land holdings of the Red Cliff Company in the Alberni Valley. Red Cliff was owned by an American syndicate of lumber manufacturers, the Red Cliff Land and Lumber Company of Duluth, Minnesota. The timber rights were for the best timber on Vancouver Island. The deal also included property with a deep-sea wharf. Both the provincial government and the British government were convinced the property was being purchased by the German Empire to serve as their North Pacific naval base. The Germans were focused on world domination. This deal reflected the long term planning considered to attain this goal. The BC government did not allow the deal to go through as planned once war broke out in Europe.[10]

Coincidentally, at the time of this event, Mike's father, Phillip, and his good friend Peter Sidoroff were riding the Trans-Siberian railway west to fight on the German Eastern Front.

Buy some land

Mike, Natalie, and the early community in general did not concern themselves with these details of the past. Again, it is interesting to note Mike's family were oppressed people who lost their land to a Communist regime, yet here in British Columbia, another oppressed people, the First Nations, had lost their land to BC's colonization and the capitalist system.

The young, less politically sensitive Andruff family had more pressing interests than thinking about the past: they needed shelter and a livelihood. Their savings were meagre. As it turned out, however, they had enough savings to purchase a small home on David Street in Alberni.

Part of Mike and Natalie's plan was working. While staying with Vi and Sam Kalugin in Beaver Creek (a neighborhood district of Alberni), Mike organized a renovation to accommodate his family. By returning to the Alberni Valley, they received vital support from family members who already lived there to help get them started. Mike's sister Vi and her husband, Sam, and his brother Nick and his wife, Zoya, were both well established in the community with their families. Mike and Natalie hoped to find jobs in the robust forest economy of the Valley. Natalie initially worked at the local drugstore and later secured a job in the food services department of the West Coast General Hospital. Still convalescing, Mike was unable to obtain employment at this time. His therapeutic exercises helped him to regain his ability to walk in a fashion, but his right foot still dragged with each step. He had developed more mobility, but sadly, his right arm never did respond to therapy: it remained limp for the rest of his life.

The family vacation back to the farm

In the summer of 1956, roughly a year after the accident, Mike and Natalie took a family car trip back to the farm. They travelled in a British-made automobile, an Austin 30. It was a compact vehicle, but they managed to squeeze in all their personal items plus camping gear. Not expecting adverse conditions in the summer months, they were surprised by a snowstorm while camping in their tent near the Columbia Icefields. The roads then flooded, which affected their car. These types of things make family vacations unforgettable, even laughable, but much later!

Once in the Peace River district, they visited all their relatives: the Schischikowskys in Worsley; the McIntyres and Sidoroffs in Hines Creek; and the Koymans and Elena on the farm. They even had time to attend sister Doreen's wedding. She was marrying Lawrence Calvert, affectionately known as Tuffy.

Mike had to do two things not related to family visits. He finalized the sale of the Hines Creek home, and he talked to several people who saw the accident. He asked them to give evidence as witnesses. The proceeds for the home sale were to be used for his lawyer's retainer. Mr. N.C. Willson, who two years earlier had drawn up Phillip's will, was engaged to handle Mike's negligence case against the Waterhole Oldtimers' Association. Mike relied on his legal advice.

Mike's financial situation resulting from the accident was dire. He believed the operators of the fairgrounds were negligent because they did not use reasonable safety protections like bunting on the fencing, which could have prevented his life-changing accident.

While Mike had hoped he would be well supported in his legal case by family and friends, he had an uneasy sense that some seemed to offer less than enthusiastic support. The Waterhole Oldtimers' Association had a long history and strong community support. Some in the community viewed the couple's conduct on the day of the accident as irresponsible.

Natalie had relatives who were cynical of her conduct. Some already viewed her as an irresponsible mother. Rather than their dwelling on her weakness for alcohol and their criticism of her failings, she could have used their compassion and their help to lift her up. Sadly, those who could have been most helpful looked the other way. Empathy, the cornerstone of emotional intelligence, had not yet emerged in some people's self-awareness.

Before Mike and the family left northern Alberta, he was greeted with some promising news. He was contacted directly by a member of the Association who indicated that yes, he would vouch that Mike's allegations had merit. He further mentioned he was aware of a Mr. Ritchie, formerly of Berwyn, now living in Kelowna, who had filmed the race during which the accident happened. That film, he contended, would corroborate Mike's contention of negligence by the Association.[11] This helpful information was forwarded to Mike's lawyer, Mr. Willson. Mike had hoped, naively, that the trial would take place after the farmers' harvest time in the fall. His statement of claim was not submitted to the Supreme Court of Alberta until November 14, 1956, over a year after the accident.

The David Street years

Renovations at the home on David Street in Alberni were completed by the family upon their return from Alberta. The house would be well suited for the family's requirements. It was situated a block and

THE PORT ALBERNI YEARS: 1956-67

a half from Alberni Elementary School. A soon-to-be-built shopping plaza would be two and a half blocks away. Next to the shopping plaza was St. Andrew's United Church, which became the family church. Mike's brother Nick and his family lived on Margaret Street, about four blocks away. By all accounts, this was a good family home in a convenient location.

Playmates for me and my sister Kathleen lived on the same block, and a reliable babysitter for Laurie, Granny Fletcher, lived across the street.

The community lacked recreational facilities in those days but had numerous organizations and clubs in which to engage socially. The true amenities were the great outdoors: fishing in the Somass River; swimming at Paper Mill Dam or in Sproat Lake and viewing the petroglyphs; and hiking Mount Arrowsmith or along Kitsuksis Creek.

It rained a great deal, except for the summer months. The Beaufort Mountain Range stopped the clouds from passing over this part of Vancouver Island, making the Valley a natural repository for buckets and buckets of rain. Rubber boots, a waterproof jacket, and an umbrella were important for staying dry on walks to and from school.

The year of 1957 was a big one for the local economy. Two new paper machines were under construction for MacMillan Bloedel, as was a nearby junior high school named A.W. Neill.[12]

Now thirty-six, Mike was the same age as Phillip had been when the family had started life over in Homeglen. Mike, too, was forced to start over once more. His young family was counting on him. He had his deficits. He was no longer a labourer. He had limited mobility. He lacked education, and his work experience was no longer applicable. He had to rely on his wits now. He had to think like a grandmaster chess player, three moves ahead. Drawing on his relationships from his previous work at the pulp mill, Mike gained employment with the mill expansion, managing rentals and parts supplies on the project.

It had taken Mike a year to find employment after the accident. He was stressed about his lack of employability. He had never asked for financial help, not one nickel, because he was independently minded, just like those prairie farmers in Homeglen.

With his relatives and former colleagues at the pulp mill offering much-needed support his plan to find employment had succeeded. But in his personal life, things were difficult. The previous year had been ruinous in terms of his relationship with Natalie; the couple had their issues behind the scenes. The family's finances were bruised, and so was Natalie. Relying solely on Natalie's earnings the previous year had proved unsustainable. Natalie was troubled with the stress of being the breadwinner for the family, in addition to providing all the home care to Mike over the last year and a half. Consequently, she was smoking and drinking above and beyond acceptable norms. The children would hear loud arguments in Russian; these signalled mayhem was soon to follow.

Mike was dealing with several stressors himself. He was determined to follow through his lawsuit against the Waterhole Oldtimers' Association for negligence. By this time, the Association had retained the firm of Friedman, Lieberman and Newson. They filed a statement of defence dated January 21, 1957. Their statement denied any wrongdoing on the part of the Association. Additionally, Mike's medical costs, home renovation costs, and the cost of feeding and clothing three kids were overwhelming. He, too, was hitting the bottle a little more frequently. It is cold comfort to know that many a young family in the Valley coped with finances in the same way as the Andruffs—hence the numerous beer parlours in the community, including the King Edward, the Somass, the Beaufort, the Barkley, and the Arlington. They became social centres for the many down on their luck.

The kids

We kids lived in a different world from our parents, thankfully. Kathleen (Kay) attended the A.W. Neill Junior High School. I started school at Alberni Elementary, while Laurie, too young to be in school, was cared for by Granny Fletcher. The kids on the block and in the surrounding area played together, playing games like British bulldog; knock, knock; ginger; hide and go seek; Chinese jump rope; double

Dutch jump rope; hopscotch; and the telephone game.[13] Sometimes we invented our own games. Those heavy, heavy rains happened frequently in the fall and winter, so we played board games or card games in our play time. In summer season, we enjoyed an outdoor pool, and next to the elementary school there was a park with a wading pool. In those days unsupervised wading pools were not forbidden by health laws. This is where late one summer night, having the pool all to myself, I taught myself to swim: it was a night to either learn to swim or drown.

In the summer, we camped at the Edgewater Resort in Parksville. This resort featured a long tidal beach that was a great adventure land for beachcombing and sandcastle building. At the time, oysters could be collected from the beach. We would usually eat those for breakfast.

In the fall, the Valley residents enjoyed the Alberni Valley Fall Fair at the exhibition grounds. The fair was lots of fun and not to be missed! It included fun rides for the kids at the midway, 4-H exhibits and contests, prizes, merchants' stalls, and service displays. It was always several fun days of community engagement.

At Christmas, the kids were entertained at the annual Christmas party for kids put on by Mike's fraternal organization, the Independent Order of Foresters.

Mike's brother Nick and his family were close by, and the two families visited together often. A typical Sunday meant kids playing softball in the backyard in the afternoon while the women made a favoured Russian food, *pelmeni* (dumplings), for supper. It was always a game among the kids to see who ate the most. After dinner, sometimes Nick would give the young boys a haircut, the bowl cut in fashion at the time, with his electric clippers as they sat in a chair in the middle of the kitchen. The last pleasure of the evening was gathering everyone in the living room to watch the *Ed Sullivan Show*.

While this idealistic portrayal of family life might have seemed normal on the surface, at home the reality was woeful.

Kay's approach was to distance herself from home because of its dysfunctional nature. She did experience domestic violence first-hand, occasionally sporting a shiner. It was not that she did anything wrong; it was more likely that, as a teenager, she was beginning to assert herself.

I immersed myself in sports and was often out of the house. However, I was not immune from "the buckle." I recall two strappings from Mike.

The quiet one had it the worst: Laurie experienced loneliness, abandonment, abuse, and depravity. Neither her brother, three years older than her, nor her sister, eight years older, were at home to care for her. Before attending school, she was passed from babysitter to babysitter. Once in school, she nurtured and valued her friendships with those on David Street. (One friendship lasted sixty-five years, until her friend's death.) But she often was home alone, frightened, and sad. More than any others, Laurie was Mike's right hand. He relied on her to help him on all his projects around the house.

A parent's duty is to care for and keep a child safe. Laurie's parents abrogated this fundamental responsibility. She was repeatedly left alone and placed at high risk in a world that exploited such vulnerability.

Laurie's saddest day happened when she was ten years old. Her mother needed money, so she took Laurie's two-wheeled bike, her only means of freedom, and despite Laurie's protestations, sold it. "My bike kept me in touch with my dear friends in my old neighbourhood. Without it, I was cut off from them," says Laurie.

"As the years went on, my understanding of my life and my family became clearer. I wondered if my parents' behaviour was a result of their upbringing, their struggles, their parents, genetics, or was it because they were simply bad parents. They could have been good people, but maybe should not have had children."[14]

Justice delayed is justice denied

Mike was relying on his lawyer and the Canadian justice system to prove his accident was a result of negligence on the part of the owners of the fairground, while the Waterhole Oldtimers' Association was relying on their lawyers to prove he was a trespasser.

From 1956 to late 1959, the case was delayed. After the statement of defence was filed in January 1957, there was no further action for over a year. The case was next to be heard in Grande Prairie by Judge Greschuk in May 1958, but the judge was assigned elsewhere at the last minute.[15] Finally, in September 1959, more than four years after the accident, the case was scheduled to be heard in front of a justice of the Supreme Court, the Honourable Neil Primrose, in Edmonton.

The proof of negligence requires that if there is a contract between a body charging a price for use of its facility and a person pays the price for usage, then there is a duty of care owed by this body to its invitees. If that duty is breached in some manner and damage is incurred, then negligence exists.

In his statement of claim, Mike, the plaintiff, sought general and specific damages of some $51,000.[16] Now, Mike had a very limited education. He relied upon his lawyer to steer him professionally through the subtleties of the law. He did have concerns about the quality of service he was receiving from his lawyer. Why was hearing the case taking so long? What was his lawyer doing to ensure proper evidence was being collected? Mike had other concerns as well. He heard that some Oldtimers and their lawyer, Mr. Friedman, had viewed the alleged film of the accident. But it was not available for his lawyer, Mr. Willson, to view; it was now alleged to have been destroyed.

Expenses were piling up as time passed. Now living in Alberni, Mike had to pay for getting all his witnesses to Edmonton in addition to paying the costs of his legal team. The witness who supported Mike's allegations of negligence and supplied the details of the film was not available, because Mike could not cover his costs to testify. Another blow to his case was having to change his lawyer for his day in court. Gone was Mr. Willson. It is unclear whether fees or other considerations were the cause for this change. Mike was now represented by Mr. J.R. Dunne and Mr. G. Forbes. Had this been a case of a David versus Goliath? A country lawyer out of his element versus a savvy downtown insurance legal team?

Justice Primrose heard the evidence and listened to the case law for the plaintiff. He also considered the defence's arguments, that Mr. Andruff was not in fact an invitee but a trespasser on the property. In his decision, the judge placed responsibility solely on Mike for his misfortune because he did not properly care for his child.

In concluding his judgment, Justice Primrose found for the defence and denied the plaintiff's claim with costs, including discovery (costs associated with determining each parties' arguments). The judge qualified his judgment, saying if he erred in law, he would assess damages at $23,000.[17] This latter step is used in the case of an Appeal of the Decision. It is fair to say Mike had no financial ability whatsoever to consider any further litigation. He would have to accept the court's decision, with no appeal. Disappointingly, he had to let go of any further reliance on the justice system of Canada.

The costs were significant for Mike, but so, too, was the trauma for his daughter Kathleen. As a twelve-year-old, it was burdensome for her to give testimony at the trial. This alone was a traumatic event, yet she had also witnessed first-hand her father damaged in a tragic accident. The trial forced her to revisit a very painful time in her life. Her pain and suffering as a young person were beyond what anyone should have had to bear at such a tender age.

The power to choose

No matter what life throws at a person, they always have the power to choose how to react. For Mike, with his legal, financial, personal, and marital issues roiling in his head, his choice was therapeutic... to build a boat.

Incredulous-sounding as it was, particularly with the recent failure of the lawsuit and his physical deficits, Mike announced to his family in 1960 that he had decided to build a twenty-four-foot, inboard-powered, cabin cruiser. One of Mike's greatest personal losses was his ability to create with his hands as he had done in his welding shop. This project was his own personal challenge to come back from his sense of loss.

He enlisted his brother Nick to join him in his project. Nick lived on Margaret Street, and the large warehouse they rented for this project was just a few doors down from his house. So, meeting at "the shed," as they called it, became an evening ritual.

It is possible that his employment with Alberni Engineering had a bearing on this choice of an outlet. (Alberni Engineering built boats. They had hired Mike after a lengthy bout of unemployment to care for their parts department.)

Mike's craftsmanship was uncanny for a left-handed right-hander. His technique was to use clamps to hold fast pieces while he worked on them. Nick also lent his skills, and together they made a good team. They applied the planking to the hull after soaking it in water. This gave the bow of the boat its attractive curves.

Day after day for over a year, the brothers toiled on this project. They had obviously learned a lot of woodworking skills from their father. He would have been rightly proud of his sons' finished work. Just as the neighbours in Homeglen had come by to view Phillip's work with his axe, Mike and Nick also had their share of Alberni neighbors coming by to marvel at their craftsmanship. Their labour of love could only rightly bear one name, their mother's, Elena. The *Elena* was to ply the waters of the Somass River and the Alberni Inlet for several years. When Nick later moved to Saltair, near Chemainus, BC, with his MacMillan Bloedel transfer, the boat was moved to an open-water mooring next to his property. *Elena* was eventually sold to the brother of my school chum Ray Parks. It was renamed *Dewitis* and moved to the valley's Sproat Lake.[18]

The brothers invited all the family and their friends to use the boat. Their brother-in-law Sam Kalugin loved to fish with them in the Somass River.

It turned out that the timing of Mike's project coincided with a boom in Alberni and Port Alberni's economies. The unionized forestry workers in the Valley had wages comparable to those in Canada's highly paid auto industry, among the highest paid in the country.[19] While Mike's work was not directly tied to forestry, if MacMillan Bloedel was booming, the Valley's economy was booming. Times were improving again.

CANADIAN IMMIGRATION DURING this time was starting to turn away from overt racial discrimination in its selection practices. In 1962, new regulations looked at independent immigrants being admitted according to their skills and means of support, without regard to national origins.[20] Port Alberni was seeing its share of international workers as the community opened its doors widely to seek teachers, retail clerks, journeymen, and administrators.

The TV era

It started with the kids spending a lot of time at the neighbours' homes. It quickly became clear that the more affluent homes were buying televisions. Everyone was keen on viewing the news and entertainment offered on the set. In the earliest days of television in Canada, shows were intermittently scheduled through the day. One or two shows, including kids' shows, were available to view in the morning, and some news shows later in the day. In between the morning and evening programs, the TV screen showed a test pattern, which in the mid-1950s was a picture of an Indigenous chief in full headdress regalia. Seeing this test pattern at least demonstrated the antenna was working!

As is often the case in a small town, every family just had to have one. The Andruffs were no exception: whether they could afford it or not, the family had to keep up with their neighbours.

The Phillips console-box TV arrived on its metal stand from Jowsey's Furniture and Appliances in the early sixties. (Black-and-white was the only option for TVs then.) In the days before cable was available, reception could be quite sporadic, and the only way to adjust it was to reposition the rabbit-ears antennae on top of the TV or the roof of the house. In the early years in the Valley, only two channels were available: the Canadian channel CBUT and the American channel KVOS, out of Bellingham. Remote controls had not been invented yet, so a trip to the set was required to change channels or control the volume—quite a different experience from today.

Every Saturday, the kids watched *Bugs Bunny* cartoons just before the *Hockey Night in Canada* broadcast at 5 PM. My mom and I rooted for the Montreal Canadiens, whereas Mike and Laurie were Toronto Maple Leaf fans. Kathleen (Kay) was often out with friends, so she was not focused on sports at this time of her life.

Hockey was and still is Canada's national game, almost as powerful as a religion. Back then it even had its own hymn, the "Hockey Song," sung by the Canadian legend Stompin' Tom Connors.

Everyone had an opinion on the teams. Who were the best players? Who started that fight? Who would win the Stanley Cup? After the telecast, it was common for the keenest fans to drive over to the rink in Port Alberni and watch the senior men's hockey team, the Port Alberni Luckies, play their weekly game. The local team went so far as to recruit players of good quality by rewarding them with well-paying jobs at the paper mill. It felt like the whole town showed up, as each game was packed to the rafters with fans.

November 22, 1963, brought terrible news to the Valley and to everyone around the world who saw the events play out that day on their TVs. Schools and businesses suddenly closed just after noon. Everyone was sent home, and all eyes were turned to their TVs, trying to learn and understand what was happening in Dallas, Texas. The shooting of John F. Kennedy was a seminal moment for viewers as they witnessed the assassination of an American president and its aftermath. Viewers were left to ponder how such a bright, young, promising leader could be cut down in the prime of his life. His wife, Jacqueline, described his presidency as a brush with Camelot, quoting from the musical of the same name.[21]

Television had created a new awareness of the bigger world outside the Valley. Life was unfolding on the biggest stages of the world. While the screen brought a variety of sports and entertainment, it also laid bare war, death, crime, and violence in living rooms daily. The world seemed a scarier place.

Another dose of reality happened on TV every Sunday night just before supper. It was the *Walter Cronkite CBS Report*, which often focused on the status of the ongoing war in Vietnam. Television brought these events of the world into viewers' homes: TV film footage was a lot more immediate and vivid than newspaper articles. The speed of life was increasing through television, even in small, tranquil Canadian communities like Port Alberni.

The tsunami

Early Saturday morning, March 27, 1964, Mike was driving me to the ice rink in Port Alberni for a hockey practice. Unbeknownst to us, three enormous waves of water had rolled up the Alberni Inlet following an earthquake in Alaska. The damage was immense. As we drove along Third Avenue near the paper mill, all types of strange sights left us aghast. A car was positioned standing on its front grill, and a sailboat was abandoned on the street. Mike had to drive his car around all these many oddities. I asked my father, "Is this the Twilight Zone?"

Good planning or good luck, the family home and property on David Street was three feet higher than the adjacent, lower Spenser Street, where the wave had stopped. But while Mike's family home was spared, Nick's home was not. Nick and his family had just been transferred across the Island to work in Chemainus the month before. Their house in Port Alberni was vacant and for sale. Sadly, their house took a direct hit from the tsunami. The Canadian army was called in to help clean up the community.

After Mike's previous bad experiences with fate, he finally caught a break during the Port Alberni tsunami. His home was safe.

Keeping up with the Joneses

No one wants to feel or look inferior in one's community. The nature of one's home, the type of car owned, or the length and location of vacations are thought by some to speak to the level of one's social standing in the community. Any self-respecting immigrant would do their utmost to appear to be keeping up with the fictional perfect family, the Joneses.

It was at this time that Natalie suggested they foster a child to add to the family's finances. Doreen was a fourteen-year-old Indigenous girl who arrived at David Street's cramped quarters from the Alberni Indian Residential School. This was the family's first direct experience with an Indigenous person. She and Natalie had a strained relationship at first, but they eventually became affectionate with one another. Living with Doreen, the family realized how badly children were treated at the residential school.

Mike and Natalie, whether they wished to or not, were drawn into a vortex of debt as they tried to keep up. Outwardly, they appeared to be part of the "haves" group, but had they been honest with themselves, they would have admitted they were "have nots" with a debt problem. The bill problems grew every month, until they finally reached a point where they needed debt counselling. "Natalie, the spending has got to stop!" Mike exclaimed.

Armed with helpful ideas on how to turn their financial ship around, they decided to use the equity in their home to help extinguish their debts. Their daughter Kathleen, or Kay, as she was now known, was leaving home to study at the University of Victoria. So, in 1965, Mike sold the David Street property and consolidated his debt. He next arranged for a new mortgage on a yet-to-be-built home on 11th Avenue North in Port Alberni.

This plan was based on the hope that the booming economy would continue to do well and grow. But shortly after contracts were written to buy the land and build a new home, the first economic wobble occurred. Boat-building contracts at Alberni Engineering were sharply reduced. The company needed to cut back its overheads. Mike was let go from his job.

However, Argyle Machine Works was a company more allied with projects related to the pulp-and-paper mills. Good fortune smiled on Mike. They needed a parts manager, and he was hired.

From the post-war time into the sixties, unions played a large part in the forest industry. The demands they made of employers were similar: a forty-hour work week, union security, union dues check-offs, and wage increases. Internal struggles within unions also existed. Communist leadership of some unions were pitted against union leadership with the social democratic party, the Co-operative Commonwealth Federation.[22] While a union would have provided Mike with a more secure job, his lifelong disdain for unionism, particularly for a communist-led union, made such a connection impossible. He was a proud Canadian whose family had suffered under communism. As Mike shared with his family, "I'm not joining any damn union, no matter what!" Being in a union impugned his traditional independent family values.

Natalie wanted to make my birthday special. With the help of my friends, she planned a surprise fifteenth birthday party. I arrived home after a skating session at the arena and was surprised to find my friends, including Claire, Lon, Nancy, Charlie, Myra, and Henry, all there. Natalie had prepared a turkey dinner with all the trimmings for this very happy birthday gathering.

At the same time, Laurie had continued with her friendships back on David Street, riding her bike from 11th Avenue, but that changed when Natalie cruelly sold her bike. Making new friends in their new location was not easy for Laurie due to her shyness.

Yet again, on the surface, life was good now. Mike had income, the debts were consolidated, daughter Kay was now training to become a nurse at the Royal Jubilee Hospital in Victoria, and a brand-new house had been built for them. It was exciting for the family to live in the new house. Everything was bright and clean. Could this be like living like the Joneses? If Mike and Natalie had hoped for a better life than farming in Gage, after all they had been through with Mike's accident, then they had finally achieved their goal.

The bountiful Canadian economy of the 1960s had raised the standard of living for all. Mike and Natalie always took pride in being Canadian, and for all their efforts, despite all their setbacks, they had something to show for themselves.

THE PORT ALBERNI YEARS: 1956-67

CANADA CONTINUED ITS evolution as an advanced nation with the introduction of the Canada Pension Plan on January 1, 1966. The CPP offered a more promising future to Canadians in their retirement.[23]

Others among their relatives also felt more prosperous than they had in the fifties. In 1966, over a few beers in Campbell River at a family gathering, Mike's brother-in-law Tuffy (Lawrence Calvert) encouraged three other Andruff families to start an investment club. They would each put ten dollars a month into a joint account, and when there were sufficient funds, they would invest in real estate. Here, with their limited educations and even more limited business experience, were novice investors planning to use financial leverage to grow wealth. They had all come a long way from those Hungry Thirties. Mike Andruff, Tuffy Calvert, Sam Kalugin, and Nick Andruff established ACKA Enterprises Ltd., with Mike as their president. The family gatherings continued, and the funds grew.

The tale of two cities

Both Alberni and Port Alberni were towns economically driven by the forest industry. Mike and his family had lived in both towns. The obvious question of the day became, why have duplication of municipal services and administrations? A civic referendum approving a merger of the two, now to be called Port Alberni, passed. Fred Bishop was elected the new mayor of the amalgamated city in 1967. Echo '67 was built: a beautiful community complex with an indoor swimming pool and leisure centre to commemorate the amalgamation and Canada's centennial. Port Alberni was becoming a more attractive place to live.

The leisure centre was approved by the community through a referendum. Mike and Natalie voted in every election, and they participated in this referendum. Their parents' generation had always valued their freedom to vote in Canada and had passed this sentiment down to their family.

Looking back

Overall, Mike and Natalie's move to Port Alberni for an easier life was partially successful. Having joined the agrarian exodus to urban centres, they had both good and bad experiences living in an industrial town.

The call to well-paying jobs brought a broad mix of people to the Valley. Both skilled and unskilled labourers came from other provinces. Many professionals and well-educated people migrated there from outside Canada. For example, as the community school's student population increased, teachers arrived from the United Kingdom and Australia to fill the school board's staffing requirements. All these new people added to Mike and Natalie's new experiences and helped broaden their perspectives on the world. They had their own home, jobs, and a social life outside their extended families.

The forestry industry had enjoyed significant profitability in the early days. In these times, MacMillan Bloedel management could control all aspects of their enterprise, and in the case of Port Alberni, the entire community. As time passed, labour unions recognized they had the power to take some of this control away from business managers. As production costs were no longer under the sole control of management, business plans countered by constricting the amount of labour used through increased mechanization.

Through 1967, temporary layoffs at various production plants occurred. It was like waiting for the other shoe to drop. Who would be next? Those with technical skills were relied upon to keep the places running. Those in support positions were typically the first to get the pink slips terminating their employment.

After enjoying their new house for just over a year, and with a big mortgage to service, Mike lost his job. His next step was to either stay at home or retrain.

Mike was not alone; the overall employment levels in the forest industry were being reduced. Along with others, he was encouraged to take job retraining at the BC Vocational School in Nanaimo. In January 1968, the Andruffs moved to Wakesiah Avenue in Nanaimo.

CHAPTER 5

THE ACKA YEARS: 1968-75

IN 1968, MORE violent world events unfolded. On April 4, Reverend Martin Luther King Jr., the key figure in the American civil rights movement, was murdered in Memphis, Tennessee. Black people across the US rioted in the cities. On June 5, the Democratic presidential candidate, Robert F. Kennedy, one of John F. Kennedy's younger brothers, was assassinated in Los Angeles. This violent turmoil created an air of uncertainty in everyday living. Canadians, too, were affected, given their proximity to the US.

Canadian immigration policy was changing drastically as well. Canada had mostly taken in Europeans in the past but now was open to immigrants from Asia and developing countries. Its policy for screening immigrants was said now to be "colour blind," that is, free of racial bias. Canada needed people to fill the labour market to keep its economy moving forward.[1]

In Nanaimo at this time, Laurie and I attended school and Natalie worked part-time in the community. Mike's course load at the vocational school included accounting, business law, business machines (pre-computer age technology), and timekeeping (methods for calculating employees' payroll). He received good marks.[2] After he completed the program in the fall of 1968, the family moved to a two-bedroom apartment at Tenth Street in New Westminster.

Armed with his new business studies, the initial plan was for Mike to secure employment and then look for investment opportunities for ACKA. New Westminster was likely selected for two reasons: real estate values and rents were lower than in Vancouver, and I had my sights set on joining the New Westminster Junior A hockey team.

New Westminster

The Qayqayt First Nation inhabited the land before all others. They were never invited to negotiate a treaty for their land, probably because the British colony was not a part of the Dominion of Canada when New Westminster was being settled. They were effectively moved out of the way, allowing early settlers to advance their economic agendas.

The current site of New Westminster was selected by the British Royal Engineers in 1858. It was selected because of its defensibility. New Westminster soon developed a rivalry with Victoria for recognition as the capital of the colony of British Columbia. For the most part, the people of Victoria kept a strong sense of British traditions, whereas the New Westminster folks were largely French Canadians and Maritimers.[3] Victoria prevailed.

Much of New Westminster has a grid system of streets and avenues. The land rises steeply uphill from the river and plateaus above, making for some steep roads. The hills also provide excellent vistas of the Fraser River.

As the family settled in at their apartment Tenth Street, Mike searched for work. Eventually, he landed a job with a high-pressure vessel manufacturer in North Vancouver. This meant commuting through rush-hour traffic on a busy highway. Mike was unaccustomed to busy streets after living in a small town. He was a one-armed, left-handed, handicapped driver using a column shift. Laurie and I were enrolled in secondary school, and Natalie secured a job at the Royal Columbian Hospital.

In the summer of 1969, there was great excitement in the air. President John F. Kennedy had predicted that before the decade was out, America would land a man on the moon. On July 20, 1969, this goal became a reality.[4]

All the world seemed to be watching the event on their televisions, including Mike's seventy-five-year-old mother, Elena, back on the farm. From her early farming days in Russia to watching a man landing on the moon was an incredibly long span of human ingenuity. The immensity of this human achievement had to be overwhelming!

The new decade: The 1970s and the era of ACKA

The American actor Will Rogers once said, "Don't wait to buy land, buy land and wait." His comment reflected a well-known fact: owning real estate is the key to building wealth. Now it was time for the founders of ACKA Enterprises Ltd. to advance their objective of building wealth through real estate.

On August 19, 1969, Mike and Natalie, acting on behalf of ACKA, bought a house at 311 Devoy Street in New Westminster by way of an Agreement for Sale for $14,000.[5] This transaction offers two contrasting observations.

First, ACKA Enterprises Ltd. was recognized as a limited company. Was it registered with the BC Registrar of Companies? If it was, why did Mike and Natalie assume liability for the transaction? This era was fortunately pre-capital gains tax, which began in 1972. However, it was a misstep to not effectively use the corporate body for the transaction. This demonstrates the ACKA group's lack of planning and business discipline to track financial assets and record deductible expenses.

A second observation was the very impressive method of making their purchase. Using an Agreement for Sale allowed them to buy real estate without having to qualify for a mortgage and to avoid a 20 to 25 per cent down payment (which they did not have). The founders had likely saved no more than $1,500 by 1969. By using this method of purchasing real estate, they bypassed strict banking regulations and secured a piece of property. As it turned out, they used $1,500 for their initial deposit, followed by another $500 one month later. The seller financed $12,000, requiring payments of $100 per month, at 8.5 per cent interest.

An Agreement for Sale is a way to buy a property with the seller financing the transaction. The agreement typically establishes a purchase price and sets a time period for the purchase and, upon completion, the seller is obliged to convey the title to the buyer. The seller retains their mortgage and title, but a notation of an RP (Right to Purchase) is noted on the title's list of charges, liens, and interests for the buyer.[6]

This method of purchase suited ACKA because they initially envisioned a quick fix-and-flip strategy. The plan was to use a "sweat equity" approach to renovating the property, meaning no one would charge for their labour. Materials needed to be carefully purchased to fit a thrifty budget. Mike, Natalie, and the family moved into the property. They worked on the renovations more consistently because their other relatives needed to commute from the Island to do their "work bees." The Andruffs paid one hundred dollars per month for rent while continuing to work on the renovations.[7] For a brief period, Mike's nephew Danny lived with the family while he attended the BC Institute of Technology (BCIT).

This residential family home at 311 Devoy Street was in The Heights, on the upper side of the Sapperton neighborhood. It featured a wonderful view of the distant Port Mann Bridge and the Fraser River. The house was a two-storey, three-bedroom home with a carport.

All appeared to be perfect on the surface. A property had been strategically acquired, and a program was in place to move forward with renovations. But for Mike, the pressure was on. He had to work at his regular job to provide for the family, as did Natalie. He had to work evenings to advance the renovations. Also, as the leader of ACKA, he had to be thinking about the company's next moves. It didn't help that his work fatigue and Natalie's dependency on alcohol led to more physical abuse in the home. At this time, Laurie and I were in high school, and I was playing junior hockey. Kay had graduated from nursing school in Victoria.

In 1970, the ACKA group made another house acquisition on Tenth Avenue in New Westminster. The home was vacant, allowing renovations to be done swiftly. Few details on this transaction, or the purchase of a fourplex in Whalley, were maintained. Laurie continued attending high school at New Westminster Secondary School (NWSS). I had already graduated from NWSS. Kay moved to live in Vancouver and worked at the psychiatric hospital at the University of British Columbia (UBC).

A significant event happened on December 25, 1970. Tuffy Calvert, a founding member of ACKA, died unexpectedly. This created the first wobble in the company, as Tuffy's wife, Doreen, asked for permission to cease involvement in ACKA Enterprises. Her request was granted.

By all accounts, the ACKA Enterprises real estate machine was in full operation. In 1971, Mike, Natalie, and Laurie moved to an apartment in Surrey. Mike worked as the manager of this apartment building while he continued to work on renovations on both Tenth Avenue in New Westminster and the Whalley fourplex in Surrey.

While all this ACKA business was unfolding, I was headed on a completely different path in my life than my father and his relatives. On September 4, I married Claire Brewster. Claire and I were both attending UBC and lived in a Kerrisdale apartment in Vancouver. Mike maybe had pangs of disappointment, as Phillip had felt about him, regarding his son leaving the family home. I could certainly swing a hammer by this point, and I had helped my dad a great deal, but I was on my way to getting a university education. Mike had always encouraged education for his family. It was likely a bittersweet experience for Mike as he continued his quest with his shrinking family unit.

On October 22, 1971, the property at Devoy Street sold for $27,957.[8] Pre-capital gains, this sale yielded almost a hundred per cent increase in value over the purchase price and provided a hefty return on ACKA's initial $2,000 investment. (Tuffy would likely be smiling down from heaven. He was ACKA's spiritual guide, no doubt about it.) Other family members, noting the strong advances of

ACKA, wanted to participate. Two new shareholders were admitted to the fold: Nick's son Dan, and Natalie's brother-in-law, Hugh Cook, joined ACKA as investors.

The Devoy Street house transaction reflected the power of financial leverage. Using other people's money, they managed to ride the market upward, use sweat equity, and gain a handsome reward for their efforts. Property by property, ACKA was developing an asset base.

Amid ongoing renovations, Mike and his ACKA colleagues were on the lookout for a larger acquisition. After weighing their options, they decided to find an income-producing property. As renos were completed on the properties, each was sold. Mike had certainly been pushed to his limits with all the sweat equity work he had provided. The local real estate market had provided a fortuitous upward swing for ACKA. Their investments had been well timed, and the company was on a roll.

MEANWHILE, KAY HAD worked hard to develop her career. In the fall of 1971, she decided to pull up stakes and move with her South African friend, Dianne, to Durban, South Africa. She was now free to pursue adventure.

The Castlegar Hotel

With the sale of the fourplex in Surrey, ACKA had enough cash to provide a down payment for an income-producing property. It is unclear how this investment was selected. Options included motels, apartment buildings, trailer parks, and industrial properties. Six years earlier, the Andruffs had started saving forty dollars a month for their future, and it appeared now, in 1972, they were on the verge of buying a significant investment.

After a detailed search, the members decided upon the Castlegar Hotel in the Kootenays.

Castlegar is a town in British Columbia's Interior. It had a pulp mill, an airport, and a community college. Many who lived in Castlegar worked in Trail at the smelter to the south of the city. No doubt many of these attributes influenced the ACKA group's decision to invest in this region.

The Castlegar Hotel was built in 1909 by William Gage, a station agent for the Canadian Pacific Railway.[9] It had twelve hotel rooms, a bar, and a restaurant. The hotel had lots of potential for upgrading.

Mike had a host of new challenges. He needed to find staff for the bar, the restaurant, and housekeeping. He needed to establish the scope of his renovations. Lastly, he had to plan strategies to compete for customers with the Marlene Hotel, located across the street.

It is likely that the Industrial Development Bank (the name changed to the Federal Business Development Bank in 1975) chipped in to help with the $25,000 renovation costs. The upgrades were mostly in the bar; attractive signage was also added to the building.

During the flow of beer and the borscht at the hotel, Laurie was finishing up high school. She graduated from high school in Castlegar and entered Selkirk College for her first year.

By now, Mike had his trusted family running the bar, the rooms, and the restaurant. Natalie, Kay (who returned to Canada late in 1972), and Laurie worked tirelessly to do whatever was required to make the business a success. Because of the strong ethnic Doukhobor influence in the community, the restaurant featured traditional Russian foods such as borscht (two kinds, a thick vegetable soup and a beet vegetable soup), served with an optional dollop of sour cream; *vereniki* (pyrogies), made of mashed potatoes and cheddar cheese; *kotletki* (hamburger patties); *halupki* (cabbage rolls); *piroshki* (hamburger meat and rice covered in bread dough); and *kulich* (a seasonal sweet bread eaten at Easter time).

Living together and working daily side by side was not easy. The girls did their best, but it never seemed to be enough for Mike. He was as tired as they were, and, as a result, he couldn't muster any empathy or be supportive. Natalie's alcoholism was raging (living over a bar was not helpful). Their working relationship morphed into management by chaos.

During this chaotic time, Mike and Natalie desperately needed a break. They went on a two-week Hawaiian holiday, their first-ever trip outside Canada. Laurie, now a dependable nineteen-year-old, was called upon to manage the business in their absence.

When they returned from Hawaii, Mike and Natalie were greeted with an announcement: Kay and John Johnson planned to marry. They were married on June 1, 1974, at our uncle Nick's restaurant, the Tahitian, in Chemainus, on Vancouver Island.

Mike's family was burnt out. They had had no assistance from any of the other ACKA members since leaving New Westminster. They worked tirelessly for a limited wage. None of the Andruffs got rich working as staff at the Castlegar Hotel.

In early 1975, the ACKA shareholders wanted answers. What was happening with the business? It's important to remember that the shareholders had no true sense of what was involved in running a business. They offered lots of advice but had little understanding of what it took on the ground to make the business profitable.

A meeting was held in the hotel restaurant. All the current shareholders were present. The meeting was recorded so that Jim Kalugin (a non-shareholder) in Brisbane, Australia, could listen to it so he could counsel his father, Sam. Kay, a valued employee, was asked by a shareholder to leave the meeting. The request astonished her. She had useful ideas and helpful comments about the business, but certain shareholders were uninterested. To be clear, the acrimony in the room was palpable. Shareholders did not like management by chaos. They were not receiving any type of regular return on their investment, nor were they receiving appropriate periodic communications. There appeared to be a negative view of Mike's effort at this stage of the investment program.

The shareholders had options to consider: Should they sell their renovated hotel and re-invest? Should they hold on for the longer term? Or sell and call it a day, and wind up the ACKA partnership?

The hotel had been updated, but there was no way of knowing if the value had been increased by the renovations. No alternatives were considered for any future investments for ACKA Enterprises.

Holding onto the hotel for the longer term did not seem viable, given the disenchantment of the shareholders. Nor did it seem the Andruff family had the legs to continue without further support from their relatives.

In the end, the group decided to sell the hotel and wind up the company. They offered no reasons. This was a soul-destroying decision for Mike. He was being let go for the umpteenth time in his life, after building a successful enterprise. Now fifty-four years old, he had toiled for six years for ACKA. The formula was working. Natalie's drinking problem had been a serious problem for him, but on a broader scale, the investments were progressively effective. Mike had found his niche, but his brother, sister, brother-in-law, and nephew nixed him. Mike would say the company was wound up "due to misunderstanding."[10] He had returned to that lonely status he had known before in his life, "unemployed."

It was during the sale transaction of the hotel that Mike and Natalie were required to confirm with legal documents the legal validity of their surname, Andruff. They had none. It was at this point that they legally filed for a change of name from Andreeff to Andruff.[11]

For ACKA, the truth of the matter was that none of the shareholders had any business acumen. They could not understand financial statements. They had no sense of market trends, and, most illogically, they based their decision-making on their emotions. No one, including Mike, made a business plan for the next decade for ACKA. The real estate market continued its upward trend well into the eighties, sadly without ACKA as a participant. The group's earlier notion of building shareable wealth was lost over time. The shareholders' giddy enthusiasm at the outset, had been replaced with envy, mistrust, and anger. Their emotions alone, they discovered, were not enough to run a successful enterprise.

Many years later, Nick Andruff admitted in his book, *Now What?*, that they had made a big mistake in not continuing the business. He wrote, "Why we ultimately proceeded with the latter, I do not know, but I do know that a couple of years later, real estate skyrocketed, so we missed an incredible opportunity. That mistake stays with me to this day..."[12]

Amid all this turmoil it was Laurie's turn to step out of the family unit. On August 2, 1975, Laurie married Paul Buck, an RCMP constable in Castlegar, and they moved to Grand Forks. On October 21, 1975, Elena Andreeff, wife, mother, and grandmother, passed away. She was buried in Gage in the Holy Trinity Cemetery, next to Phillip.

Back in Castlegar, Frank Webber, a local investor and part-owner of the Marlene Hotel, stepped up to relieve ACKA of their final investment by purchasing the Castlegar Hotel. Someone could say upon reading published news stories that Frank had long-term designs for developing the hotel site into a new plaza. Two years later, in 1977 on Christmas Day, the Castlegar Hotel was devastated by a fire. The main-floor bar was never reopened. The owner used the main floor for his turkey-gizzard pickling business. In the summer of 1982, a second suspicious fire led to the complete destruction of the building.[13] The origins of each fire could not be determined by local officials. A current Google Earth view of this location proves that Frank was indeed a man of vision.

So ended the ACKA real estate investment adventure. However, the principles they employed proved that building wealth is possible through real estate. Money (even a meagre amount), time, patience, a business plan, and a certain amount of collegial participation is all it takes to create wealth. Even a refugee like Mike could do it.

CHAPTER 6

THE LATER YEARS: HOSPITALITY, SERVICE, AND SOLITUDE

LIFE IN CASTLEGAR had not been all bad for Mike and Natalie. Both their daughters had married while they lived there. I had graduated from UBC with a commerce degree. Most importantly, they had gained valuable new work experience in the hospitality business. Faced with the crossroads of their careers and as empty nesters, they were now set for a new chapter in their lives.

The motel business

Travelodge International was an American company. In 1939, it started selling licences to motel owners wanting to use the Travelodge brand. This brand featured low-cost accommodation close to downtown centres. In downtown Vancouver, Travelodge had an opening for a night auditor. In early 1976, Mike and Natalie were offered the job, as a couple, and accommodation was included. They soon proved they had the right experience to run the operation, which, in addition to rooms, included a café and a swimming pool.

The hours were long and challenging. Mike was thriving in his new managerial opportunity, but the enticement of the bar in the café proved appealing for Natalie's drinking habit. Sadly, the same old headaches of managing Natalie's drinking problem had returned.

On the family front in 1976, two new granddaughters were born: Kay gave birth to Andrea in March in Castlegar, and my wife, Claire, gave birth to Thea in July. These new experiences as grandparents revitalized both Mike and Natalie. Up until this year, they had lived with a lot of negative realities in their lives. Now they had two incredibly positive events to enjoy: they had grandchildren to spoil!

In 1977, Mike and Natalie decided to drive to El Cajon, California, to see the head office of Travelodge. They had recently acquired a sporty 1974 Pontiac Le Mans. They asked Paul and Laurie to join them on their trip. By picking up Laurie and Paul in Grand Forks, they could easily swing by Castlegar to see more family, including their new granddaughter Andrea.

One of the perks of working for Travelodge was a discounted room rate when staying at other Travelodge motels. This made the trip a lot more reasonable on the travel budget.

The experience of this trip must have encouraged them to travel more. Shortly after their return, Mike opted to trade in their trendy Le Mans for an older-model camper van. In the years ahead, work was their priority, but when they had a chance to take holidays, they took off for excursions in the camper van.

Mike and Natalie's work experience with an international motel chain reflected the evolution within the Canadian workplace. Labourers were still significant in the labour force, but a new work force was growing in the service sector. This type of employment was well suited to Mike with his disability. It was also notable that Mike's disability was perceived as less of an employment barrier to his employer. His self-worth was restored in this era, although he had always preferred to be the employer than the employee. He was playing the hand he was dealt, and he seemed to finally be on the winning side.

In the big scheme of things, the employee is the last to know important news. The Travelodge was in Vancouver's downtown

THE LATER YEARS: HOSPITALITY, SERVICE, AND SOLITUDE

district. Rapid change was occurring in the growing Vancouver population and the surrounding landscapes. There was a high demand for condominiums. A development company approached the owner of the Travelodge, and their offer was too good to refuse. So, in mid-1979, Mike and Natalie were advised their services were no longer required.

They needed to reset, again. Claire and I, along with Thea (almost three by then) and our newborn, Matthew, who had arrived in May, lived in Kerrisdale. Mike and Natalie moved in with us in June while they reset. They lived there until the end of August (conveniently, Claire and I spent summers at Crescent Beach in the summer, so Mike and Natalie had our house in Kerrisdale to themselves). In September, Mike and Natalie rented an apartment. Laurie and Paul had moved to Morinville, Alberta, where baby James was born in November, a fourth grandchild.

At fifty-eight years old and too young to retire, Mike and Natalie tried to find another opportunity in the hospitality business. Their opportunity presented itself in 1980. Managers were required at the Craigflower Motel on the Gorge, in Victoria. Mike and Natalie were returning to Vancouver Island living. The Craigflower Motel was similar in nature to the Travelodge. It had rooms and a café. All they had to do was simply manage the affairs of the motel. However, the ol' demon from the bottle interfered again. At this point in their lives, it would be fair to say Natalie was a hopeless alcoholic. She could not control herself, and Mike could not help her. It was evident to Mike this type of work was not viable for them. It created too many opportunities for Natalie to drink on the job. Reluctantly, in August, he went to the owners, apologized for wasting their time and patience, and handed them their resignation.

For thirty-eight years, drinking had been a part of their lives. Mike had managed to keep control of his drinking. As his consumption decreased over time, Natalie's increased. The cost of this untreated illness was increasingly taking a toll on them as a couple and on their extended family.

It was evident that their family and friends had had enough of their drama. It was probably the cause of their being in debt in Port

Alberni. It was a contributing factor in ACKA's demise. It was evident in their lack of employability now. How were they to carry on?

They decided to move back to the Lower Mainland so they could be closer to the grandchildren in Vancouver. They selected the community of White Rock to live in and rented an apartment on North Bluff Road. They had space to sort themselves out and proximity to my family in Vancouver. Kay and Laurie were living in Castlegar and Morinville in Alberta, respectively. Mike was desperate to get Natalie help for her alcoholism.

In April 1980, Mike's sister Doreen married Pieter Riedijk. He and Mike became lasting friends. In October, Claire gave birth to our third child, Gregory.

Natalie and her alcoholism

What was the deal with Natalie's drinking problem? Did Mike's accident put her over the edge? Was it her hard-working life? What caused her desire to drink insatiably?

Her drink of choice was beer. She became inebriated at every opportunity. This caused all around her to suffer emotional pain. At family celebrations, engaging people outside the family, at home, or working on the job, Natalie's drinking shrouded all her social exchanges with abhorrent behaviour.

How did she become addicted to alcohol? Roughly four per cent of Canadians become alcoholics.[1] Family history plays a part in this matter. From accounts of the extended family, Natalie's drinking began at home, when she lived with her parents.[2]

There were many risk factors present in Natalie's early life that may have contributed to her illness. Alcohol was always available in her family's home. Neither her father, Fred, nor her mother, Palagaya, could be classified as excessive drinkers, although there was a culture of drinking in the home. Another family member offered this impression: "There were alcoholics in the ancestors of these folks."[3]

Natalie and her sister made *braga*, a poor man's vodka. This was an alcohol-based derivative made from potatoes. She had limited

THE LATER YEARS: HOSPITALITY, SERVICE, AND SOLITUDE

parental supervision in her early days. Her father had come to Canada earlier than the rest of his immediate family. He worked, saving up for their later passage to Canada, which took some time. From early on, her family was poor. Natalie left home at seventeen or eighteen years old to provide for herself. She had limited education and was not exposed to opportunities to develop critical thinking, which a broader education offered.

She was a lively party girl. Mike had agreed with his father's pick for a wife, as he also liked to party. The partying was fun, but then the children started to arrive, bringing new responsibilities. But the partying didn't stop for Natalie. Life became a series of highs followed by a series of lows. And the lows included lots of physical abuse of Natalie by Mike. All in all, these were not ideal conditions in which to raise children. We naive little souls did not comprehend the scale of this misconduct at first. However, over time, we couldn't help comparing our lives with others, and realized our home situation was not how others lived. Life could have been better.

Regardless of all the mayhem at home, the family did attend church regularly, which included the children going to Sunday school. Also, the children were always encouraged to get a "good" education. We were all involved with extracurricular activities in the community. Family dysfunctionality aside, both Mike and Natalie did their best to nurture their family. Manners, respect, and caring for others were important to Natalie. She worked hard on instilling these virtues in her family.

Apartment building management

The Horizon House on Balsam Street in Vancouver was a large Kerrisdale apartment building. Mike and Natalie were hired as residential managers in 1981. Mike's jack-of-all-trades skills set were suited to this type of work. He was hired to save the owner money by screening for good tenants, bookkeeping, banking, and doing many different kinds of repairs: plumbing, appliances, electrical, heating, and general cleaning. In return, the couple were offered a one-bedroom ground floor unit. Of course, the question was, could he keep a lid on Natalie and her problem?

Claire and I and our family lived in a single-family house on 42nd Avenue. Conveniently, it was located three blocks west of Mike and Natalie's apartment building. Claire and I often walked over with our kids and baby carriage to visit them. We would park the carriage on the outside patio.

Mike may not have been able to give his kids financial support, but he had construction and design skills to offer instead. For us, it was a partially renovated kitchen, a new back deck, a new basement bathroom, and an awesome treehouse for the grandkids. For a "left-handed right-hander," Mike did utterly amazing work. Everything he built was straight and true, while I, by then an accountant, looked on with admiration.

By 1983, the extended family had a regular cadence of seasonal parties and Sunday dinners. But one Sunday dinner at their apartment "knocked the wheels off the buggy." Natalie was in her usual state of intoxication. Our family had arrived for dinner. Natalie was baking salmon in the oven in a black cast-iron frying pan, and she burnt her hand quite severely on the handle because she didn't use a potholder. Claire noticed Natalie barely reacted to what must have been a severely painful burn. Natalie brushed off all concerns for her.

This incident was a wake-up call. Claire and I had reached a threshold, and we decided this was too much bad exposure for our children. Our children were three, four, and seven, and we realized our kids could not be safely left alone with their grandma. Anything could go wrong. It was apparent there was just too much risk. I voiced, again, my long-felt opinion that my mother needed to dry out. This was the last straw, and she was banned from any further contact with her grandkids. Natalie tried to gloss over the event. She apologized and promised to rein herself in. But Claire and I remained firm. For months, phone calls were ignored and requests for visits were declined. Kay and Laurie heard what was happening and they agreed, for they shared concerns for their own children. (Laurie and Paul had welcomed a second son, Jason, in November 1981.)

This enforced absence of grandchildren ultimately persuaded Natalie that changes in her life were needed.

This was an event long overdue. Maybe Natalie herself recognized she could not continue to live as an alcoholic. So, in June 1983, Laurie came down from Morinville, like an angel coming down from a golden cloud, and accompanied sixty-two-year-old Natalie to her first Alcoholics Anonymous meeting. It is ironic that having been caused so much pain and grief, Laurie would graciously lead Natalie to her first step in a long journey to sobriety. It took some time before the guards were let down by the family. It was her actions, not her words, that mattered to all of us.

Mike joined Natalie in her sobriety. For the next twenty-five years, their standard response to an offer of a social drink was "Water is fine." The family learned to never ask, "Do you want a drink?" but instead to say, "Do you want a cup of coffee, a soft drink, or cold water?" Many of the relatives in Natalie's orbit retained a certain amount of skepticism, hidden below the surface, about her accomplishment. The big winner, of course, was Natalie. She was finally sober, and now she had her grandkids to enjoy. She remained true to her word to leave alcoholism in the past.

As part of their new-found life, Mike and Natalie rekindled their faith. As members of the Holy Resurrection Russian Orthodox *Sobor* (church), Mike got involved as a church warden and Natalie became the president of the ladies' auxiliary. They had a new motivation to lift themselves up.

The last of their grandchildren, Geoffrey, born to Laurie and Paul, arrived in March 1984. Mike and Natalie were overjoyed to have seven healthy grandkids. The only snag was that just one of their three offspring, now all with young children, lived in the Vancouver area. Over the years, they did their best to visit the other two families.

In the year of Mike's and Natalie's sixty-fifth birthdays, Vancouver invited the world to visit Expo 86, a world fair. Expo 86 was formally opened by Prince Charles and Diana, the Princess of Wales. It opened in May and ran until October. Mike recalled, "It was like having our very own Disneyland!" The colourful pavilions of each country were stunningly beautiful. The monorails travelling overhead gave a sense of a futuristic mode of transit. The Andruffs all bought season passes, and many an evening was spent picnicking on the fairgrounds. With fifty-four countries exhibiting, including the USSR, this was a wonderful international event.

AROUND THIS TIME, Canada's immigration department embarked on a business immigration program. Essentially, prospective immigrants with wealth could invest in Canada and through this program receive a visa, in exchange for their promised participation in the program to create jobs for Canadians. Immigrants from Asia and the Middle East were most prevalent in this program. Many Canadians were skeptical of whether the objective of job creation was met.

Demographers were also sounding the alarm that Canadians were not reproducing in sufficient numbers to support a growing aging population. Immigration again seemed to be the answer. Clearly, from the time of Mike and his fellow Russian refugees' arrival, covering nearly one hundred years to the present, Canadian immigration policy has been continuously evolving. It may not always have had the right solutions, but it did create a multiethnic, multicultural society. The composition of Canadian society, sometimes described as a "vertical mosaic," was transforming into more of a multidimensional "Rubik's Cube" society.

Kay, John, and Andrea moved from Castlegar to Walnut Grove, Langley, in 1987, which elated Mike and Natalie. Langley was about an hour's commute from Vancouver.

Mike and Natalie had an eight-year run of building management in Kerrisdale. In 1989, the building sold and their job was terminated.

In that summer of 1989, a call went out to all the Andreeff family members, complete with their families in tow, to meet for a family reunion in Osoyoos, in the Okanagan. It was the first of six reunions over the years. This was a happy time for the brothers and sisters, now all retired, to spend time reminiscing and enjoying being together again.

THE LATER YEARS: HOSPITALITY, SERVICE, AND SOLITUDE

This also seemed like a fitting time for Mike and Natalie to take a break and enjoy a little travel. They decided on a train trip across Canada in September. Aside from trips to California, Chicago, and Honolulu, Mike and Natalie had not travelled extensively. This was a wonderful opportunity to sit back and enjoy the country they loved with the family they loved. They had worked hard all their lives; now it was time for a well-deserved holiday.

Retirement years

Mike and Natalie were now sixty-eight years old. Since they were now retired, they agreed to build a basement suite in Kay and John's new house in Langley. It seemed like a good project for Mike, and it gave them an opportunity to be close to Kay and her family.

Meanwhile, in Alberta, Laurie and Paul were pulling up stakes and transferring from Morinville, near Edmonton, to Ottawa, where Paul's new job was. They bought a house in Orleans, a suburb outside of Ottawa.

The real estate market, which had done so well for ACKA, continued to move forward positively. Kay and John saw an opportunity to upgrade their home, and in 1991, they sold their house and moved to a new home in the area. In turn, Mike and Natalie decided to move back to Kerrisdale, to an apartment with a view.

The next family reunion took place in Sylvan Lake, Alberta, in 1992. This site was chosen because it was close to Homeglen, the original homestead of the Russian refugees. Here was a chance to walk in the paths of their forefathers and to talk about family history. Mike took time to look for his brother Philipe's grave at the old colony site. After a good deal of searching, they found it; it was a solemn, melancholy moment.

Mike and Natalie now lived a simple and enjoyable life. Natalie worked part-time at Moore's Bakery in Kerrisdale. In the evenings, she loved listening to the Vancouver Canucks' hockey broadcasts. Perhaps this was a holdover from the *Hockey Night in Canada* days on David Street in Port Alberni. She also liked to talk on the phone with her daughters and her church friends. Both Laurie and Kay enjoyed Natalie's new, sober self.

One aspect of her life had become expensive for her: her visits to the dentist. If Natalie could have had the advantage of better dental hygiene in her earlier days, her particular need may have been averted later in life. Unlike medical services, the costs of dental services were borne by the individual in these times, unless they had a privately funded extended health plan.

Mike continued to faithfully serve his church in heart and in person. But the hundred and one jobs he did for the church were starting to become too strenuous for him.

Although I was a residential realtor now, I was still qualified as an accountant, and I prepared Mike's tax returns. In collaboration with Mike's doctor, it was decided Mike should be entitled to a disability credit. This application process illustrated the very worst of government bureaucracy. The tax department wasn't convinced Mike was disabled. His doctor reconfirmed his physical disability, but the government hesitated and delayed. Eventually, they relented. However, after three years, they again asked him to again prove his disability. This was all quite stressful for Mike, and it reflected very poorly on the tax department. It should be remembered that Mike never, ever took money from any government. He never took welfare for himself or his family, and he always paid his taxes. He was a proud Canadian. Even with all the employment discrimination he had endured, and with his low-paying jobs, he still paid his taxes.

Lac la Hache was the site of the next reunion, in 1995. It featured the usual ball game of BC versus Alberta, mixing and reacquainting with distant relatives, and enjoying a big potluck dinner on the Saturday evening. These events had to be in late summer because the Alberta farmers still had crops to harvest. Some stayed in local motels, while others camped in tents or rested in their RVs.

In retrospect, these were the best times for learning and recording family history. The brothers and sisters had their full faculties and they communicated effectively. Sadly, from a learning point of view, more time was spent enjoying each other's company and catching up on family stories than with the younger generation talking with the older generation about the past.

The big heart attack

In 1997, seventy-six-year-old Mike had a heart attack. Cholesterol management was not part of Mike's early medical health care. He had suffered with angina. When the big event happened, his cardiologist said a quintuple bypass was immediately necessary to set Mike back on his feet. The procedure was a success, and he did feel much stronger with a better-functioning heart. The family was grateful to have Mike alive and recovering.

In the lead-up to and during the convalescence after Mike's surgery, he prayed a lot. He was obviously anxious. He had been in hospitals before and had bad results. This time, he had highly experienced, professional, well-qualified surgeons with good medical staff providing this vital and life-saving operation. British Columbia's health care within the Canadian universal healthcare system provided Mike his operation at no cost to him personally. Had he been an American, it is questionable whether he could have afforded to have this procedure. Canada's humane universal healthcare system is aptly illustrated by comparing Mike's heart surgery experience to his 1955 hospital experience, when he had to pay personally for his medical treatment.

The family rallied around Mike during this health episode. Claire and I wanted to care for him and Natalie in our home, now in Dunbar. We had a basement suite (which Mike had previously developed), so we invited them to move in. They were pleased with this invitation, and they lived with us for five years. They enjoyed many aspects of living in a house again, especially having their own vegetable garden. We shared dinners, sometimes upstairs, sometimes down, and joined together on lots of weekend outings. Happy times were back.

Claire and I offered to drive Mike and Natalie, along with the kids, to the next family reunion at the Koyman farm, near Fairview in northern Alberta. In 1998, we had a chance for the next generation to see the origins of the Andreeff farm life in Canada. It was a triumphant experience. The spirit of kinship was high. Mike's brother Nick and his sisters were grateful to see him at the reunion and in good shape after his surgery.

Family history

The Andreeff brothers and sisters were getting older. They had gotten together for many years at these reunions, but little was done by way of sharing the folklore of the family. In 2000, the group decided to meet again in Osoyoos, but this time, Fi's daughter, Susan McIntyre, coordinated and edited a booklet called *Our Heritage, Our History: Andriev Family Stories.*

The booklet's introduction reads as follows:

> This booklet is dedicated to the memory of Philip and Elena Andruff, who with their faith, their dreams and a propensity for hard work, left all they knew to come to Canada and build a new life for their family. Herein are stories of the family who laboured, took risks and made sacrifices so that the next generations could live in freedom and prosperity. Throughout it all, there is a testimony to a family's enduring faith in God. For these gifts, may we be eternally grateful.

Each family member contributed reflections of their past as they remembered it.

In 2001, all of Mike's sisters and his brother assembled at our home to celebrate Mike's eightieth birthday. They came from far and wide just to give their birthday greetings to the eldest of their family. Mike was very humbled by their gestures.

Natalie's episode

Mike and Natalie were now in their eighties.

Their continued use of medical services had helped them to lead better lives. Natalie had chain-smoked cigarettes for many years.

THE LATER YEARS: HOSPITALITY, SERVICE, AND SOLITUDE

Later, she was diagnosed with chronic obstructive pulmonary disease (COPD), which used to be called emphysema. In 2002, she spent three weeks in the UBC hospital. Her condition was so serious that Mike called Father Michael of his church and asked him to come immediately to her bedside at the hospital and prepare to administer last rites.

Her physician strongly urged her to live a restful lifestyle. Sadly, Natalie had too much trouble climbing up and down stairs from the basement suite. It was time for the couple to move to an assisted-living facility that had elevators and prepared meals. They took a beautiful suite at Sunnyside Manor, a private assisted-living facility in south Surrey.

The assisted-living lifestyle suited Mike and Natalie. With all meals and services provided, it was like living in a hotel. This all came at a huge expense, of course. What savings they had managed to preserve were quickly draining with this level and style of care.

In the BC system of socially supported seniors' care, one's assets determine the type of care received. A portion of an individual's Canada Pension and Old Age Security pension, and the Guaranteed Income Supplement are used to pay rent at a facility. This was the next direction for Mike and Natalie.

The last reunion

Qualicum Bay on Vancouver Island was the site of the last reunion attended by Mike and Natalie, in 2003. Having to take a ferry to the Island may have diminished the turnout. In the party room at the campsite, the noise and rambunctiousness of the younger generations drowned out the conversations of Mike and his siblings' older generation. Perhaps this was a portent of the changing of the guard.

It was noticeable to more than just the oldest generation that the Andruff elders were approaching their physical limits for attending and travelling to future reunions.

Evergreen Heights

The Baptist Housing Senior Living organization built the Evergreen Heights assisted-living facility in White Rock, BC. They had staff to check daily on the seniors. They offered meals and activities. Mike and Natalie's one-bedroom unit had big bright windows and a kitchenette for added meal flexibility. A guest room could be booked in advance so visiting relatives could sleep there overnight. Mike and Natalie no longer had to worry about their finances. Their lives were now essentially in the hands of the Lord.

At this stage of their lives, they were both in very delicate health. Natalie's eyesight was very dim. She had advanced macular degeneration, causing diminished sight and colour blindness. At best she was seeing grey shadows. Mike had significant hearing loss. If Natalie was near a stove and used the wrong heating element, when she called Mike from the bedroom to help her, he couldn't hear her calls for help. Still, they helped each other as best they could. One set of good eyes and one pair of good ears, and they magically worked together as one, seamlessly. It was remarkable.

The day Mike agreed to sell his car was a sad one. His car was essential to his independence. He had never been dependant on others before, despite all he the hardships he had endured in his life.

Early in January 2008, our daughter, Thea, and her husband, Leandro, presented Mike and Natalie with their first great-grandchild: a beautiful baby girl, Chloe. Her great-grandparents were both eighty-six years old. The smiles and the joy on their faces signalled truly a happy moment for all who were there.

In 2008, both Mike and Natalie were struggling with their declining health. Both had been in several ambulances, in and out of hospital. Mike was very touched by the compassionate care he continued to receive from the health-care professionals who treated him.

During this time, they both became particularly dependent on family. Mike was moved to palliative care in the summer. This was in the same Evergreen complex, in a neighbouring building and close to where they were living. His memory was failing him. It was not

THE LATER YEARS: HOSPITALITY, SERVICE, AND SOLITUDE

uncommon for him to call me or Claire sometimes twice a day to satisfy his whims. Our round-trip commute to help him took one and a half hours by car.

This change meant Natalie was now alone in her suite. It was difficult, but possible, to wheel Natalie over to visit him. On July 15, a small family group helped Natalie to visit Mike for their sixty-sixth wedding anniversary. It was a quiet affair, with little to celebrate under the circumstances.

The next day, on July 16, 2008, Mike died. He was eighty-seven years old. I was with him all night at his bedside.

Delicate Natalie carried on, but she was a smaller, weaker, shrinking picture of her former self and very vulnerable. In early September, she did a self-styled pirouette in her kitchen and fell, breaking her hip. A surgery ensued at Peace Arch Hospital. Claire and I visited her in the hospital on her eighty-seventh birthday, September 8, 2008. She died the following day. Her heart, once strong as an ox's, had weakened over time. She had a history of high blood pressure and COPD and died from congestive heart failure. Prior to hip surgery, she knew her chances were 50/50 for success. Every day after visiting Natalie in the hospital, Claire and I silently wondered if she would make it through another night. Kay came to her bedside, and Laurie was present by speaking on the hospital's cordless telephone the day she slipped away.

Mike and Natalie died less than two months apart, just fifty-five days. They were both laid to rest at Forest Lawn Memorial Park in Burnaby. Natalie used to joke about their burial plots with a view, already picked out! This burial site was a long way away from Grandfather Gregori's Holy Trinity Cemetery. However, Mike and Natalie had made their peace.

Their lives were made better in British Columbia, Canada.

PART TWO

CHAPTER 7

NEW CANADIANS AND THE BABY BOOM ERA

Beginning with the end

When I converted to Catholicism, I was taught that to care for the sick and elderly was an act of grace. My father was a patient in the Evergreen Baptist palliative care unit. For his last two weeks, Mike had been preparing to meet his maker. His whole life had been dedicated to his faith in God. All the family and his priest had come by for prayers and to pay their last respects. Now it was just Mike and me together.

Mike had an esophageal obstruction and could not eat solid foods. Talking was hard for him.

I thought he might be ready to pass on the day before this visit, but he had hung on. When I arrived at the care facility around noon, I was greeted by the compassionate nurses and shown to his room.

Natalie was already there. She and I talked. She felt the end was coming soon and was now at peace, as they had said their goodbyes. She asked me to see her back to her apartment.

The afternoon was quiet. The nurses came and went; making their patient comfortable was their concern. I sat by my dad, holding his left arm. From time to time, I would leave the room for some fresh air and then come back.

We were less concerned about talking with each other now, although I still wanted to carry on the conversation. We were both waiting. We had told each other in the late afternoon that one had been a good father and the other a good son, and that we loved each other. Neither of us was teary-eyed now.

In the evening, I started to focus on Mike's breathing patterns. His breathing cadence had slowed. I watched as his chest movement matched his breathing rhythm. The room was still.

Breath in, breath out, pause. Breath in, breath out, pause. Breath in, breath out, silence. Breath in, breath out, pause. Breath in, breath out, pause. His body was spent. His breaths became fainter.

At 3 AM, I felt I had done my duty for Mike that day. I thought perhaps he wanted to be alone. I left the room and went home.

Around 8 AM, a nurse called to say that Mike had slipped away during the night. So ended our unique relationship, one that few understood. Mike could be vicious toward his family, but his uncanny ability to do extraordinary things despite his physical disabilities was always awe-inspiring to me. Plus, although I was too young to remember the terrible accident that had happened to us, I always felt an overwhelming sense of gratitude to my father for his selfless act that saved my life.

Mike's elegy

> You saved your son from certain death, Mike,
>> But was it worth it?
>> Your body was diminished, and your once good life had ended,
>> Was it worth it?
>> You survived on the crumbs off the table of others, while your debts piled up,
>> Was it worth it?
>> Enduring shame and sorrow, as the boozer claimed your reputation,

Was it worth it?
Now, after your last breath, while you look down from above,
Was HE worth it?

David Street, Alberni, BC

Standing in the kitchen and looking through a partially opened bedroom door, I found my attention caught by the sound of a squeaky metal pulley. I could see my father sitting on his bed, pulling a handle down with one hand, while his other arm, in a felt cuff, was raised. I could not understand why my dad's arm couldn't move up and down by itself like mine could.

When I was four years old, I'm told I was about three feet, four inches tall. My brown eyes matched my brown crew-cut hair. I had a port-wine stain above my right eye (caused by a vascular anomaly—a capillary malformation in the skin). It resembled an upside-down map of South America, from my eyelid to my hairline. (In later years, I called it my "Gorbachev"—the former leader of the USSR had a similar birthmark.) In an old photo, I am wearing a striped T-shirt, corduroy pants with an elastic waistband, and soft leather moccasins with white fur linings on my feet.

I was too young to remember past events. My first memory was that kitchen on David Street.

I didn't know that a year earlier, my mom, dad, and older sister, Kathleen (her job had been to hold the nails for her dad), had substantially changed the former house to make it into what it was, as I remember it.[1] They added three bedrooms on the north side, and a bathroom and utility room on the west side. If you walked out of my bedroom and through a small hallway and past the bathroom on the right, the kitchen was next. Passing through the kitchen, you came upon the dining area. To the right was the utility room and back door, and to the left was the living room and the front entrance to the home. The floors were finished with linoleum, which my mother waxed every Saturday. The street side of the living room featured three picture windows.

As I was the only boy, I had my own room. Sisters Laurie and Kathleen shared the middle bedroom, and Mom and Dad were in the front bedroom, street side.

The front yard had a lawn, and we had a large vegetable plot in the back. The north side of the property had a driveway and a carport, and Mike's toolshed was beyond the carport. Many of Mike's tools from Andruff Iron Works were stored in the toolshed.

Behind our backyard was a gravelled alley, and in front was a paved sidewalk on the even-numbered side, a gravel transition, and a single, unmarked, blacktop roadway. Houses of a variety of sizes and vintages were on both sides of one-block-long David Street. Beyond the view of the houses on the street were the great mountains of the Beaufort Range. These majestic behemoths were visible from everywhere in the Valley. Unfortunately, they served as great cloud catchers, bringing us more than average rainfall compared to other Island communities.

In my eyes, our house was a perfect little three-bedroom bungalow in the middle of the block. Taking my tricycle from the carport, I could ride it in one direction to Pierre's house or in the other direction to Jerry's house. Both were at the ends of the block. Along the way, I could wave at some girls two houses north, or stop by Keith's, or go further along at Sinky's. Some of the houses didn't have any kids living in them. Old people lived in them, and they never seemed to come outside. Around the corner from Jerry's house, on Lathom Street, was a neighbourhood grocery store. This was where a kid could buy, among other things, penny candy, if he had any pennies. When I was a little older, I was often sent to the store for "a quart of milk, a loaf of bread, and a pack of smokes, Sportsman filtered." I was also sent to pay our account periodically.

For the first few years, my tricycle was my social connector. I had lots of fun with my friends, and I saw very little of the adult world. My dad was at home, but he was always busy around the house. After supper, I was put early to bed.

Kathleen was five-and-a-half years older and was always with her set of friends. Laurie was a sweet little three-year-old; she was often cared for by others, since she was so young.

I would not know this, of course, but right off the bat, my simple life was so much grander than my father's had been in his early years. The David Street house had hot and cold running water and the plumbing was inside the house. Electricity warmed the home, provided lighting, and made cooking and keeping food easy with a four-burner stove, oven, and a refrigerator with a freezer compartment. There were no chickens to feed, no cows to milk, and no tree stumps to pull. All I had to do was play with my friends, attend my multi-room grade school when I got a bit older, and eat the food that my parents provided for us.

For a young tyke like me, time seemed to go by very slowly, particularly in the summer months. There were no community centre or recreational programs available. I enjoyed playing cribbage with my friend who lived up the street, Ian Sinclair (Sinky). Ian was several years older than me. We would play five to ten games at Ian's house; I loved Ian's little Chihuahua named Beeboo. Then we would change our venue to my house for another five to ten games. I felt lucky to have Ian as a friend. He was kind, smart, and friendly.

New arrivals

As agreeable as Alberni was for the Andruffs, so it was for a new wave of immigrants. After the Second World War, dozens of newcomers arrived in the Valley. Dutch, Norwegian, Swedish, Danish, Hungarian, and German people came looking for well-paying jobs. Many spoke only their native languages. Quick to remedy this problem were local housewives, who set up English-language classes at the hall of St. Andrew's Church.[2]

However, it was not easy to remedy the shortage of jobs, something Mike had experienced first-hand. Mayor Loran Jordan lamented that more immigrants were arriving in Alberni than could be handled. The jobs and the accommodations were not as plentiful as Canadian immigration officials had promised.[3]

In 1956, Hungarian refugees came to the Valley after their country's revolution. As the Russian refugees had before them, they sent their children off to schools to learn how to speak English, though the schools did not specifically offer English as second language (ESL) classes for the children. This small community, enriched with an international mixture of people and cultures, was helping to create a young Canadian society.

Alberni Elementary School

In the fall of 1958, my life was about to change. I entered Grade 1 in Alberni Elementary School. The school was located a block and a half from my house: I walked south on David Street to Arrowsmith Road, walked one block east, turned right onto Helen Street, and then reached the school grounds. Just north of the school was a small community park with a wading pool, swings, and teeter-totters. Between the park and the school were bike racks. I noticed there were no tricycles parked in the covered bike racks. All schoolchildren made their own way to school, either on two-wheeler bikes or by walking. The community was a very safe one.

On the east side of the school was a soccer field; on the west side were two baseball diamonds.

Mrs. N. Johnson welcomed me and all her Grade 1 students with a smile and a calm, gracious manner. I had looked forward to going to school, and I loved my Grade 1 teacher. My subjects included language, spelling, writing, reading, health, physical education, arithmetic, science, arts, and music. Mrs. Johnson described me in my first-year report card as "very energetic and the life of the class."[4]

Moving through Grades 1 to 7, my teachers were Mrs. Johnson, Miss Wong, Mrs. Gill, Miss Lang, Mrs. Oddy (grades five and six), and Mr. Black. All had arrived in Alberni on the promise of well-paying teaching jobs. They established a solid foundation for my future education. By the mid-sixties, the Alberni School District had nineteen schools, 170 teachers, and 4,800 students.[5]

One of the great benefits of going to Alberni Elementary was that I could go home for lunch. Mike prepared a hot lunch for me every day:

toasted open-faced sardine sandwiches and a bowl of chicken noodle soup was a typical midday meal.

I experienced numerous milestone events that shaped me as a person when I was at school. Assemblies, sports days, science fairs, and club days were among them.

Assembly consisted of all the students meeting by division in the large hall. It was always fun. We would meet for seasonal events like Remembrance Day, as well as film strips, fairs, concerts, and Christmas Hamper days. I recall at least three memorable things that affected me in assembly.

Every Christmas, each division would prepare a hamper for assembly. Each student had brought a can of food to put in the box, collected for several weeks before Christmas break. Just before the final assembly before the break, the class would have a couple of students decorate the box with wrapping paper, just like it was a present. When all the boxes were delivered to the assembly hall, it made an impressive showing of giving to the portion of the community in need. A haunting thought occasionally crossed my mind: "Is one of these hampers destined for my house?" (We weren't always eating prime cut at our house.) My lifelong spirit of giving was inspired by the Christmas hamper program.

The day I displayed my photography project on club day was also memorable for me. My presentation was in a dark corner behind the stage curtain of the assembly hall. I had crafted a plywood photo-development box. It consisted of an electric light bulb, an on/off switch, glass windows, and a mirror. Using a negative, a piece of photography paper, and trays of developing chemicals, I demonstrated how I created pictures from negatives. My exhibit was very popular, and I enjoyed a keen sense of accomplishment.

When the opportunity was right, the school occasionally had entertainments in the assembly hall. One such event was an afternoon of tumbling, pyramid building, and drill displays presented by the physical education department. A young Hungarian lad was prominent in the afternoon's event.[6]

My involvement in the assembly was as a member of the drill team. What exactly was a drill team?

According to Wikipedia, "Drills need to be second nature to an individual, being able to act and react to given circumstances in a predictable way. Foot drill teaches individuals to work effectively in a group. In this way, the group becomes a single cohesive entity, with limited words of command."

The quality of our drill performance team rested with the gym teacher, Mr. Pavey. Mr. Pavey was a transplanted Brit. He was of slight build, with Coke-bottle glasses festooning his nose and fair hair that was slightly thinning. When he looked up, his Adam's apple protruded noticeably. He wore a tie with a white pin-striped shirt, with the sleeves rolled up to his elbows, and a houndstooth patterned vest matching his pants. He wore loafers on his feet. My school chum Charlie was convinced he was a former drill sergeant in the British army.

Mr. Pavey's students, whom he called "nig-nogs," were challenging to drill, being ten and eleven years old. Teaching these student drills required patience and an aptitude that some of the students did not initially seem to possess. He placed the students in four lines of six, equally spaced. They had to make fists with both hands and place them on their chests just over their nipples (this caused snickering all around). Next, students had to jog in place, in unison. This was a problem for many. The purpose of being in unison was to draw to the ear a cadence of sound. He instructed the students to move one line forward, with the next following, until all moved around the room into a circle. That very sequence took at least two sessions to complete successfully with the helter-skelter cast of minions.

My drill team's year-long work ended with a command performance in the assembly hall in front of the entire school. The experience thrilled me. The audience was dazzled. Mr. Pavey's drill team was honed into a single unit, performing with disciplined military precision. The spontaneous applause and cheers were elating. Being a part of a big team was valuable experience, not only because everyone could celebrate a common success, but also because it fostered many strengthened friendships.

WILLIAM MAJERCSIK SPOKE English with a noticeable Hungarian accent. He was my school chum and one of the hundreds of Hungarian refugees who now lived in the Valley. On the same day our drill team performed, William surprised his fellow schoolmates with a solo performance of his gymnastics skills. We could tell he was an accomplished gymnast because he even had appropriate footwear for the event. William tumbled over eight boys kneeling on their hands and knees, he walked on his hands, and he did cartwheels and back flips. In Hungary, he had lived with his mother and father in one room of a house in Budapest. They knew in 1956 that life was intolerable under communism, so his father planned their escape across the border to Austria. They ended up in a refugee camp near Linz. After being accepted to Canada (which took in 37,500 refugees in 1956 and 1957), they went by train to Oostende, Belgium, then by ferry to Dover, then by train to Liverpool, then went really far to Halifax, Nova Scotia, aboard the *Empress of Britain*. Then they travelled by train to Abbotsford, BC. His father found work in Vanderhoof, and after that job ended, he moved to a sawmill job in Alberni. William learned his English from his schoolmates. He brought a new skill set that his schoolmates had never had the opportunity to witness. This refugee was teaching his new friends that there was more to athletics than hockey and baseball.

One life event indelibly etched into my memory happened on a particular Friday in late November of 1963. Students were advised by a special announcement over the loudspeaker system in each classroom that the president of the United States had been assassinated, and students were to pack up their belongings and proceed home. Why does an eleven-year-old boy need time to process the assassination of the leader of the United States? I wasn't sure, but this event caused me a great deal of angst. As the TV reported on the event and its aftermath, my heart felt heavy because President Kennedy was the one who had promised to put a man on the moon before the end of the decade and to end racial discrimination in America. I sensed the loss of this young leader who exhibited a better vision for the future of the world than the stodgy old men who preceded him. Television was providing my young self with perspective on politicians.

New friends were made during school days. Among those who became lifelong friends are Charlie Gailloux, Lon Miles (now deceased), Daryl Brown, Ray Archibald Parks, Claire Brewster, and Nancy Weaver.

THE SOCIAL INSURANCE number was introduced in 1964. As my parents claimed theirs, they also procured numbers for Kathleen and me. The number was intended for use in the unemployment insurance program, but in 1967, it was also used for identification on income tax returns. I, along with many others, was now a number in Canadian society.

The boat

Mike's circle of friends liked to fish. They would talk about "catching their limit" and about "the big one that got away." He could not cast a line with one hand, but with his indomitable spirit, that didn't hold him back. In the late 1950s, a resort on the east side of Vancouver Island called Beachcombers rented out fishing rods and dinghies with inboard motors. Mike wanted to fish with me. It was a lovely bonding opportunity. He would take a few treats for our outings, including my favourite, Oh Henry! bars.

The two of us figured out how to run the boat, and then Dad instructed me on how to put my line in the water.

For the first couple of expeditions, we were "skunked." Mother would ask, "How many fish this time? None?"

Then one day, I witnessed for the first time my father's genius. Mike had adapted a fishing rod to house a small motor. He could let his weighted line out, troll, and then retrieve the line by pressing a button that activated the motor to reel in the line. The motor was powered by a twelve-volt car battery sitting in the bottom of the boat. Yes, a little unconventional, but Mike was experiencing his own brand of fishing.

Our fishing proficiency soon improved, and we began filling the freezer with fish. "How many fish this time?" Natalie would ask. "We caught our limit," I would proudly report.

I was happy to spend time out of the house with my dad. Times in our home were not always happy. Arguments and fights between my mother and father were both terrifying and embarrassing. Mother was hard-working and caring when she wasn't drinking too much. The problem was that she was always drinking. I would find open beer bottles in my toy closet. I found it best to overcome my mental anguish by living two lives. One at home with the chaos, and one outside my home, where people seemed happy.

I was unaware of the trial attended by Mike and Kay (Kathleen) in Edmonton. Either the disastrous end result was left back in the courtroom, or my memory of this time was repressed. How could a twelve-year-old process an unfavourable court decision?

Mike began another incredible project when he started building a boat later named the *Elena*. I knew my father had trouble doing a lot of things with only one hand, but building a boat?

Good fishing days were ahead!

Scouts

My parents enrolled me in Cubs in 1960. The Scouting movement was a very popular boys' activity in the Valley. The local papers often reported on each troop's activities.[7] My cub pack met in the basement hall of St. Andrew's United Church (the church our family attended).

The program was tied to *The Jungle Book* by Rudyard Kipling, with many of the characters in the book personified by the leaders. The young wolf cubs were encouraged to "Do Your Best"—DYB, DYB, DYB! Good turns to others were encouraged by the leaders. This program offered a creative outlook that engaged Cubs in the community and outdoors.

My friend Charlie also was a member of the pack.

After two years, we moved up to the 2nd Arrowsmith Scout Troop. The Scout motto was "Be Prepared." This was where former

Cub Scouts really improved their outdoor skills and confidence. Set against the backdrop of the Beaufort Mountains, we often had our meetings outdoors. Proficiency in knot tying, building shelters from natural materials, lighting fires without matches, making rope, and camping in the forest were typical activities. These experiences led to my appreciation of nature: the trees, the streams, and the silence in the woods. Living with nature began to take on a new meaning for me.

The annual Father-Son Banquet was a welcomed experience. The boys could show their resourcefulness to their fathers by preparing the meal and the entertainment. Games and a singalong capped the event, which was held every spring.

Since 1961, the city's main employer, MacMillan Bloedel and Powell River Limited, had an agreement with all the troops in the Valley to operate their own Christmas tree farm.[8] The 2nd Arrowsmith Troop contributed to managing the farm. In return, we harvested trees and sold them in the vacant lot next to St. Andrew's church before Christmas. We pitched a tent (sales proceeds were kept in a metal box in the tent, and it was a good place to stay dry), organized the lot to offer a broad selection of trees, made a campfire in a metal drum, and helped customers locate and buy their desired tree.

Each Scout had a six-foot wooden staff as part of his kit. The pole was marked in one-foot segments. During the selling of trees, the staff was used to measure the height of the tree and hence assign its price. The trees sold for twenty-five cents per foot![9]

The Scouting experience focused on good citizenship, teamwork, leadership, and planning. These were valuable building blocks. I enjoyed being a Scout, but other activities were demanding of my time. Charles continued on moving even further up the Scouting ladder to become a Queen's Scout.

St. Andrew's United Church

Port Alberni did not have a Russian Orthodox church. The alternative church chosen by Mike was St. Andrew's United Church on Johnston Road. The family attended church every Sunday. This is where the young Andruffs nurtured their moral and spiritual foundations. In the early days, Laurie and I attended Sunday school in the basement under the main activity hall. In 1962, Don Redman, the church organist and choir leader made overtures to Mike and Natalie to have me join the Sunday church choir as a junior soprano. Sing? Me? Mr. Redman recognized a young boy could fill the air with the sweetness of sound.

To my horror, my parents thought it was a splendid idea. It meant choir practice and then sitting in church on Sundays, captive in front of the congregation. It went even further. On festive holidays, Mr. Redman thought it nice if he could show his musical skills by having certain members of the choir offer solos. This stressed me to no end. Solo? What if I made a mistake? What if my voice cracked? Both of those circumstances likely occurred during my singing career at St. Andrew's. But standing up in front of a crowd was now something I could manage confidently.

Toward the end of my choir singing career, I would place my bike next to the sidewalk guard rail on the church property. Coming out of Sunday school, I could run out the door, jump onto my two-wheeler, and be halfway home before Mr. Redman came out of the church looking for me.

Nurturing by proxy

Activities like Scouts, sports, or church activities at St. Andrew's were positive forces in my life, and my parents encouraged my involvement in them. Perhaps they understood they needed help from their village to raise their son. I could have gone in a different direction, given my dysfunctional family environment. I did not get involved in taking drugs or using alcohol.

Some immigrants may have an interest in a higher standard of conduct by virtue of being permitted to participate in Canadian society. My parents recognized they didn't have all the answers in child rearing. They were doing the best job they were capable of; however, they needed help.

Papers

Charlie Gailloux and I shared a strong friendship. We had started school in Grade 1 together, we were in Scouts together, we played hockey together, and we shared a paper route. We delivered the *Daily Colonist*, which was published in Victoria. It was a unique newspaper because it had a Sunday edition.

We delivered the papers, collected our customer's payments, and then paid our own monthly bill to the *Daily Colonist*. The balance after collections was ours. Delivering the papers was one thing, but chatting away together on the route was another. Our route was three kilometres long. We would pick up our papers at around 3:30 PM on Gertrude Street. We rode north to Compton Road, past A.W. Neill Junior High to Grandview Road, and then north until the end of the road, and depending on how long-winded we were, we would finish around 5 PM. Some days, if we were arguing about something, it was not uncommon for one of us to ride his bike into the other's. This was not done in malice, but in frustration with each other. Even after a bout of bike joisting, we'd often ride a little farther down Compton Road to Hickey's store, where we would each buy an ice cream.[10]

We were both reliable, trustworthy, and hard-working. This work had to be done in sunshine or rain. In Alberni, outside the summer months, the rain was plentiful.

We carried on with the paper delivery for about a year and a half. For unknown reasons, I ended up finishing my delivery career without Charlie. My biggest payday came on Sunday, March 29, 1964. The day before, the Valley was hit by three tidal waves (tsunamis, caused by an earthquake in Alaska). The first was 12.7 feet high and struck near midnight. The second was 14.3 feet and hit the beach at 1:15 AM, and the clean-up round was 13.6 feet at approximately 3 AM.[11] (My dad drove me up 3rd Avenue at about 6 AM that morning for my weekly hockey practice at the arena.)

Everyone was stoked with adrenaline. What had happened? How many people had died? Where were the answers?

The *Daily Colonist* had the answers—well, at least partially. The headline read "In Wake of Waves—Albernis Seek Disaster Aid."[12] That Sunday, I was given a double order of newspapers with the instruction to sell the extras and keep the money. My future memories of the tsunami were more often related to my profitable paper day than the actual event itself.

The *Daily Colonist* was a fine newspaper. It provided the reader with ample stories from across the country and around the world. It was a good way to stay in touch. The name of the paper indicates that it had been available to colonists even before they had joined Canada as a province (the paper was established in 1858).

A.W. Neill Junior High School

Stepping up to junior high school in the fall of 1965 was a big deal for me. Being in Grade 8 meant I had a locker, a schedule of classes, and a rule that one must never go up the down staircase. The flow of students in the building was important to the principal. Being caught at one end of the second level and going in the wrong direction on the staircase to save time meant a sure detention.

My French teacher, Monsieur Benvin, was my homeroom teacher. His classroom was on the second level of the school overlooking the playing field.

I was now a feisty thirteen-year-old, and I had never really noticed girls before. In homeroom, I sat at the back of the class next to the door. Right in front of me sat a girl named Claire Brewster. She was very nice to talk to and she always had a lovely smile on her face. I later learned she was an elite swimmer. While in Grade 8, Claire competed in the Canadian National Synchronized Swimming (now called artistic swimming) Championships in Toronto. She was the BC champion three times and the Western Canadian champion twice.[13] Her mother had earlier been approached by an American swimming coach who offered to continue Claire's training in southern California. She declined because Claire was only twelve.

THE RUSSIAN REFUGEES

Once a year, in the gym, the students did a fundraising event called the Penny Race. It was the boys against the girls. Each group would bring pennies from home and line them end to end on the gym floor. At the end of the contest, whichever line was longer was declared the winner. The money was then donated to a community cause, and the winners got to be the "masters" and the losers had to be the "slaves" for the afternoon. That year, the boys won the contest. I asked Claire to be my slave. I then meekly asked her to carry my books. From that point forward, I thought Claire was just wonderful. Now we talked all the time.

Claire commuted from Port Alberni to Alberni by school bus. The junior high school in Port Alberni was under construction. During one of our chatty times after school, Claire lingered too long talking and missed her bus. I offered to walk her home. During that walk, I introduced Claire to my friends' ritual of "twenty-five on two." This involved buying a half dozen day-old cinnamon buns from the Adelaide Bakery for twenty-five cents and eating them together at Roger Creek Park. After we'd eaten the cinnamon buns, I carved an "M" and a "C," surrounded by a heart, into a nearby tree.

We talked the whole time as we continued our long journey to Claire's home. At one point, nearing the A&W drive-in on 3rd Avenue, I asked Claire if she would like a drink. I was a man of means, of course, because I had a paper route. On that day, unfortunately, I didn't have as much money as I thought I did, so I bought one orange drink and asked for two straws. Rather than to confess to not having enough money for two drinks, I explained to Claire that it was more romantic that way.

From the school in Alberni, we had walked over five kilometres to her house on 6th Avenue in Port Alberni. Afterward, I walked another five kilometres back to my house. It didn't matter to me; I was smitten.

Hockey

No one knew how the fire started, but when it finished burning, there was nothing left of the former drill hall on the fairgrounds, which doubled as a curling rink.

I started skating in 1962. At the end of the curling season, the curling rink manager briefly offered the ice for public skating. I loved skating and wanted to try hockey.

The good news was that the curlers had a passion to curl again, and soon. Within six months of the loss, the City of Port Alberni announced its plans for a new curling rink and hockey arena. It would be located in Recreation Park on the former soccer field. The insurance money from the fire was $125,000, and the City appealed to the community for a $250,000 money referendum. The community supported the bylaw, and a new ice rink complex was built at a cost of $318,450.[14] Duncan Russell was the new manager of Parks and Recreation.

My passion was spending every available hour on the ice in the new hockey arena. Public skating sessions usually had a roped-off area for beginners. The open ice was for those who could skate unaided. Mr. Russell hired me to be his skate patrol for general skating sessions. My job was to keep the beginners safe from falling.

In the mid-1960s, there was a Saturday afternoon general skating session that drew my friends, including Claire. My heart would skip a beat whenever she was on the ice. Asking her to hold hands while skating was both thrilling and scary for me. What if she didn't want to hold hands? When she said yes, I was elated. The Beatles were all the rage at this time, and their music was played during the skating sessions. Songs like "She Loves You" and "I Want to Hold Your Hand," were perfect for a young couple skating together in the Port Alberni Civic Arena.

From 1963 to 1967, hockey mattered a lot to me (I hoped Claire would understand my commitment to my sport). I played at the pee-wee, bantam, midget, and juvenile levels. In January each year, the local hockey association featured a hockey jamboree in celebration of

Hockey Week in Canada. Games for each division, starting with the youngest players, were played continuously on a Saturday. The finale of the day was the senior men's game.

I played on the teams that represented my hockey association for each division and travelled regularly throughout the season to other communities to play. The local paper often carried stories of the games. My friends and I were often mentioned as prominent in our team's success.

In the summers, I went to hockey training schools, twice to Chilliwack and once to Esquimalt. These ventures probably strained the family purse, but my dad always supported my quest to be an elite player.

In 1965, Mike co-coached the Sons-of-Norway-sponsored bantam team I played on.[15] He drove me to all my practices and games regularly and offered me his advice after each game, even though he had not played the game.

In September 1967, the *Alberni Valley Times* reported that my good friend Lon Miles and I were invited to a junior hockey team tryout in Victoria.[16] I didn't make the team, but Lon did. Two weeks later, our family moved from Port Alberni.

Leaving the Valley meant saying goodbye to many friends, most of all to Claire. I was very fond of her, and I promised to stay in touch. Her family had a summer place in Crescent Beach, outside of Vancouver on the Mainland. During the summers, when I had time on my hands, I mailed little notes to her.

Timing is everything

There had been no recreational facilities in the early years when I was growing up in Alberni because there was no public funding available for them. MacMillan Bloedel had enjoyed a twenty-year property tax freeze on the 1940s' $800,000 assessed value of its plant and facilities. The provincial government, hearing protestations from the City Council, stepped in to ameliorate the City's position. In 1958, the corrected assessed value for the mill's property was $24 million. By 1960, the company was required to pay a fair property tax, allowing the community to collect more tax dollars and pay for needed services.[17]

The Valley was also preparing plans for Canada's Centennial celebration, which coincided with the amalgamation of the twin cities under one name, Port Alberni. Government grant assistance was being offered for the first time to help with these projects, including the Echo Centre, a community centre ($685,000) and indoor swimming pool ($460,000), a civic works yard ($335,000), public safety works ($266,000), and a new fire hall ($240,000).[18] Don Brewster, an executive for MB in Port Alberni and Claire's father, was also president of the BC Summer Swimming Association. He had considerable experience with swimming pool facilities. Mayor Fred Bishop asked Mr. Brewster to lead the initiative for the plebiscite vote. He did so successfully.

These new facilities were big improvements for the community. These changing times reflected a trend happening across the country, as governments now realized they could incur public debt for infrastructure spending. This was also useful politically to obtain votes for the governing party of the day.

The blowing winds of change

The newly amalgamated population of Port Alberni had grown to approximately twenty thousand residents. MacMillan Bloedel was approaching its zenith as an employer, creating significant wealth in the community. Sadly, there was no room for the Andruff family and no time to enjoy that new house or the new community improvements. Perhaps overall it was a good thing we were leaving now, because a rocky economic future for Port Alberni and MB lay ahead.

Union memberships had strengthened, as had union leadership, and unions exercised their power for improved conditions and higher wages, pushing down the profitability of all the product lines. World markets were focusing on the globalization of labour costs to acquire cheaper products. Others in the community at large were concerned about all industries' impact on the environment. Environmentalism was in its formative stages. The vast tracts of timberlands and harvesting methods such as clear-cutting were under scrutiny by environmentalists. The blowing winds of change were coming to the Port. One can't see wind, but it brings change. Sometimes the change is as unwelcome as the ever-present rain in Port Alberni.

Reflecting back

This was a much different world than Mike had ever known. Growing and selling grain as a farmer had been so simple. But the farming life had changed with time as well. Marketing boards, freight rates, foreign markets, and changing crops had made farming as complex as the forestry industry.

In time, even environmental issues like carbon taxing began to plague the farmer. In an article written in 2020, a farmer near Red Deer remarked, "I have been farming 38 years and my family has farmed some of the same land for 114 years. But I am beginning to feel that government policy is a much greater threat to my livelihood than Mother Nature."[19] The same land for 114 years? Despite the issues of the day, that family has shown its commitment to working the land.

In this rapidly changing world, my father had to move on to keep up.

NAME AND SURNAME	AGE Men	Women		
6. Stephan Danuilov	45		$500	Bee-keep-
his wife Agnia		40		ing
" son Eugene	16			horticult-
" relative Haidar Popov	38			ure.
his wife Capitolina		38		
" daughter Eutania		5		
7. Stephen Lebedkin,	26		500	
his wife Thecla		24		
" son Eugeny	5			
" aunt Agripina Belousov		38		
her nephew Anna Shabelnikov.	23			
8. Elias Vodotiko	40		500	Lockmith
his wife Anastasia		36		Engine-
" son Vitaly	16			driver
9. Gregory Andreev	38		700	
his son Philip	25			
his wife Helena		30		
" son Iochim	5			
" " Nikifer	1			
" daughter Valentina		1/5		
" " Basil	30			
his wife Helena		27		
" daughter Olga		1		
" " Ivan	29			
his wife Anna		25		
" daughter Elizabeth		2/3		
" " Hilarion	19			
his wife Pelagia		18		
10. Luca Sidorov	25		900	
his son Hilarion	28			
" wife Sophia		27		
" daughter Elizabeth		8		
" Agripina		7		
" Irina		4		
" Anfisa		1		
" son Procopius	32			
his wife Elyhoria		25		
" son Michael	5			
" daughter Anna		8		
" relative Athanasius Sidorov	46			
his wife Anastasia		47		
" son Ivan	21			
" " Abraham	14			
" " Nicklas	9			
" daughter Anna		10		
" father-in-law Ephraim	85			
Kosmov				
11. Zachar Lefener	29		400	
wife Anastasia		29		
		18		
brother Malafey Savin	56			
Xenia	25		500	
		22		
		45		
son Agaphia	15			
	9			
	2			

Page 2 of the list of thirty families presented for vetting to the Canadian Department of Immigration and Colonization. No. 9 on the list is Gregory Andreev and family. No. 10 is Luca Sidorov and family. **PUBLIC ARCHIVES CANADA**

Gregory Andriev's Declaration of Passenger to Canada document, which granted him entry into the country. **PUBLIC ARCHIVES CANADA**

This uncredited photo is believed to be of the first encampment in Homeglen.
COURTESY OF LAURIE BUCK

116 newly landed Russian refugees disembarking from their train in Wetaskiwin, Alberta, bound for their new home in the Canadian Pacific Railway colony of Homeglen. **PHOTO BY C. WALIN, JUNE 20, 1924**

The young Andriev (Andreeff) brothers. Clockwise from the top: Phillip, John, Bill, and Lawrence. **ANDRUFF FAMILY ALBUM**

This photo is of the infamous "Bolshoi Dome." With winter approaching and building funds now dried up, the roof was never completed. **GLENBOW ARCHIVES NA-2828-9**

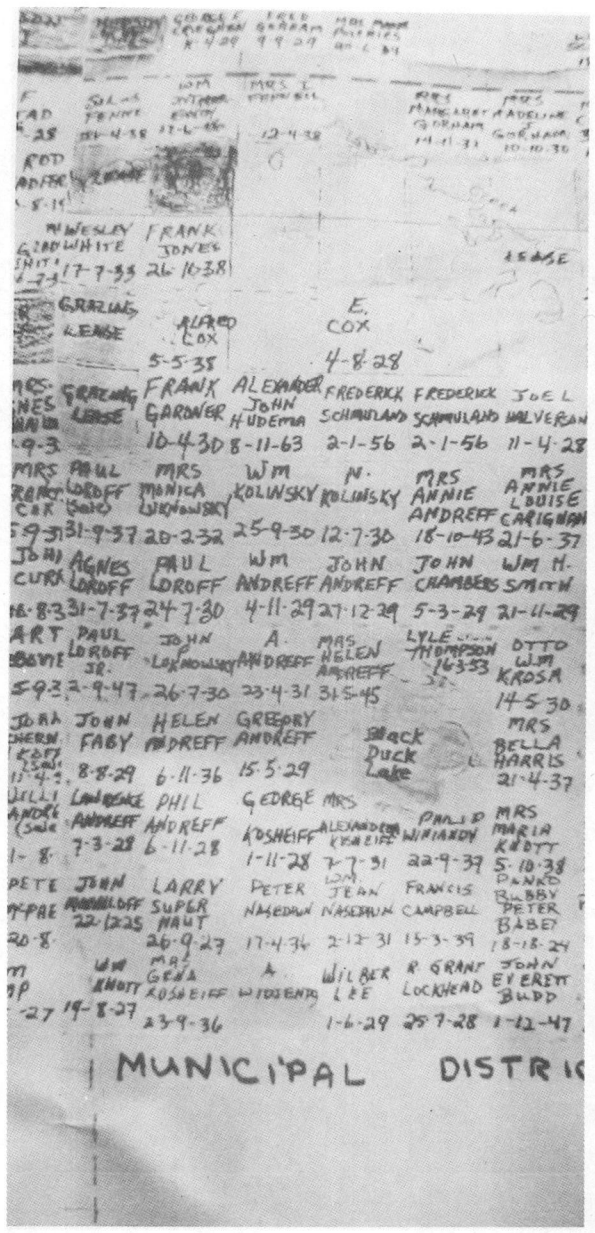

This is a hand-prepared cadastral map showing for whom, when, and where Lawrence Andreeff bought quarter sessions of land near Fairview as early as 1928. SHANE KOYMAN

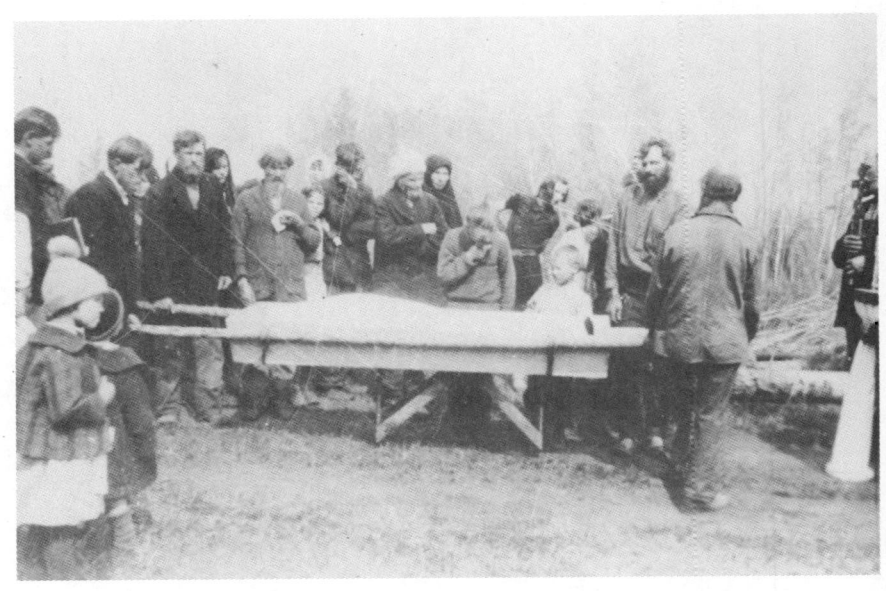

Lucaria Sidoroff's post-Mother's Day funeral, 1931. **POLLY ELDER**

The Andreeff family, circa 1931: From left, Akim, Nikifor, Philip, Zinayeda, Valentina, Anesya (smallest), Elena, and Constantine. **ANDRUFF FAMILY ALBUM**

Natalie being welcomed to the family by Elena and Phillip.
ANDRUFF FAMILY ALBUM

Mike Andreeff on his favourite horse.
ANDRUFF FAMILY ALBUM

Kay Sidoroff, Vi Andreeff, Anne Sidoroff, Nick Sidoroff, Lucy Slyshack, Natalie Sidoroff, Zina Sidoroff, and Sam Sidoroff. **POLLY ELDER**

The Massey-Harris Model 101.
ANDRUFF FAMILY ALBUM

The beginning of Mike and Natalie's romance. **ANDRUFF FAMILY ALBUM**

The Gage Cemetery. **COLLEEN REID**

Mike and Natalie Andreeff's wedding day in Edmonton. Constantine (Cons) Mishukoff was their witness. **ANDRUFF FAMILY ALBUM**

The Andreeff family, circa 1953. Back row (left to right): Fanny, Zina, Jean, Nick, Vi, and Fi. Front row (left to right): Doreen, Phillip, Elena, and Mike. **ANDRUFF FAMILY ALBUM**

The two Mikes: Sidoroff on the left, Andreeff on the right. **ANDRUFF FAMILY ALBUM**

The old Greek Orthodox church of Saint Pokrovsky near Hines Creek, Alberta. Seated on the stairs are Natalie Sidoroff, her sister, and one other. **COURTESY OF LAURIE BUCK**

Michael (Muka-shoe) Andreeff. **ANDRUFF FAMILY ALBUM**

P. Andruff, Gage Farmer Dies

Residents of the district were saddened by the news of Mr. Phillip Andruff's death at the Fairview Municipal Hospital on Friday, October 2nd, at the age of 65 years, after a lengthy illness.

Born in Moscow, Russia in 1888, he served in the first world war for 4 years during which he received the George Cross.

He came to Canada with his wife and family in 1924, and settled in Homeglen, Alberta. In 1929 he moved to the Peace River Country and settled on a homestead at Gage, where he farmed until the time of his death.

Left to mourn are his wife, 2 sons, Mike of Hines Creek, and Nick of Port Alberni, B.C., and six daughters, Mrs. S. Kallugin, Mrs. R. W. Clark of Port Alberni, Mrs. L. Shishikowsky of Stettler, and Jean, Fiena and Doreen at home, also 3 brothers, Lawrence, of Port Alberni, William and John of Gage.

Funeral services were conducted by Rev. Salovieff, from the Greek Orthodox Church in Hines Creek, on Monday, October 5th.

Interment was made in the family plot of the Holy Trinity Cemetery.

Front-page story in the *Fairview Post*, published October 8, 1953. Phillip's Certificate of Naturalization bears the name Phillip Gregory Andreeff. **FAIRVIEW POST, OCTOBER 8, 1953**

Seated on the Pontiac is Kathleen Andreeff with brother Michael. **ANDRUFF FAMILY ALBUM**

Front-page news in the *Fairview* Post, August 11, 1955. **FAIRVIEW POST. AUGUST 11, 1955**

A young Mike Andruff. **ANDRUFF FAMILY ALBUM**

The David Street house in Port Alberni. **ANDRUFF FAMILY ALBUM**

Family picture in the David Street home. From left, Kay, Mike, Laurie, Natalie, and Michael Jr. **ANDRUFF FAMILY ALBUM**

Kay, Michael Jr., and Laurie. **ANDRUFF FAMILY ALBUM**

Laurie beside the tent pitched at the Beachcombers resort in Parksville. ANDRUFF FAMILY ALBUM

Laurie with Granny Fletcher. ANDRUFF FAMILY ALBUM

Michael poised for multiple sports. ANDRUFF FAMILY ALBUM

Ian Sinclair and Michael playing a casual game of marbles on David Street. ANDRUFF FAMILY ALBUM

The tidal wave of March 1964 was front page news. *DAILY COLONIST.*
MARCH 28, 1964

Michael's first dance with Claire in the new house on 11th Avenue in Port Alberni. **ANDRUFF FAMILY ALBUM**

Natalie and Michael Jr. on the deck of the 11th Avenue home. **ANDRUFF FAMILY ALBUM**

Laurie, Kay, and Michael in the front yard on David Street. **ANDRUFF FAMILY ALBUM**

Mike Andruff, President, ACKA Enterprises Ltd., in front of the Castlegar Hotel. ANDRUFF FAMILY ALBUM

Claire and Michael in university. ANDRUFF FAMILY ALBUM

Michael romancing Claire. ANDRUFF FAMILY ALBUM

Claire and Michael's wedding day. ANDRUFF FAMILY ALBUM

Three generations. From left, Claire, Thea, Leandro, Michael Jr., and (seated) Natalie and Mike, holding their great-granddaughter in 2008. ANDRUFF FAMILY ALBUM

CHAPTER 8

LEAVING THE VALLEY

Nanaimo

I viewed the move to Nanaimo in 1967 with mixed emotions. Port Alberni had been a wonderful place to grow up. I had experienced good schools and teachers, active sports with my valued school friends, activities in the forests, fishing in the ocean, and wholesome friendships. I had done my best to avoid the adult world by keeping busy with my numerous activities.

Nanaimo had always impressed me as a great sporting town. I wanted to be a part of the hockey scene. I resolved to excel in the forthcoming hockey season so that I could reach my goal of playing at the junior level next season.

Nanaimo was a coal-mining town in the old days and was the capital of the world-famous Nanaimo-to-Vancouver bathtub race. The mayor of Nanaimo, Frank Ney, promoted this event by donning a pirate costume to look amazingly similar to Disney's Captain Hook character.

Nanaimo also had a MacBlo pulp mill, two ferry terminals, and several shopping centres. It was known as the "hub city" of the Island.

Enrolling in school meant making new friends, and I was fortunate to be able to blend in. I was also able to keep up my reasonably good grades at John Barsby Junior Secondary School. A teacher named Mr. Thiessen encouraged me to join the school volleyball team. It was a different sport than I was used to, but Mr. Thiessen imparted skills and training. The school team won the Mid-Island Volleyball Tournament.[1]

I learned to drive a car in Nanaimo. In 1968, one had to be sixteen years old to take a driver's licence test. The written test was straightforward for me. The next step was a road test that including curbside parallel parking. Wentworth Street was challenging for young drivers. This was the steepest street in Nanaimo's downtown area. Parking a car, facing uphill on Wentworth, required nerves of steel because the full weight of the car taxed both turning and braking skills to avoid damaging the vehicle and failing the driving test. Fortunately, I was driving an automatic.

My 1967-68 hockey season in Nanaimo went well. My hockey skills were better than average. This proficiency helped my credibility in the dressing room with my new team. My midget-level team won the Vancouver Island Championship.[2]

The National Hockey League expanded to twelve teams during the 1967-68 season. Expansion meant more opportunities for draftable hockey players. The path to professional hockey started at the junior level. In order to get recognition by professional scouts, one had to be a standout. Like every young Canadian boy, I wanted to be on this path to the "Bigs." I had to play at the junior level in the next season to start this journey.

Leaving the Island

The summer of 1968 was a big milestone for the Andruff family. Mike had completed his retraining courses during this summer. Both he and I were eager to turn the page and move on. Mike needed a job, and I needed a team.

Another positive aspect to leaving the Island was that we no longer had to deal with the BC Ferries system.

For fourteen years, every excursion off the Island was subject to the BC Ferries' schedule. On busy holiday weekends, the ferry system did not have enough capacity for all passengers to travel between the Island and the Mainland. This meant waiting in the lineup. In short, the ferry system was a pain. It was a relief to leave it behind.

New Westminster

New Westminster was perfect for me.

The British Columbia Junior A Hockey League consisted of teams in Victoria, Kamloops, Vernon, Kelowna, Penticton, and New Westminster. The New Westminster Royals played at the Queen's Park Arena.

I entered the Royals' training camp in the fall of 1968. Coach Bobby Love was a local hockey legend.[3] He played eleven seasons of semi-professional hockey for New Westminster in both the Pacific Coast and Western Canada leagues back in the 1940s and 1950s.[4]

During a pre-season game at the Vancouver Forum arena, Coach Love approached me and said the words I had been yearning for: "We'd like to sign you, Mike." What a big day!

The first game we played was in Victoria. The team flew there on an Air Canada Vickers Viscount turboprop-engine plane. This was my first plane trip. The Victoria team won the game 10 to 5; I scored a goal at 2:20 in the second period.[5]

Junior hockey was very competitive. As a sixteen-year-old, I spent a lot of time sitting on the bench. The first season, we only won ten games. I did not have as good a season as I expected. Coach Love changed his view of his young Nanaimo prospect.

The next season, in 1969, three of my front teeth were smashed out by a hockey stick. The grinding life of a hockey player was demanding in other respects too. The team bus would leave Friday morning for, say, Kamloops. Saturday night, we might have played

THE RUSSIAN REFUGEES

in Vernon, and Sunday afternoon, in Kelowna or Penticton. Then the team bus typically drove home on Highway 3 back to the Queen's Park Arena in New Westminster.

I visited the dentist as soon as I could and was fitted for a partial denture.

The second season, we won only two games. I had the third-highest points on the team, but the team lacked the muscle of the other teams. It was becoming clear to me that my path to the "Bigs" was leading to "Nowheresville."

During this time, I attended New Westminster Secondary School (NWSS) for Grades 11 and 12. Natalie drove me and my sister Laurie to school from Devoy Street each morning. Again, I was meeting new people. I was able to handle my courses and my hockey schedule, which often meant studying for tests while riding the team bus. While at school, I also participated in the NWSS hockey team.

In Grade 12, weariness from my excessive hockey playing and travelling likely manifested itself in my French course being terminated. I thought my French teacher seemed to have it in for Michael the hockey player. More to the point, he was telling me that my efforts in French studies were not adequate. (French was a required course for university entrance.) My teacher and I had an unfortunate exchange of words one day in class. I got up from my desk, walked out of the classroom, and never returned. My wise old counsellor, Mr. Wright (Hooker Wright—an apt name that described a basketball move for which he was renowned), organized an alternative class for me to complete my graduation requirements.

While attending NWSS, in Grade 12, I worked a graveyard shift at a local roof-truss manufacturing plant in Sapperton. This provided me with a paycheque and the means to add to the family grocery budget. I also bought myself a French-made car called a Simca.

When I graduated from NWSS, I decided to have an after-grad party at Devoy Street. With my folks' permission, and asking Kay to be the chaperone, I invited my friends to attend. I also asked my old friend Claire to come, and, to my delight, she did. The party was a classic one, with assorted levels of drunkenness, long searching

LEAVING THE VALLEY

conversations among friends, and endless LPs playing through the night: the Stones, Creedence Clearwater, Led Zeppelin, The Who.

Claire was once more a beautiful vision to me.

We started dating again and were invited by our early school chums back to Port Alberni for a reunion of sorts. I picked Claire up on a Friday from her summer job in my Simca and off we went to Port Alberni for the weekend. This was the beginning of our summer romance.

Over the course of the summer months, I realized there were other things to think about as well: should I pursue my hockey dream and try out for a junior team on the prairies accepting a nineteen-year-old, or should I consider going to university? Claire told me she was going to UBC in September. I could not stop thinking about Claire. She simply intoxicated me. Besides, in practical terms, if my hockey career plan was to be moving toward the "Bigs," then people would be approaching me by now, and they were not.

After work in New Westminster, now at a paper-packing plant in Burnaby, I would drive every day to visit Claire. She worked for many summers at the Crescent Beach Swimming Club, eventually as the head coach. We were now going steady.

In August, I paid a visit to Dr. Bob Hindmarsh, a former Nanaimo resident and now a professor at UBC and the UBC Varsity hockey coach. The Royals had played the UBC Braves the season before.[6] Did Dr. Hindmarsh know me as a player, I wondered? I presented myself to Dr. Bob and asked him if he could help me register at UBC. He said he could, and furthermore, he wanted to help me select my curriculum. I was to be enrolled in first-year physical education, and I would play hockey for the UBC Braves Junior Varsity team. I was still able to follow my hockey dream, and I was now going to UBC! Hockey had become my passport to higher learning. Dr. Hindmarsh was one of those individuals who shaped many lives, and I felt indebted to him for putting me on the path to a university education.

Three months earlier, it had seemed as though I was not qualified for university. Now I could tell Claire that I was joining her at UBC in September.

At this point in my rather self-indulgent life, I was not close to my family. My parents were busy either working in their jobs or for ACKA. My older sister, Kay, had a nursing career and was working and living in Vancouver.

Laurie, my youngest sister, was a devoted fan of mine. She attended all my home games in New Westminster, but I offered very little of my time to her due to my hectic schedule. From my perspective, family life on Devoy Street was modestly dysfunctional, so I didn't much care to stay there. This was indeed unfortunate, because I should have been aware that my youngest sister was suffering in silence. She had no outlet to avoid the strife at home. Over the course of her childhood and adolescent years with our parents, they moved thirteen times and she attended five different schools. Her life was a living hell.

Later on in my life, I realized that my lack of family attachment was a dereliction of my duties as a brother, especially to Laurie. I owed her more attention than she received. Into our adult years, we understandably drifted apart. With Laurie, her husband Paul, and their boys living first in Alberta, and then later in Ontario, it was difficult to keep the ties strong when we lived so far apart. However, as our children became adults, our relationship rekindled as weddings drew the family together again. Later in life, Laurie shared her early life experiences. To say it was an awakening for me would be an understatement. Her capacity to move on, with the joy that her devoted husband and her boys brought her, aided her in leaving her past behind. For me, my empathy and love for Laurie and our shared dysfunctional childhood has rekindled the happiness of a stronger, more honest relationship.

IN 1969, THE Canadian government passed the *Official Languages Act (1969)*, making French and English the two official languages of Canada. The act requires all federal institutions to provide services in English or French on request and for both languages to be used for all purposes of Parliament and the Government of Canada.[7]

CHAPTER 9

THE UNIVERSITY OF BRITISH COLUMBIA

The student's life

One of the first lessons learned at an institution of higher learning is that your identity as an individual is reduced to an eight-digit student number. All transactions with the university require this student number for identification. Examinations, exam results, year-end transcripts of marks, and student loans all carry one's student number.

I was in the Physical Education faculty, and Claire was in the Arts faculty. I had rented a basement suite in an area called Marpole in Vancouver. Later, I moved closer to campus to reduce my commuting time. My sister Kay stepped up generously to pay my rent for the balance of the year. Kay's help was unsolicited, and I was genuinely grateful for her support.

One of the many things Dr. Hindmarsh had imparted to me was how to deal with student finances. He strongly encouraged me to get a part-time job and to apply for as many bursaries and scholarships as possible. It was still a challenge to make ends meet in that first year.

My rigorous schedule included daily hockey practice with games on weekends, daily classes at university, meals, and studying time, plus a part-time job. I valued my study time, because at least I could be with Claire in the same study hall.

Our romance blossomed. I felt that we were old soulmates in young bodies. We were kindred spirits—so much so that I asked Claire if she would consider marriage. She wanted to marry as well, but her mother and father strongly objected. Living together before marriage was unacceptable to them. They eventually agreed to our marriage on the condition that we wait one year until we were the legal age of nineteen.

Claire started classes at UBC at the same time as I did, but in late October, she dropped out. She enrolled in the Pitman Business College and earned a business diploma. She reckoned she should work to help our financial situation.

After I did reasonably well academically in my first year, I considered my future moves. I didn't see a career in physical education for myself. After my first year, I met with Assistant Dean of Commerce Colin Gourley. Gourley explained that it was possible to open the door to a bachelor's degree in commerce if I would take and pass a calculus course. That summer, I successfully passed the course while working full time.

The wedding

Our wedding was planned for September 4, 1971. The academic year usually started in mid-September. This timing permitted us the chance to get married, take a short honeymoon, and return to register for second year.

At 1 PM, Claire and I were married in St. John the Apostle Catholic Church. We hosted 235 guests at our reception,[1] which was held at Hycroft Manor on McRae Avenue in Vancouver. A long-time friend from Port Alberni, Mayor Fred Bishop, toasted the bride. A buffet dinner for some special guests followed at the Vancouver home of Claire's parents, Don and Joanne Brewster.

THE UNIVERSITY OF BRITISH COLUMBIA

After the receiving line and all the speeches were completed under the jocular guidance of Master of Ceremonies Kevin Alker, Claire changed into a flaming-red hot-pants suit with a navy-blue hat, purse, and shoes. We waved au revoir to the assembled guests at 4:30 PM, and then left for the airport. We flew to San Francisco for a week-long honeymoon. Upon learning that we were newlyweds, the airline bumped us up to first-class seats. This taste of the high life was well beyond our student budget, but being young and in love, we couldn't help but savour these luxurious moments.

Back to the studies

As soon as we got back home, it was indeed back to the studies, with just enough time to manually register for second year. The university required students to gather IBM punch cards to enroll in each course desired. Full classes, or a tardy registration, left one's planned schedule of courses in disarray.

Returning to Claire's family home after registering at university, we opened a bountiful number of presents from our family and friends who had attended the wedding. We rented an apartment in the Kerrisdale area, which happened to be close to Claire's family home.

Second year proved to be a renaissance of learning for me. English literature, law, economics, and sociology were but a few of the eye-opening subjects. Freedom, especially academic freedom, was a priceless experience for me. I relished the opportunity to discuss a Yeats or Wordsworth poem, to learn about the dynamics of supply and demand in economics, or to examine topics like the pending population concerns noted in Dr. Paul Ehrlich's *The Population Bomb*.

My hockey and commerce buddies and I liked to party. Life was good, but it was also intense. In my heart, I knew Claire belonged with me at university. She had worked for the previous eighteen months. During the summer of 1972, I pleaded with her to return to university. She could obtain an Arts degree and graduate in the class of 1976 if she returned. After my summer job had ended, we both returned to university in September.

THE RUSSIAN REFUGEES

Life insurance was something that was important to me. If anything were to occur prematurely or unexpectedly, as it had in the case of my father, I wanted Claire to receive some money for her needs, in the event I was somehow seriously hurt or, God forbid, died. I took out a $10,000 life insurance policy with a triple indemnity feature. The cost was minimal compared to the peace of mind it offered me.

Following my third year, several milestone events occurred. Hockey had been a huge part of my life for the previous ten years. Now, however, I realized that the time needed to obtain good grades was competing with the time required to practice and play hockey. My future success depended on my academic training more than my hockey training. I chose to not start the 1973-74 hockey season. This signalled the end of my hockey-playing days. The end of a lifelong dream causes a great deal of sadness. It was an emotional time for me as I shifted gears in my life's plan.

Student governance became a new interest for me. I explored my leadership opportunities, and in February 1974, the student body elected me as the president of the Commerce Undergraduate Society.[2] The previous year, as the Commerce Undergraduate Society External Affairs vice-president, I had held a seat at the table of the Alma Mater Society—the university student government. This was a microcosm of civic government.

This involvement in student governance carried with it the usual trappings of representing my faculty at numerous the faculty club and Cecil Green socials (Cecil Green, a former alumnus, purchased and donated the mansion as a town-and-gown centre for campus life). One notable event hosted by the Commerce faculty was a dinner with the future prime minister John Turner. Other notable people from this time were former MP Svend Robinson (the Alma Mater Society Science representative) and Vaughn Palmer (editor of the student newspaper *The Ubyssey*, and now a journalist at the *Vancouver Sun*).

THE UNIVERSITY OF BRITISH COLUMBIA

Up periscope

Life on the UBC campus was a world unto itself, but other events were shaping the world at large. In 1973, the Arab oil embargo caused major economic upheaval worldwide.[3] The price of oil quadrupled, causing price inflation of most consumer products.

My family was at this time living in the Castlegar Hotel, working for ACKA Enterprises.

Many of Claire's high school friends had experienced travelling in Europe since graduation. I became proficient at obtaining bursaries and scholarships, and now had most of my school costs covered. With work after classes, summer jobs, and easily obtainable student loans, we decided to buy a new two-door hatchback, a 1973 Ford Pinto—yes, that car noted for exploding gas tanks in rear-end collisions (fortunately our car was recalled for this problem before it happened to us). With trustworthy transportation, we hatched a plan to take our hatchback in the summer of 1974 and drive across Canada. Europe could wait while we explored our own country first.

At 2:45 PM on April 19, 1974, we embarked on our cross-Canada journey. We travelled over 10,000 miles in thirty-eight days, filling the gas tank sixty-one times. The trip cost approximately $1,200.[4] We experienced and learned a great deal about Canada. One of our most memorable experiences was driving into Quèbec City late one evening from Campbellton, New Brunswick, having driven around the Gaspé Peninsula. In the early hours of Thursday, May 16, 1974, we arrived fortuitously at a small hotel on Dufferin Terrace, next to the Château Frontenac. Awaking the next morning to the clip-clop sound of horse-drawn carriages, we discovered we were staying next to the historic Plains of Abraham.[5] It was the very place where history lessons taught of a great battle between French and British forces in 1759. The British victory at the Battle of Quebec led ultimately to the French ceding control of Canada to the British.

The Canadian Broadcasting Corporation (CBC) radio was a constant companion on those long stretches of highway. We both appreciated and valued this Canadian institution, as do many Canadians.

Later in June of that year, my sister Kay was married to John Johnson at my Uncle Nick's restaurant in Chemainus, BC. They returned to Castlegar to live.

Sex, drugs, and rock and roll

The pace of life was accelerating in the 1970s. The challenges and complexity of our student life occasionally seemed overwhelming. As young people, we were cautious to avoid an unplanned pregnancy. We had planned to wait five years after being married before having children. The mantra in partyville during these times was "It's all sex, drugs, and rock-and-roll, baby!"

Indeed, the seventies was a decade of liberation in a number of respects. For example, men and women were moving toward equality more than ever before. Women had access to the contraceptive pill, usually called "the Pill." The pill form of contraception had been developed in the 1950s. However, given health side effects during initial trials, it wasn't until dosage refinements were made that the women of the seventies could place the benefits of the Pill above the risks.[6] The Pill's widespread acceptance caused a sexual revolution. It allowed women to educate themselves and gain employment more easily than previously. American studies, with findings likely comparable to Canada, showed that between 1960 and 2013, the percentage of women completing four or more years of college increased sixfold,[7] and the labour participation rate of married women nearly doubled in that same time frame.[8] By 2012, twenty-nine per cent of women in dual-income families earned more than their husbands.[9]

Drug use was another liberating factor of the seventies. Students under pressure typically want to avoid tension, stress, and boredom. Some choose to find an altered state of consciousness through the use of drugs. While a wide range of drug choices existed, on campus marijuana was the most widely used. It was glamourized both in lifestyles and in the movies. For Claire and me, who were former athletes, smoking, snorting, or swallowing drugs was not for us.

Lastly, in the realm of rock and roll, the music of the Beatles and psychedelic rock was surpassed by the age of disco and pop rock, including hard rock and heavy metal. The idolized performers of this later musical sub-genre were the main exemplars of the sex, drugs, and rock and roll lifestyle prevalent in the seventies.

Finishing up at UBC

Claire chose to study sociology, psychology, and English. I was working toward a commerce degree with a double major in finance and urban land economics.

In our Kerrisdale apartment, we studied in side-by-side desks that I had built for us. I often relied on Claire's excellent typing and editing skills, developed at business school, to enhance my term papers. Not only did I appreciate her help, but as the years progressed, I realized that, aside from making my papers look and read better, she received higher marks on her papers than I did. We had always had an egalitarian relationship, but this learning experience left me with the impression my wife was a lot smarter than me academically. I was very proud of Claire's academic accomplishments, and I respected her and valued her input as an equal partner.

As the academic year was coming to a close, I was now interviewing for employment opportunities. In a sign of the times, I received thirteen offers of employment. They included job offers from companies in the fields of land development, life insurance, manufacturing, finance, and forestry. I decided to accept an offer from Crown Zellerbach, a large international forestry company that represented a great career opportunity for me. They had a condition that stipulated I become a qualified accountant, so I joined the Certified General Accountants (CGA) program at their expense.

Before the second term had ended, Claire and I were revisiting plans for travel to Europe. At 9:15 AM on April 15, 1975, we left for England. We used a bus pass to travel through England and Scotland, and then a Eurail pass to visit France, Spain, Italy, Switzerland, Germany, the Netherlands, and Belgium.[10]

On this trip, a memorable event occurred on May 6, 1975, in Madrid, Spain. We had spent the day in the Prado museum and then gone out for dinner. Dinner in Spain is typically after 10 PM. After dinner was a flamenco dance show. At three in the morning, we arrived back at our hotel to find the main door locked. In Madrid at the time, each neighbourhood had a night watchman who carried the keys to the buildings on his watch. He came when he heard hand clapping. After getting a mere four hours' sleep that night, we met up with newly found friends from the flamenco dancing show the night before, and it was off to Toledo by car.[11]

Upon our return from our stimulating European vacation, our families joined together at my graduation ceremony. Later that summer, my sister Laurie married Paul Buck in Castlegar.

The first half of the seventies was unique to the junior Andruffs. At twenty-three years old, I was the first in the family to earn a university degree. Claire and I had already travelled outside our province and the country. For both of us, the university experience and travel had broadened our perspectives on life and the world. We were living an urban lifestyle in an apartment in a bustling city. We were free to come and go as we pleased and had our own transportation. Our starving student days had been worth it, and our lives were full of potential.

In October 1975, Baba Elena passed away at age eighty-one. Mike asked me to join him for her funeral in Gage, Alberta. We had a long-overdue visit with relatives, and I was asked to help dig my grandmother's grave in the frozen ground with other cousins. I had never dug someone's grave before. To do so for my grandmother was an honour. As we came to the graveside in the Holy Trinity Cemetery, I was touched to see the bright Canadian flag over the entrance to the cemetery. Patriotism can be expressed in a number of ways, but in this manner, it seemed so fitting for the family members buried there. I felt a satisfying kinship among my folk that day.

In late 1975, after a wonderful summer, Claire and I decided we were ready to start a family. If we timed it right, Claire would graduate with a Bachelor of Arts degree in sociology in May and our first child would arrive in the summer. Right on cue, our daughter Thea Michelle was born in July 1976.

Marguerite Claire Brewster

Claire had grown up in a strictly traditional, conservative Catholic household. Her mother, Joanne, was born in 1915 in Revelstoke, BC, the fifth child of six (four brothers before her, and then Joanne and her younger sister). Her family were railroad people. Joanne's granddad had worked for Cornelius Van Horne, and her father was a section manager for the Canadian Pacific Railway. Five generations of the family worked on the railroad, up to Joanne's great-nephew Chris. Joanne was a public health nurse: she first worked in Cloverdale, then in the Peace River district, and then in Fernie, BC, where she met her future husband, Don.

Don was born in South Fort George, a suburb of Prince George, BC. He proudly told his children that he was among the first ten children of European descent born there. His father, Claire's grandfather, had built the first Prince George Hotel (years later, it burnt down). In his later childhood and teenage years, he lived with his mother and a younger sister and brother in Victoria, BC.

Times were hard for them. Abandoned by their father, their single mother took in washing to help make ends meet. Don was a teacher when he met and married Joanne; he then joined the Royal Canadian Air Force and was sent abroad to serve in the Second World War. Don survived the war, and his distinguished service record was recognized with an appointment as an Officer of the Most Excellent Order of the British Empire (OBE).

Claire's parents were not immigrants. They were hard-working Canadian-born folks who shared a dream for better days, both for themselves and their children, after the war ended.

Returning to civilian life, Don's many abilities were recognized by H.R. MacMillan, who hired him to expedite supplies for his new mill in Port Alberni. Don moved his young family to eastern Canada for his work assignment. While living in Montreal, Quebec, Claire was born.

THE RUSSIAN REFUGEES

Joanne wanted her to be called Margaret, after a favourite maternal aunt, Auntie Marg. As she was baptized by a French-Canadian priest in Montreal, Claire's birth certificate had Margaret in French, Marguerite. Joanne didn't like it and insisted from then on that their daughter would be called by her second name, Claire.

It was ironic that while Don was organizing production equipment shipments to the mill for assembly in Port Alberni, my father was welding the structure to house this equipment.

In the early 1950s, Don was relocated to Nanaimo to expedite equipment manufacture for an extension at the Harmac mill. After this assignment and a brief stint at the head office in Vancouver, in the mid-1960s the family was transferred again to Port Alberni for four years. Don's mandate was to restore good interpersonal relations in the company and settle a prolonged strike, mending the impasse between the unions and management.

Claire is an intelligent, quiet, and reserved individual. She has an infectious laugh, a lovely smile, and bright-blue twinkling eyes. I love her laugh.

Perhaps like many of the mothers we have talked about who lived on farms, she has a vast capacity for nurturing. She has cared lovingly for her children, grandchildren, both sets of parents, her extended family, and of course, her adored husband. Her kindness is a virtue that she naturally exudes. She always thinks of others before herself.

Claire isn't a vegetable gardener like, say, Lucaria, my paternal great-aunt, but she likes to grow roses and raspberries, tend her apple trees, shop, bake, and cook for her family. Stylish clothes are somewhat important to her, but, particularly in the early days, she had to shop within a tight budget.

Claire gave up her volunteering hours at our kids' school when our youngest was in Grade 2. She was pleased to be hired in a neighbourhood business for two days a week, from 9 AM to 2:30 PM. Her job was editing, resumé consulting, typing university students' essays, and doing miscellaneous paperwork as required for small business owners. "Typing" was soon to become known as "keyboarding." We were in an era of computer monitors, printers, and primitive scanning capabilities. Typewriters had become extinct, like the dinosaurs.

Claire negotiated her schedule so she could pick up the kids, be home after school, and take July and August off to go to Crescent Beach with the family. Later, when the kids were in their teenage years, she spent hours driving them to the Vancouver Aquatic Centre pool, North Vancouver, Richmond, Surrey, and Port Coquitlam for their assorted sports of speed swimming, rugby, soccer, water polo, and hockey. She liked working outside the home, and the maximum number of "outside workdays" was preferably three days a week, but the demands of family meant a full schedule from the time she got up until she went to bed. She enjoyed watching rented movies at home on the weekends. Once our teenage kids were independent, she "retired" from outside work, in 2000. I worked in real estate by then, and I convinced her to become a licensed realtor. She did, and we worked together as real estate team. She retired from being a realtor in December 2010, just before Madison, our second granddaughter, arrived in January.

Claire's keen, enquiring mind was a great asset in all her roles. Her parents knew she was a special daughter, and I know she is a very special wife.

CHAPTER 10

JOINING THE WORKING WORLD

Living in inflationary times

Ever since the Arab oil embargo, the cost of living rose rapidly in the seventies. By the mid-1970s, the Canadian government implemented wage and price controls (1975 through 1978).[1] The effectiveness of such controls as an economic brake was debatable, but it showed that the government was trying to do something to help control runaway prices and wages.

Having lived in an apartment through our university years, and now with a newborn, it was time for us to consider buying a house. In late 1976, we found a two-bedroom house with a partially finished basement in Kerrisdale on the traditional, ancestral, and unceded territory of the Squamish, Tsleil-Waututh, and Musqueam Nations. We bought our house for roughly twice my annual salary.

The urban land economics course I had taken had taught me that buying "old," close to the central business district, was a stronger move than buying "new," farther out in the suburbs. Time would prove this to be a wise choice.

I was busy working during the day and pursuing my studies to qualify as an accountant in the evenings. It was a grind, but I was an

JOINING THE WORKING WORLD

experienced and dedicated student. In May 1978, I completed my course work and earned my CGA designation, as Crown Zellerbach had requested.

The student debt that Claire and I had accrued at university was retired in eighteen months after graduation—a tribute to our frugality, my earning capacity, and the government of the day's commitment to education.

We were now enjoying our summer months of July and August with Claire's parents, Don and Joanne, at their summer home in Crescent Beach. We lived in their back two-bedroom suite, and little Thea enjoyed the warm weather, the sandy beach, and of course, the doting attention of Don and Joanne. Among married couples, it is not uncommon to spend more time with the wife's family, and so it was with us.

In May 1979, our first son, Matthew, was born, followed closely thereafter by another son, Gregory, in October 1980.

After I earned my CGA designation, I was asked to teach a management auditing course in the CGA program at UBC. This new income aided our family finances. One of our financial objectives was to pay off our mortgage as soon as possible.

My employer paid me well, and it was common for me to receive a ten per cent annual raise in the late 1970s. I also received employee benefits like life insurance, long-term disability insurance coverage, a defined benefit pension plan, and an extended health plan that included medical and dental coverage. Still, after living costs, including our mortgage and a top-up on the mortgage, there was little left over for Registered Retirement Savings Plan (RRSP) contributions. Our goal was to crush the mortgage first and then worry about retirement plans.

One of the biggest concerns for our contemporaries was the interest rate on mortgages. Depending on when one bought a home, it could end up that, upon renewing a mortgage for another term, the new rate of mortgage interest would be more than the income required to cover monthly payments. During the times of highest interest rates, some homeowners were forced to just walk away from their properties, leaving the bank to salvage the remaining equity, if any.

Fortunately, we were able to cope with our thirteen per cent mortgage. However, in September 1981, a typical five-year term mortgage interest rate peaked at 21.46 per cent.[2]

My corporate experience

The forestry industry in the 1970s and 1980s was an economic powerhouse in British Columbia. It built entire communities and sponsored libraries and community amenities; paid significant taxes; and drove the provincial economy.

I worked as an accountant for seventeen years. I was well paid, but I wanted to progress to a higher level in the corporate world. Over the course of my career in the forestry industry, I worked in six different accounting positions in four different companies. Moving up the corporate ladder required changing companies every two to five years.

Many of my university colleagues had made similar career moves. Some gained a higher level of career success, while others were less interested in corporate success, instead focusing on interests outside of their work. I received excellent compensation for my work, yet I recognized that the industry was not as strong as it used to be. It had provided a good life for my family. I worked an 8 AM to 4:30 PM day, my weekends were my own free time to enjoy, and I received three weeks of paid vacation.

The one drawback for any accountant is a little something called "the month end." This is that time of the monthly financial cycle, usually four to five days before the month actually ends, when the books have to be closed for the period. Month to month, this is the life of an accountant. The standards require results to be tabulated for one division so it can be consolidated with other divisions. There is no excuse to not close the books.

If the accountant is a family man and a baby is soon to arrive, then the discipline of the month-end schedule becomes a test of one's loyalty to his wife and kids. However, if one has an exceptional wife who guides appropriate family planning, she will have her children before or after month-ends. With tongue in cheek, I can say Claire was adroit with the timing her deliveries so I could avoid this test of my loyalties.

At this time, the Canadian workforce was moving from manual labour to more clerical work. Production plants were mechanizing to reduce the cost of labour. Workers were having to redefine themselves in this era, as noted by my parents.

I had never driven a tractor, pulled stumps, or harvested crops like my father, but I did commit myself to hard work. When he was in Grade 8, my son Matt, for a poetry project on the theme "why," characterized his father thus:

My Dad
Works
Every where
Every day
He wants to be the best[3]

The corporate elite was not immune to cutbacks. For example, in the mid-1980s, the US determined that softwood lumber in Canada was less costly to produce than American lumber. To protect their domestic lumber industry, the Americans demanded a softwood lumber agreement to levy tariffs on Canadian lumber.[4] The resulting agreement had a profound economic impact on the Canadian lumber business.

Over my time in the industry, my accounting colleagues also faced several economic cycles, and many were terminated with severance packages, which often included pension benefits, to ease the financial pain of the proverbial pink slip.

The once-unassailable forestry industry was being challenged by, among other things, environmentalism. Old-growth timber in the Carmanah Valley was being clearcut by MacMillan Bloedel loggers. The Western Canada Wilderness Committee and First Nations successfully protested that the Carmanah should be saved from the chainsaws. In return for surrendering its timber licence, MacBlo was compensated by the provincial government.[5]

A second environmental issue in the mid-eighties was led by the Greenpeace environmental group. They focused on the problem of organochlorides discharged into adjacent water bodies from the pulp production process. Fish stocks were affected by these chemicals. The BC government quickly enacted the strictest environmental regulations in the world.[6] Companies were forced to remove all organochlorides from their production process.

The capital expenditures required for compliance with the regulations were significant. From the shareholders' point of view, this was non-productive spending, a negative impact on the returns of their investment.

My last accounting assignment was as a project controller for a division that managed pulp-and-paper capital-spending projects, including these organochloride projects. Over the seventeen years of my experience in the forest industry experience, I came to believe that the forest industry was weakening. As noted in Chapter Four, the early BC colonists had taken a strident position on the use of land and its resources, suggesting that "the betterment of humankind lay not in harmony with nature but in its conquest and transformation." Local environmentalists and First Nations had successfully, in the court of public opinion, reversed this perspective of living with nature.

With the forestry industry in decline, my career path seemed uncertain; a dead-ended career was more likely to be the case. My boss had announced he was planning to retire from the business at the end of 1991. Sensing the moment was right, I asked him to help me obtain a severance package and he agreed.

Canadian political turbulence in the 1980s

In 1980, French-Canadian politicians, echoing the views of many Quebec Francophones, held a provincial referendum proposing to establish Quebec as a sovereign country that would still have some association with the rest of Canada. The suggested arrangement was known as sovereignty-association. Feelings of alienation toward English Canada had been brewing since at least the early 1960s. The proposal was rejected by sixty per cent of the population. Nonetheless, it was clear that the recognition of Quebec society through only the *Official Languages Act* was insufficient to satisfy their rights and freedoms as a society.

In 1982, Canada repatriated its constitution from the United Kingdom. The *Constitution Act, 1982* was complemented with the Canadian Charter of Rights and Freedoms. This was a broader application of the *Canadian Bill of Rights* that was enacted in 1960.

The government of Quebec did not approve the enactment of the *Constitution Act, 1982*. Perhaps this reflected the soured relationship between Quebec and the rest of Canada.

The repatriation of the constitution allowed the country to get on with amendments that could solve some of the provincial jurisdictional issues. The Meech Lake Accord was written to create the first amendments. Public sentiment was divided on the proposed accord, regardless of the initial approval by all of the provincial premiers. Legislation required ratification within three years. The changes of all provincial governments over this period caused the accord to time out. A second effort to amend the Constitution in the form of the Charlottetown Accord similarly failed.

CHAPTER 11

THE GOLDEN ERA OF FAMILY LIFE

All in the family

Each generation refines its views and philosophies on all manner of things. Like some baby boomers of our time, Claire and I shared the view that she would stay home to nurture the children, and we agreed never to use corporal punishments with them. As well, the notion of physical or mental abuse toward my wife, the woman I dearly loved, was inappropriate and alien to me.

Claire was and is a great mother. She chose to stay home, nurturing her children, rather than starting her career after obtaining her university degree. We often laughed when people asked Claire if she worked.

Raising a family means sleepless nights, caring for sick children, feeding and clothing them, providing stimulating activities, reading them stories, arranging play dates, shopping for groceries with them in tow, and keeping a household functioning. My sentiments toward my beautiful wife were that she possessed incredible talents, was organized, and was a loving mother and partner. She embodied the philosophy of Confucius, "The strength of a nation derives from the strength of the home." We were dedicated to building a strong family together.

Debt management, so much a part of our family history, was guided by our desire to live debt-free. We viewed our education, and therefore our potential earning power, as a gateway to this goal.

Binding and drawing our extended families together was also something we wished for. We recognized that the seventies had been a self-indulgent period as we nurtured our relationship and attended university. Now that we had our young family, we were broadening our awareness of the value of extended family.

A fun event we started in the late eighties was our Christmas party, which we called Sing for Your Supper. We invited family and friends to a pre-Christmas buffet. The evening started with a social gathering, then came the carols, skits, poems, stories, and jokes. After some good-natured fun, Claire produced an outstanding buffet dinner with all the trimmings. This annual event went on for thirty-three years. My dad keenly videotaped these often-hilarious performances.

The Arbutus Club

In 1981, we became members of a private, family-oriented recreational club. The facilities included a swimming and diving pool; spa facilities with a steam room, dry sauna, and whirlpool; a gym; a hockey arena; an eight-sheet curling rink; squash and racquetball courts; outdoor tennis courts; and a cafeteria, bar, and dining lounge.

Claire and I enjoyed playing tennis together. The club also had a child-minding centre, which freed up couples to enjoy sports together. Our family used the pool, skating rink, and cafeteria regularly. I liked to curl and play tennis. Claire enjoyed tennis, fitness classes, and swimming.

Claire's parents were original charter members of the club. She was familiar with the place, as she had been a lifeguard and taught diving and synchronized swimming there in her late teenage years.

When a program like hockey or swimming ended, there was usually a team banquet for all the participants and for families to get to know each other better. The club was a happy place to visit.

School

Our home was three blocks from our kids' school. Claire usually walked with them to school in the mornings and back after school until they were in Grade 4.

In the early days, the kids started their friendships with children in the area. (One of our neighbours had three children around the same age.) They played T-ball and soccer together. Kerrisdale Annex offered kindergarten to Grade 3. Kerrisdale Elementary, also nearby, offered Grades 4 to 7.

Of our three children, one had reading difficulties. This was of great concern to me and Claire; we frankly expected all our kids to go to university. In this era, specialized education resources were available to aid students who needed help. These educators assured us this reading latency would not affect the prospect of higher education for our child.

Our neighbour

Claire and one of our neighbours often walked to the school together with the children. (The neighbour's family is concerned that if her name is used, there could still be repercussions, even in this day and age.) Over time she shared her story with Claire. In 1966, she lived in Brno, Czechoslovakia. She had trained as a doctor. A communist-ruled country like Czechoslovakia had limited personal freedoms. Our neighbour resolved that she did not want to live or raise a family under communist rule. She and several friends planned to cross the border to take refuge in another country.

When the time came for their departure, she walked into her living room and took two valuable candlesticks from the fireplace mantel. She could sell these to provide money during her escape. Her resolve was so strong that she hadn't told her mother of her escape plan for fear of upsetting her mission.

The group left after nightfall. Over several days, they walked and skied toward a mountain pass. It was a harrowing experience. One of their friends did not make it, but our neighbour succeeded in crossing the border. If this was the cost of her freedom, she thought, it was a terrible price to pay. She ended up in a refugee camp near Vienna.

She applied through the Red Cross to emigrate to Canada. Her qualifications were likely an asset in her application. She flew to Toronto, where she worked as a nanny for a family for a number of years. While living in Toronto, she met her husband. They moved to Vancouver, eventually living on the same street as us.[1]

Catholicism

Claire's mother, Joanne, was a devoted Catholic all her life. She attended mass every week. If she had to be somewhere on Sunday morning, she attended the Saturday evening mass. At Crescent Beach, she attended the 8:30 AM Sunday mass regardless of how late any parties went the night before or how early Sunday swim meets started. She was strict and a very good Catholic role model.

Back in 1971, when Joanne learned I wanted to marry Claire, she made it clear it would be a Catholic Church wedding. Additionally, when Father O'Brien of St. John the Apostle interviewed me, he offered a compromise in order to proceed. He would marry us, knowing Joanne was a devoted parishioner, if we agreed to raise our children in the Catholic faith. Both of us wanted our children to be raised with faith, so we were happy to agree to this commitment. St. John the Apostle was a mere three blocks from our home in Kerrisdale.

After many years of attending Sunday mass with Claire's folks, it became evident that Don did not receive Holy Communion. Joanne had also married a non-Catholic. Given that the children were to start their catechism lessons, I decided to convert to the Catholic faith and took a twenty-week program offered by the archdiocese. Joanne sprang into action, suggesting Don join me in the program. This was a positive bonding experience for the whole family.

All of our children were baptized; one of the boys was baptized at Crescent Beach with water in a golden clamshell to anoint his forehead.

During the children's catechism lessons, signals of dissatisfaction about attending their lessons became evident. As the years went on, it was determined that the nun teaching catechism was striking the hands of the children with a ruler to discipline them. This conduct was finally exposed by the parents and the nun was removed. Clearly this was inappropriate behaviour shown to the young ones.

Ultimately, in the 1980s, all of our children were confirmed. However, as the next several years passed, our attendance at mass became sporadic. Yes, activities like swimming, water polo, Cubs, soccer, and other activities were on the increase to account for some of this, but there were other concerns.

Like many congregations, the church was always wanting to raise funds for various programs like building schools and improving existing properties. Every year, Project Advance was promoted from the pulpit. Some years, greater projects were planned and therefore more money was called for. There was pressure for all attending church to donate ten per cent of their incomes. This was a significant challenge for a single-family income.

On May 12, 1975, Claire's European journal records us visiting the Vatican in Rome and the papal treasury. Claire wrote about viewing the treasury, "Vatican jewels are brilliant & worth millions. I see now why the Catholic Church is the biggest business in the world, as Mike would say."[2]

The experience did leave one wondering about the incongruity between the extreme poverty in the world and these stockpiled papal rings, jewellery, and other treasures. The intransigence of the Vatican holding on to these priceless relics, instead of converting this wealth to help the needy and feed the starving, offers a study in contrasts. The Church exhorts, among other things, love for its fellow human beings, but holding these priceless treasures does little to help those in need.

The more significant concern about the Catholic Church for Claire and me came with the emerging revelations of the sexual abuse of children by the clergy. The Church was too slow in handling the issue. A poll conducted by the Angus Reid Institute in 2019 suggested seventy-eight per cent of Canadians thought the Church did a poor or very poor job. Furthermore, forty-two per cent identified themselves as spiritual but not religious.³

Sadly, this is the position we found ourselves taking after making our commitment to Monsignor O'Brien many years before. He had asked us to follow the Christian faith but our family failed to do so.

Given that my parents were so devout in their Orthodox faith, it was a hard decision to close the door on the family's churchgoing. Perhaps this was similar to the experience that the Old Brothers felt as their children left the congregation of Saint Pokrovsky.

Technology

I recall from a third-year commerce course I took in 1974 on computing that the instructor was explaining something called "the Internet," which the military had developed, and another thing called "email," which we would all use one day instead of snail mail.

In my early business career around the mid-1970s, teletype was the medium of business communications. Then, my company got the first commercial fax machine. This alone was a profound change for business communications.

I was enamoured by computers from the very start. I bought a British computing system called a Sinclair Z80. The Z80 was a low-cost home computing system. A TV was required to be the monitor and a tape recorder was used to load programs written in the Basic program language. The big draw on it was Pong, a form of computer tennis.

The next computing system I acquired was a luggable system called an Osbourne. A small suitcase would describe its size. It featured a keyboard that covered the monitor for transporting it from place to place. It was heavy and slow. I had started using an accounting program called Accpak and a spreadsheet program called Lotus 1-2-3.

A desktop computer running on the Microsoft operating system was the next level of home computing.

In the mid-1980s, I confounded Claire by suggesting we buy a VHS video cassette recorder. We could get one from the department store on a 30-60-90-day payment basis: use now and pay one third each thirty days. After I convinced her it would be great for the kids, we brought it home. It came with the video *Annie*. It was an instant success.

Cordless phones were now the rage—no more twenty-foot phone cords to trip over! It worked better when the antenna was extended. Next came the telephone answering machines.

Cubs

I had raised a couple of my own wolf cubs. The Knox United Church in Kerrisdale happened to have a Cub pack that our son Matthew first joined. As I talked with some of the leaders, it became evident they wanted to move on with their boys to Scouts. They asked me to step in as a new leader just as our son Greg began his experience.

This was a wonderful bonding experience for us. I enjoyed the program because it offered the young lads a stimulating experience. Having been a part of Scouting myself as a boy, I was able to give the pack enthusiastic leadership. Many of the other fathers joined in, and we made a memorable experience for all.

The Crescent Beach Swimming Club

The Cresent Beach Swimming Club (CBSC) is not just a swimming club, it is a tribal experience. Claire has been a part of the CBSC her whole life, with her family. Even when her father was transferred to Port Alberni, Claire's mother ensured they still came over for July and August. Claire took lessons as a child in swimming, tennis, lifesaving, diving, and sailing. She taught diving, swimming, and synchro and became a head coach for the swim club.

It became optional to attend church on Sunday in Crescent Beach due to weekend swim meets, but Friday evening, foot races were mandatory. The foot races are for the children of the swim club members. It is not racing for ribbons. They run races for candies! All participants are rewarded at the finish line with candy. There's no requirement for any attendee to show up with children, because for some of the adults, it was about schmoozing on the Friday night cocktail circuit.

The CBSC provides a fun-filled summer of activities, with something for everyone. It features swimming, sailing, tennis, water polo, lifesaving, pentathlon, foot races, bingo, picnics, bull head derbies, sandcastle contests, bridge for the ladies, golf, and an annual evening social fundraiser called Parents Night Out. Some summers, we had to go home in September just to rest from all our CBSC activities in July and August. Those were the best summers.

The travel bug returns

The 1980s were also notable for the amount of travel undertaken by our family.

Claire and I had knuckled down to the working-family lifestyle for ten years. In 1985, I suggested to her that we take a one-week holiday to Hawaii. The children were at a more manageable age, and both grandparents stepped in so we could have a real, long overdue adult holiday. This was our first trip to Honolulu.

Later that same year, family friends invited us to Palm Desert for a week. We spent time travelling through Joshua Tree National Park, Twentynine Palms, and Indio. I loved the poolside palm trees.

Another, more grandiose travel plan (the family equivalent of sending a man to the moon) was in the works. Claire and I had planned and saved for this for some time. It was a trip to visit Claire's sister and family in Sydney, Australia. Because of the distance and expense, we decided we would need at least one month. Each of the children's teachers would have to approve a two-week absence, as the trip was planned during the Christmas break of 1986-87. Care was required to update all the proper immunizations for the children. Lastly, we organized a daily trip planner to maximize our travel experiences.

Claire's sister Patsy and brother-in-law Kevin were wonderful hosts. Once we had arrived in Australia, we took the train to Forresters Beach (on the XPT—their express train) for a beach cottage vacation, followed by a trip to a sheep station; then we went off to ski on Mount Thredbo. Next was another train to Canberra, the federal capital, and lastly a return trip to enjoy Christmas and all Sydney had to offer its tourists. We enjoyed the trip immensely and also had the satisfaction of the new horizons we had shown our children, now in Grades 1, 2, and 4.

Just over a year later, our family made a special, magical trip to Disneyland, which seemed like the happiest place on Earth. We realized that family travel provided the best quality time a family could spend together.

Thea's trip to Belgium in 1989 was the last trip by a family member in the golden eighties. Claire's brother Ken and his family lived in Brussels. Ken worked in Europe for MacMillan Bloedel in pulp sales (some of it from that mill in Port Alberni). He invited Thea, who had taken late French immersion schooling, to visit with him and his wife. This was more cultural enrichment for a thirteen-year-old. Claire's mother's side of the family were Flemish. Claire's parents accompanied their granddaughter on the plane to Europe. Then, a few days later, they went on their own scheduled bus tour of the UK.

Moving day

Claire and I lived in a small Kerrisdale home with two bedrooms on the main floor and two downstairs. We had stuck to our commitment to eliminate our debt and had paid off our mortgage in twelve years. To me, this meant freedom to save and play the stock market. To Claire, it meant time to move to a bigger house for her growing family.

In 1988, Claire found a fabulous, brand new, four-bedroom home (with all bedrooms on the upper level) in the Dunbar area. We couldn't say no, because it was everything one could desire in a new home. It would mean the children would have a longer walk to their school, but they didn't have to change schools. It would also mean rejoining the mortgage club, but it was the right house for our family.

As the ACKA experience had shown, real estate prices were on the rise throughout the 1970s and the 1980s. The price paid for the Kerrisdale home had increased by a factor of five because it was in a prime location. This increased equity, plus a cheaper borrowing cost, propelled us into a significant step-up in the quality of our residence.

CHAPTER 12

NEW HORIZONS IN THE 1990S

Independence and self-employment

In the early 1950s, my father left a well-paying job to start up his own business, using the skills he had gained in his previous work experience. His independent stripe had its benefits. Being his own boss meant freedom of choice. It also meant bearing responsibilities and risks.

In 1992, I had considered numerous possibilities for my future direction once I'd left the corporate world. I could continue working for an employer or I could start working for myself. I chose independence and decided to become a residential realtor. I had studied urban land economics in university seventeen years earlier. The switch required me to have faith in my own abilities, but over time it proved fortuitous.

One of the daunting statistics of the profession was an eighty per cent failure rate for first-year realtors, due to lack of results. With a new home and mortgage and now three almost-teenagers and a wife to care for, failing in my new-found profession was not an option.

Hard work, patience, and persistence were key attributes for lift-off in my new career. It took me less than a year to become a viable realtor. Over time, and with an attitude of always seeking to do better, I learned three pillars for success: passion, planning, and producing. I used these building blocks and my business experience to evolve from being a realtor to a real estate team leader, then to the president of a company, and finally an investor in real estate. My journey in real estate spanned twenty-five years. Just as ACKA had succeeded in building wealth through real estate, all of my family have taken similar pages out of the ACKA playbook for themselves.

A legacy of my Port Alberni days was giving food hampers at Christmas. For twenty years, my real estate team and I organized the Dunbar community to collect food and cash donations for the Greater Vancouver Food Bank to help others in need.

Serving the public in real estate was a rewarding experience. Claire joined my real estate team as a productive realtor for ten years. We both enjoyed the many benefits of independence, including working on our own schedule, taking time off for pursuits of personal interest, and travelling. There is no greater freedom in a working life than to be self-employed. At various times, all our family members were engaged in the real estate business.

Our Dunbar neighbourhood in Vancouver became one of the most desirable and expensive neighbourhoods in Canada.[1] The affordability of a house can be measured by the formula of house price divided by annual salary. In 1976, our Kerrisdale house, also in a desirable area, was purchased at a factor of two times my annual salary. Home prices in the Dunbar area were *not* affordable during the time I was ending my real estate career. Houses at that time were trading in excess of thirteen times the average annual salary.

Capturing the last moments of family home life

As John Lennon wrote, "Life is what happens to you while you are busy making other plans." Our children were in their high school years while Claire and I were busy trying to provide a comfortable lifestyle for them. When our youngest was in Grade 2, Claire rejoined the workforce and then in later years worked with me in real estate.

Mike and Natalie—Grandpa and Grandma—occasionally helped the children with early morning rides to high school and after-school snacks. They were generally helpful with the children, in fact. My sisters felt that Mike's abhorrent conduct continued after he and Natalie had retired, but we never witnessed any unacceptable conduct during the five years they lived with us.

Our daughter, Thea, became an elite swimmer. She produced a national qualifying time in the 100-metre butterfly event in Grade 10 before a career-ending knee injury curtailed her competitive swimming.

Our sons, Matt and Greg, also had unique extracurricular activities. Matt played water polo for the Canadian National Water Polo Team, planning for the 2000 Olympics. He travelled across Canada and to Hungary and Mexico for competitions. His Team Canada did not qualify for that Olympics. Greg, in Grades 9 and 10, travelled with the school band to Harrogate, England. He also enjoyed playing hockey at the Arbutus Club.

One of our best family experiences before the children left the family nest was a Christmas time trip to Club Med in Mexico. I had kept in touch with my Alberni Elementary School friend Ray Parks. Ray and his wife, Trudy, lived in Victoria and had a similar-aged family to us, with three kids. We decided to holiday together in Playa Blanca, Mexico. Our friendships, Mexico's warm weather, and new cultural experiences all combined to create a lasting memory of how good it was to celebrate life and have fun together.

A second family-rich event came via an invitation to the Parks, family home in Victoria in 1992 to celebrate Canada's 125th anniversary of Confederation, popularly referred to as Canada 125. The Parks hosted a large gathering of family and friends. The day's events included a themed provincial and territorial obstacle race among the participants, followed by a feast featuring "roast beaver" (roast beef in disguise). The obstacles featured, among other things: for the Yukon event, participants racing around the cul-de-sac wearing snowshoes; for the Prince Edward Island event, participants peeling a potato; for the Alberta event, participants jumping over several sawhorses; and last but not least, for the Quebec event, participants striking a piñata or "swatting the Meech." The event was celebrated in good humour, with several cases of Molson Canadian and Nova Scotia's Moosehead beer.[2]

IT WAS DURING this time that Ray Park introduced his friends Maria and Vaslav Cempirek. Ray and Vaslav had been friends since their college days. They were on sports scholarships with Gonzaga University in Spokane, Washington. Ray told us Vaslav's story. He was a Czech defector. In the Prague Spring of 1968, Vaslav was in the army. This was not a good time to be a Czech soldier, as Warsaw Pact armies were now arriving to suppress the social reforms of the Dubček government. Vaslav quickly decided life could be better than it was under the communist regime. He fled to Austria, where Canada and other countries were providing a humanitarian response to the needs of the Prague Spring refugees. Canada decided to use the Hungarian model, which was to relax admission criteria, including medical examinations and security screening. The federal government chartered flights to bring 11,200 refugees to Canada between September 8, 1968, and January 10, 1969.[3]

OUR KIDS' GRADUATIONS from high school began in the mid-1990s. Our expectations for our children's education to continue at university did not happen as planned.

Sometimes our lives are interrupted by world events. This was the case in the nineties.

Diana, Princess of Wales

The world was shocked at the untimely death of Diana, Princess of Wales, on August 31, 1997.

Her elegance and keen sense of fashion made her a world-class celebrity. She became known as the "People's Princess," as the UK's prime minister, Tony Blair, referred to her after her death—a term affectionately picked up by the media. Diana and her husband,

Charles, struggled in their marital relationship; they separated and then divorced. She learned to use her celebrity to champion humanitarian causes and single-handedly uplifted the image of the Royal family.

Her untimely passing has a place in history with other beloved people who passed before her. Previously, the assassination of John F. Kennedy was an event of similar magnitude. Diana's funeral was watched by an estimated 2.5 billion television viewers, the most in the history of television.[4] It was possibly one of the greatest, globally collective moments of sadness and grief the world had witnessed. Like President Kennedy, Diana was deeply admired and loved. Her decency and understanding of human suffering touched the world community.

This loss touched Thea personally, as she had corresponded with Diana during the Expo 86 days.

Skiing, surfing, and cruises

Independence cuts both ways. One can be independent, only to find out that one's kids like the idea of independence too. Around the mid-1990s, a term called the "gap year" became popular. High school grads felt compelled to go and ski for a year at the Whistler ski resort or go surfing at Bondi Beach in Australia before pursuing a higher education. Tongue-in-cheek, this was called Whistler or Australian University. It could also be called a touch of the ol' "affluenza"—as if affected by a virus, the younger generation get by relying on money received from their affluent parents.

Thea and Greg both took a gap year. Matt went directly to a local college. Through these years, our kids did support themselves with part-time jobs. We made it clear that we were always willing to help when help was required.

A lovely surprise closing out the decade came in October 1999, when Thea provided Claire and me with our first cruising experience, a one-week western Caribbean cruise. For the previous two summers, Thea had worked in Beaver Creek, Yukon, at a lodge for Alaskan cruise excursions. A complimentary cruise was the perk offered for employees who served for two consecutive summers. This included taking parents along with you if a shared cabin was acceptable. Thus began our passion for cruising.

CHAPTER 13

THIS BEAUTIFUL LIFE

THE POWER OF a good education can never be underestimated. Used wisely, it creates a beautiful life. I greatly valued my parents' continuing advice to keep going to school. My dad recognized that his overriding commitment to his family's need for hands on the farm ended his own chance for an education. Sacrifice of this nature was for the greater good of the farming family. Fortunately, my evolved urban lifestyle did not demand this type of commitment.

Dreams realized

After gadding about for a year or two, our girl headed to university. Like her mother, Thea studied sociology. To everyone's delight, she graduated in 2001 with a Bachelor of Arts degree. As a nice reward to herself for achieving her educational goal, she asked Claire to join her on a trip to Paris in the fall of that year. Claire said, "Yes, if you'll also come with me to Italy."

In a postcard picturing Versailles, Claire wrote to me, "Thea's very good at French + the Metro. Ceilidh Parks has met us in Paris for the weekend."[1] Next, in an October 15, 2001, email, Thea begins with, "Ciao d'Italia, I am loving life from the ancient town of Vernazza, sitting pretty on the Northern Italian Riviera, in the Gulf of Genoa. We (Mom & I) arrived this morning from Paris by Eurail train. The train was so much fun. I felt like royalty because we had a first-class sleeping cabin. Upon boarding the train, they offer you a glass of French champagne. What a marvelous way to start a trip."[2]

Greg earned a Bachelor of Arts degree from Simon Fraser University, and Matt did a mathematics degree at UBC. Thea followed her BA with a Master of Arts degree. The educational foundations were laid for this generation of the Andruff family.

Wedding season

It seems like one minute parents are busy raising their family, and the next minute the family has walked out the door and down the aisle. Starting in May 2003 and within fifteen months, all three of our children were married.

It should come as no surprise that none of this new generation were married in a church. The various toasts to the couples were held at a golf club, a community centre, and a park.

Claire and I were overjoyed to share these key family celebrations with all our family and friends. We were also pleased to welcome a new son-in-law and two daughters-in-law to the family. In the fall of 2004, Claire and I officially joined the empty nesters club!

Weddings are a wonderful time to bring families together. And so, Claire and I also travelled to Australia for a niece's wedding, and to Ottawa for each of our three nephews' weddings. My sister Laurie and I built on this experience to rekindle a closer brother–sister relationship, despite the distance between Vancouver and Ottawa, by adding trips to Mexico, the US, and Cuba.

An abundance of travel

Claire and I have travelled a lot. We have visited thirty-one countries, on five of the seven continents. Our favourite destinations include Mexico (ten times), Sydney, Australia (five times), New York City (three times), Hawaii (three times), and Cuba (twice). We have taken seven ocean cruises.

From sitting on the rooftop bar of the Ferman Hotel in the old town of Istanbul, listening to the call to prayer from the Blue Mosque, to kissing the cod in a George Street pub in St. John's, Newfoundland; from marvelling at the Twelve Apostles in Australia, to gazing at the Cliffs of Moher in the Republic of Ireland; from witnessing two of the four Grand Slam tennis tournaments (New York and Melbourne) to two Olympics (Sydney and Vancouver); from St. Petersburg's gold-leaf-flourished fountains at the Peterhof Palace to the Aspedos Theatre in Turkey, where lions ate Christians; from 60°C (140°F) in the depth of the Grand Canyon to the Ice Bar in Stockholm, featuring ice harvested two hundred kilometres north of the Arctic Circle, to watching a golden sunset from a terrace during happy hour in Ixtapa, Mexico, Claire and I, along with our family, have enjoyed a beautiful life.

But wait . . . there's more

In 2008, Thea and her husband, Leandro, welcomed their first child, a daughter. Chloe was a great-granddaughter for Mike and Natalie, and the first grandchild for Claire and me. All our family members were elated by Chloe's arrival. Sadly, she was the first and last great-grandchild Mike and Natalie would hold. They both passed away during the summer of 2008, just six weeks apart.

Thea and Leandro welcomed their daughters Madison and Berkeley in 2011 and 2012, respectively. Francheska was born in 2020, followed by Anastasia in 2021, to Matt and his wife, Liz. The Andruff family tree is flush with granddaughters!

As our grandchildren grow older, they resemble the sophistication and energy of a bright-red Formula One race car. That high-pitched screaming of the engine, that burst of power, is how they move through their day. They master their lessons quickly, they handle computer applications and technologies smoothly, and they exhibit grace and intellect beyond their years. All too quickly, they will finish school and move on with their lives, just like the generations before them.

Claire and I have no greater joy than our grandchildren. Grandchildren are the best part of growing old.

CHAPTER 14

REVIEWING THE BOOMER ERA

MOST BABY BOOMERS undoubtedly had it good. Opportunities abounded. Economic growth, fuelled by the oil industry, was long and sustained. On the other hand, the extensive use of things like plastics, jet travel, and industrial processes and practices polluted the environment.

Higher education increased potential earning capacity, but many boomers still prospered without a higher education.[1] The Canadian standard of living was high. A unionized labourer or apprentice could have a very good retirement, with responsible household budgeting and planning. A person with a small business could prosper and grow happily into retirement years.

Immigration in my time included foreign workers arriving in Port Alberni, including "boat people" from Vietnam, and refugees from Hungary and Czechoslovakia. Many arrived due to Canada's humanitarian policies. Other refugees arrived in Canada from war-torn countries through private sponsorships. Family sponsorships shaped entire communities of families. Some immigrants arrived by effectively buying their residency through investor-class programs. Foreign students were granted permanent residency after completing their degrees, if they chose to stay in the country.

Bryony Lau reported in the *National Post* that in 2018 and 2019, Canada resettled more refugees through private sponsorship than any other country.[2] As in those early days for the Russian refugees, many of today's refugees were brought to Canada by private sponsorship. The federal government relies on private sponsorship to bring approximately 23,000 refugees to Canada each year. Canadians, many of whom are themselves descendants of refugees, are supportive of refugee sponsorship (see Appendix A, which addresses private sponsorship).

Some of these immigration programs led to "hits and misses" in terms of their intended effect. Some foreign investors may send their wives to Canada to have babies, use the medical system and educational systems, and enjoy freedoms and peace while maintaining their income-producing capacities and major assets in their home country, meaning the Canadian taxpayer is footing the costs for the immigrants' social safety net. "Astronauts" was the term used to describe the family members remaining in Canada, while the breadwinners returned to work in their country of origin.

The large component of student immigration also had its drawbacks. Their training, typically in white-collar career paths such as financial planning, law, or accounting, meant the trades and service sectors was unrepresented, exacerbating an imbalance in the workforce. Such policy leads to a deleterious imbalance of labourers. Most Canadians are unaware that in addition to the approximately 400,000 immigrants welcomed into the country each year, the country takes in at least that many as students and temporary workers.[3]

Civic, provincial, and federal governments were just getting on their feet to provide infrastructure spending when the Port Alberni Centennial spending program began in the mid-1960s. Over time, this spending increased to push Canadian taxpayers' commitment to the national debt to dizzying new heights.

The Canadian Taxpayers Federation states that in 1967, Canada's national debt stood at roughly $14 billion. By 2021, it had risen to over $1 trillion dollars, or by almost 75 times in 54 years.

The per capita share rose from $684 in 1967 to $27,687 in February 8, 2021.⁴ Again, future generations will be saddled with finding solutions to this.

Claire and I experienced first-hand the generous government spending on universities. We noticed, over time, the shifting of that support to other priorities. Many times, the federal government downloaded program funding to provinces, forcing cutbacks in spending for education and health care, among other programs. This explains why university educations are now much more expensive to obtain than previously.

With the economic impact of the COVID-19 pandemic, federal government spending will reach epic proportions, because jobless workers will need help to pay rent and buy food, while businesses will need bailouts to keep the economy running.

The labourers in the forestry industry (like those in Port Alberni) and other industries in Canada have witnessed their jobs being exported in the spirit of globalization. The income gap between rich and poor widens annually. New "green" jobs, and those in the digital economy, may be difficult to obtain for those with limited education. Additional entrants into the labour force such as women, people with varying sexual or gender orientation, and those of broader ethnicity, challenged traditional labourers for their jobs. This caused anxiety for those being challenged. Being abandoned by the capitalist system that had promised a dream life for those who grew up in the 1950s has led to "a season of despair" for some, characterized by suicide and chronic drug and alcohol abuse.⁵ The life of the working class has become a class struggle.

Jonathan Manthorpe, author of three books on international relations, politics, and history, suggests "economic disparity, festering senses of regional victimhood, vanishing industries, and a philosophically isolated establishment class whose vision of the country is often at dangerous variance to that of work-a-day Canadians all contribute to the unease experienced by a growing number of the country's citizens."⁶

He illustrates this in his example of the Canadian Parliament, where the centralized decision-making Prime Minister's Office (PMO) has "given too many examples of high-handed and disdainful disregard for not only backbench MPs, but also for ministers and senior civil servants." He's talking about the public's elected representatives.

Canada, as a social democracy, has numerous challenges. As the population has grown, so has the complexity of Canadian lifestyles. There are still some virtuous qualities in the Canadian "brand," however. The health-care system stands as a shining example of how collectively, society benefits right down to each individual. Canadians' ability to live without guns is another testament to being a decent society.

Racism, however, is still pervasive in Canadian society. This was highlighted in the COVID-19 experience, where a lack of tolerance, and even outright violence and hate, was expressed toward the Indigenous, the Chinese community, and people of colour.

There remains an age-old difference between the conservative right and the more liberal left—in fact, more than ever before, as Canadians look for principled leadership. They do not wish to see privileged politicians exhibiting actions and behaviors that defy common moral and ethical standards. They want accountability from their leaders.

Canadians must course-correct their country's direction through the vote. The collective will of the people, expressed through the ballot box, determines the future of the nation.

To quote Winston Churchill, "Democracy is the worst form of government, except for all the others."

The last words on the baby boomers

I, of course, am a baby boomer, and one who takes great pride in being a first-generation Canadian.

I picked up on my parents' work ethic early on. Despite the chaos at home when I was growing up, I believed that I received and enjoyed the appropriate life experiences to pursue a better life as an adult than my parents. True, I didn't achieve my hockey dream, but perhaps by the divine grace of a higher power, I was directed to live an even more fulfilling life.

I met Claire at a tender age. Our relationship has always been based on mutual love and respect for one another. Our earlier days together included travel and education, and we felt truly blessed later in life to be a family of five. Teamwork has been our secret for success.

Claire's parents, Don and Joanne, great Canadians in their own rights, were very supportive to our family. They enjoyed their grandchildren and cared for them a great deal. They will always hold a special place in our hearts.

We enjoy our quiet retirement years. We enjoy watching, more so than doing, these days. Our grandchildren amaze us every day as they grow up. Going forward to deal with challenges in our economy, like those corporations that figuratively "dine and dash" at a fancy restaurant, we foresee leadership roles for our young and talented granddaughters. Young women taking charge in the next generation will likely help mitigate the errors of the boomer era.

Reflecting over the years that have passed since the Russian refugees landed in Canada, their descendants can truthfully say that their lives and lifetime prospects have been immensely improved because of the refugees' sacrifices.

CHAPTER 15

HERE COMES GENERATION X

THE CHILDREN OF baby-boomer moms who were born between 1965 and 1980 are considered "Generation X," or "Gen X."[1] Opinion differs considerably on exactly what date ranges apply to each generation. But what is certain here is that they *are* the next generation.

Gen X children grew up after the sexual revolution era of the 1960s, with easy access to the birth control pill and other forms of contraception, was well underway. Society seemed more focused on adult life than on children. Divorce rates increased rapidly in Generation X because both parents tended to work, leaving the children at home to fend for themselves.

Fortunately for Thea, our eldest child, Claire stayed home to nurture her and her two brothers. Claire took time for her children and enjoyed them. In contrast, the next generation revealed a shifting norm in society that required both parents, or single parents, to be employed for financial survival. Thea's life experience provides a female point of view for this generation.

Gentle beginnings

When Thea was born at the hospital, the nurse turned to me and pointed at the clock and said, "Remember: 1:11 PM on July 11." It was a small gesture, but I have remembered this time (and, obviously, the date) all these years.

Thea's first memories are from when she was four and attending preschool near our home. She was a happy child and felt safe in our home in Kerrisdale, Vancouver. Blonde and blue-eyed like her mother, Thea was an active little girl. She started walking at nine-and-a-half months old, and we had to work to keep up with her energetic pace. As she approached school age, she developed a pronounced diastema, a gap between her top two front teeth. Correcting the gap would necessitate numerous dentist visits for braces. Fortunately, my extended health benefits provided for a portion of the cost.

Our house at the time, built sometime in the 1950s or '60s, had two bedrooms on the main level (twelve steps up from street level, with both bedrooms on the west side of the house, next to a shared driveway) and two bedrooms downstairs. The adjacent home was a "mirrored" twin version. Thea's bedroom was on the back side of the house, on the main level. She could look out her window, past the garden, and see the buses running back and forth on 41st Avenue. She remembers her mother telling her to count five buses before getting up in the morning!

In addition to the two bedrooms, the main floor had a bathroom, a small hall, a kitchen, and living and dining rooms. The living room and dining room featured hardwood floors with two green shag area rugs. In the living room was a piano window on the east wall, and opposite the wide south-facing windows (which opened) was a large, arched, brick wood-burning fireplace.

We had the French doors between the living room and east-side dining room removed as they took up too much space. The dining room had a lovely built-in china cabinet across the back wall (north side) with leaded windows, a mirror, and crystal knob handles. It was perfect for buffet-style serving. A large set of windows on the east wall of the dining room could be opened. If you pushed through the swinging "butler door" into the kitchen from the dining room, you would see a skylight and an eating area next to the bay window. The tiled counter backsplash carried a fruity motif matching the fruit on the Tiffany light fixture over the table. A Dutch door on the northeast end of the kitchen led to an open deck space, where summer barbecues were enjoyed. It was a lovely, safe home for Thea to grow up in with her caring parents.

I barbecued hamburgers Saturday nights all through the year on that deck. My burnt patties were legendary because I'd be watching too much *Hockey Night in Canada* instead of tending to the barbecue.

For holidays and at Christmas, the family enjoyed dinners with our extended family. Thea enjoyed the Sing for Your Supper family Christmas evening and being with her relatives at these times. Claire and I enthusiastically celebrated family gatherings, and this would rub off on Thea with her future family.

Thea played in the backyard, which featured a two-storey tree fort. The yard had apple and pie-cherry trees, and a sandbox beside the garden plot where I burned the tree leaves each autumn.

During the week, before the dinner hour, she delighted in going with her mother to the bus stop to meet the bus that delivered me home from my downtown office. I would alight from the bus wearing my raincoat and galoshes. With a big smile, I would swoop down and hug my sweet little girl, and then kiss my beautiful wife. Then we three would walk home holding hands. Filled with the joy of a happy family, we would swing our little girl in the air, which she loved.

The family enjoyed Crescent Beach in the summer. Waking up early was Thea's specialty, and to allow Claire a few more moments of sleep on weekend mornings, I would take Thea in her child seat on the back of my bike for a ride along the beachfront, or we would go onto the beach and play in the sand until breakfast time.

When Thea was five years old, she won her first Crescent Beach swimming trophy. It was a very proud moment for both her and us, the first proud moment of many to come in her life.

The school years

Thea went to kindergarten and Grades 1 to 3 at the Kerrisdale School Annex, approximately three blocks from home. The location of the Annex was south of 41st Avenue, which meant she didn't have to cross a busy street to go to school. Claire walked her to school each school day.

Her first teacher was Mrs. Pender, whom Thea greatly admired. She also enjoyed her friendships with Trisha Bromley and Monica Lui, who were fellow Annex students.

Like many young learners, her math skills were latent, benefitting from additional support from the Learning Assistance Centre. This was welcomed support that helped her educational development immensely.

In Grade 2, she got chicken pox, which she passed on to her brothers; they each had to stay at home for two weeks consecutively. (A vaccine for scheduled childhood immunization for chicken pox was not available until 1995.[2]) Sadly, this event occurred during Halloween, and the children had to stay in quarantine. I took this opportunity to introduce them to the board game called *Sorry!*. It proved to be a useful way to pass the quarantine period.

Several years later, Vancouver hosted the world fair Expo 86. Taken by the Princess of Wales's elegance (Diana and Prince Charles opened the fair), Thea wrote a letter to Diana, welcoming her to Vancouver. In May 1986, she received a reply thanking her for her warm wishes. The reply was from Alexandra Loyd, lady-in-waiting to Diana.[3]

Also around this time, when asked what she wanted to do when she grew up, Thea would say she wanted to become the prime minister of Canada. Girls could become anything they wanted.

Thea attended Kerrisdale Elementary School, on the north side of 41st Avenue, for Grades 4 and 5. She met her sidekick, Trisha, in Grade 4. In Grade 5, they had become known as "TheaTrisha." They were separated in class to quell their distracting social behaviour. Also during this time, Thea was in a Grade 4-5 split class and made friends with Sandra Healy. They attended Girl Guides together. Sandra was a year ahead of Thea and had her sights set on doing Grades 6 and 7 at General Gordon School, known for offering late French Immersion. This idea appealed to Thea as well, so she asked us to help her apply to the French program. Her sense was that she wanted a challenge, and the gift of knowing a second language was appealing to her.

The General Gordon School French immersion student population included children from across the Lower Mainland. French language learning was broadly sought after. It was here that her place in Generation X was exemplified. Her teacher asked the class of thirty students how many were living in single-parent families. Many hands were raised. The teacher stopped and rephrased the question to ask how many students lived with both their parents? Thea and one other student raised their hand. They were anomalies of their generation.

During her time at school, Thea applied herself and was on the honour roll for both Grades 6 and 7. She also gained publicity by leading a petition for her Grade 6 class to be included in a short television story about her school. The event was originally planned for just the Grade 7 class. The principal permitted the Grade 6 students to walk in a line behind the student being interviewed, who happened to be her friend Sandra Healy. It was clear that Sandra had a positive influence on Thea, because just as she was inspired to follow Sandra to French immersion, she now had her sights set on applying to the Point Grey Mini School, where Sandra was accepted to attend high school.

Only three Mini Schools existed in Vancouver, and there was keen competition to land a spot. The purpose of the Mini Schools was to advance the curriculum faster than regular high school programs so that students could pursue enriched learning opportunities within their highly motivated peer group. Each Mini School took fifteen boys and fifteen girls.

With our assistance, Thea applied to the Point Grey Mini School. The principal, Dr. John O'Connor, invited her, Claire, and me to an interview. He liked the story of her Grade 6 petition. Her leadership qualities and her honour roll standing at General Gordon School earned her a spot in the Mini School.[4]

For the next five years, her fellow students did orientation trips several times a year for five-day segments. The larger group included all grades of the Mini. The later-grade students performed leadership roles for the three learning events planned each day. They skied, observed nature, kayaked, and watched live Shakespearean theatre. The Mini School program taught leadership and life skills such as confidence and ownership of one's future. Thea described it as an awesome learning experience.

Her Mini School experience also included the first taste of teachers going beyond basic lesson plans. One teacher was an avid environmentalist and encouraged students, including Thea, to place a "Save the Stein" lawn sign in their front yards. This action was in support of stopping old-growth logging in the Stein Valley. It placed her in the unfortunate position of defending her action to me and our neighbour, who both worked for forest-product companies at the time. Under protest, she removed the sign from the lawn. The sight of two grown men badgering a little thirteen-year-old girl over an environmental issue was, in retrospect, pathetic. Were their livelihoods being threatened by a lawn sign? She may have lost this battle, but, ultimately, the environmentalists succeeded in saving old-growth forests.

Thea made the honour roll in Grades 8, 9, and 10.[5] Her extracurricular swimming program demanded more of her time in those grades as she earned elite swim times in her competitive swimming. Her commitment to swimming also affected her social life with classmates. She would receive invitations to social events but would have to give her regrets due to practice time. In the later part of her Mini School program, her disciplined life was starting to wear on her. She continued her friendship with Trisha, who attended the Little Flower Academy girls' school. They often met at the Arbutus Club. As graduation approached, she was happy to leave school behind her.

Claire and I strongly encouraged her to go to university, but Thea wanted to live a little first. Her priority was to travel.

Looking back at her class of thirty students, it is interesting to note that of the thirty, twenty-eight students stayed together until the end of Grade 12 and graduated from the program. Of those twenty-eight, twenty-six ended up with post-graduate degrees, with either a Master of Arts or a PhD.

Education for Mike's granddaughter had certainly moved into another universe from his Grade 6 experience at Ranger School in Gage, Alberta.

A last thought on Thea's friend Sandra Healy. She was like my school friend Ian Sinclair. These were the better angels of humanity whose lights shine brightly but are only seen by a few. They reach out and lift up others. Both of these past school friendships have dwindled for Thea and me, but their memories remain vivid.

CHAPTER 16

MIND THE GAP

1994 to 1997

Thea was eighteen and yearned for adventure after her graduation from high school. Her early experiences with travel likely explained her wanderlust. Before she was thirteen years old, she had already travelled to Australia, the US, and Europe.

In Australia, she visited a seaside resort in Forresters Beach, New South Wales, saw the sights and scenes of Sydney and the capital city of Canberra, and visited a sheep station near Dalgety.

Her trip to the US was to Disneyland, in Anaheim, California.

In Europe, she arrived in Brussels, where her uncle Ken and aunt Sheila took her to Rothenburg ob der Tauber, Germany, the site of the famed Christmas market, to view its medieval architecture, and then they were off to see the white cliffs of Dover, Canterbury, and lastly, Paris. When they were not having these weekend excursions, Ken arranged for a friend's daughter, similar in age to Thea, to converse with her in French.

Independence

Part of being young is discovering one's independence. The rule for our kids to abide by (after graduation from high school) was to continue with further education or pay rent to stay at home. Thea started a fall semester at a local college in Vancouver. At the beginning of 1995, her chance for independence came when her cousin Jennifer arrived from Australia. Jennifer planned to go to work at Whistler Mountain for the winter. That was all Thea needed to join the procession to Whistler U.

She was hired on in the catering department, but soon became a "liftee," someone who worked at the top or bottom of a ski hill, and was able to acquire staff accommodation. That year she skied to her heart's content. Her lifestyle was skiing, partying, and working. Because Whistler is a world-class ski resort, it offered her the skiing experience of a lifetime.

Thea met a very diverse collection of young people from all over the world. They all had ideas to share with each other. In 1996, travelling to Australia was the next objective on Thea's list.

Dreadlocks: The Greatest Generation versus Generation X

Dreads are worn by some people wanting to make a statement. For Thea, it was likely to symbolize her rebelling against conformity or the status quo. This idea was likely developed in her circle of Whistler colleagues.

In late 1996, before Thea's departure to Australia, her grandmother, Joanne, a member of the "Greatest Generation," asked Thea to cut her hair to get rid of her dreadlocks. Thea explained that she felt beautiful with them. Her grandmother offered her $250 to do the chop. Thea resisted. Time passed and her grandmother approached her again, doubling her offer. Thea further explained that her statement of beauty could not be bought. Her wily old grandmother then asked Thea, "What will it take?" Mindful that she needed funds for travel, Thea floated the amount of $2,000. "Done," said her grandmother, "on the condition that you save the hair and show me."

Her Australian family, receiving her at the airport in Sydney, noted her non-conforming appearance, with dreadlocks and overalls. She was clearly looking to make an impact on them, but it was not likely what she had expected. Respecting her grandmother's request and desire for her conformity, she visited a hairdresser in the following week to perform her part of the bargain. Perhaps she realized it was not simply her looks that defined her as an individual.

Confidence

Initially, Thea stayed with her Australian relatives in North Sydney. She had a renewable one-year work permit. She took odd jobs for a month or two at a time. After a stay in Sydney, she ventured north to the Gold Coast, eventually ending up on the Whitsunday Islands in Queensland. Youth hostels were her typical accommodation.

Later in 1997, she flew to New Zealand for more adventure. She travelled alone and made friends wherever she found herself. She had developed a self-confidence during her travels and had learned how to manage and sustain herself. As she met her fellow travellers, she often received encouragement to get on with her university education when she finished her travelling. They also shared views on different places in the world for future travels.

Over the summer, she had received overtures from her parents to consider coming home. A Christmas-to-New-Year's family trip to a Club Med in Mexico was in the planning stages, and she was invited home to join the excursion. She could continue adventuring, or she could set a new course for herself at home.

In October of 1997, her family greeted a refined and smartly dressed young lady at the airport. She had obviously gained a great deal from her time spent living away.

Conquering the gap

Had the gap years away from school been worth it, and what did Thea accomplish?

Socializing with others in her peer group had taught her a great deal. She learned how to manage herself as she travelled. She recognized that being unique was fun, but conformity was important to people, most importantly, her grandmother. Her self-reliance improved her confidence in herself. She acquired knowledge of the world from her international peer group: how they lived and where they had travelled helped her form her opinions of the value of her life.

Thea was a second-generation Canadian in her paternal ancestry, so this freedom of movement and travel as a modern woman seemed quite natural to her. However, this was a world apart from how other young women lived. A female refugee's life in a UNHCR (United Nations High Commissioner for Refugees) camp is quite different. She has no such freedom. Her world is harsh, at times brutal, and controlled by others. The real gap Thea had conquered was her free life compared to her family's refugee life of several generations earlier. She is an example of what a granddaughter of future refugees can become.

CHAPTER 17

IN PURSUIT OF CRITICAL THINKING

THEA BEGAN STUDYING for her UBC degree at a time when her Mini School friends were in the last year of their degree programs, in 1998. She took general courses such as political science and history but soon gravitated to sociology courses. She found the sociology course content felt just right. This was a path that her mother had previously taken for her degree.

In Thea's first semester, she was reacquainted with a young man named Leandro Berretta, who was in his last semester. They had previously met in Grade 10. At UBC, they had classes in the Buchanan Building and arranged to meet after class in the student union building's Gallery Bar so she could ask him to remind her of his first name. They continued to meet up there for some time.

In the summer of 1998, Thea planned to work in a job outside the city. She achieved her goal by taking a job with Holland America cruise lines, which had an inland excursion accommodation in Beaver Creek, Yukon. The cruise company offered room and board, travel costs to and from Beaver Creek, and a salary. Her job was housekeeping for the travellers. If employees were loyal and returned to work the following summer, Holland America offered a big perk: a free one-week cruise for the employee and a friend or their parents. This offer appealed to Thea.

Like many student summer jobs, it provided Thea with a rich experience. During her break periods, she was able to adventure. Located on the Alaskan border, Beaver Creek is Canada's westernmost community. She ventured as far west into Alaska as Mount Denali, North America's highest mountain peak. In her adventures, she saw moose, bears, and caribou.

A fellow worker offered to drive with Thea from Vancouver to Beaver Creek in their second summer. This provided her with the experience of travelling the entire length of BC from south to north. In the Yukon, they passed Mount Logan, Canada's highest mountain.

Also in 1998, as Thea was starting her first day in her second semester, she received word that her grandfather Don Brewster had passed away. This was crushing news for Thea. Her "Papa" was one of her biggest supporters and a big reason she enjoyed Crescent Beach for all of her summers, why she enjoyed the Arbutus Club (he was a founding member), and why she enjoyed her large family gatherings. Above all, she would miss his unconditional love. Within four months, Joanne, her dear grandmother, also sadly passed. Both of these people were the best examples of caring grandparents.

In October 1999, Thea asked one of her professors if she could write her midterm exam early because she was taking her parents on a Caribbean cruise. Naturally, he obliged her, and later that month we all flew to Fort Lauderdale in Florida to join the cruise. Like all travel experiences, the cruise opened our eyes to new places and people. It was fun for us, but for Thea, it was back to work after it ended.

At UBC, one of her favourite professors was Brian Elliott. Now close to his retirement, he was a newly arrived professor from England when Claire was studying sociology many years earlier—quite the coincidence. Thea worked hard at her studies and maintained a first-class average. For her efforts, she received a lifetime membership into the Golden Key Society. This is given in recognition of students who are the top fifteen per cent of their faculty.[1] Thea received her Bachelor of Arts degree in May 2001.

Off to work

Life was full of promise for the graduate. She took a job at the English Language Institute. The previous summer, she had worked with the Institute on the UBC campus in a bilingual role helping South American, Chinese, and Japanese students. She helped them to learn cultural aspects of Canada as they studied university-level English. She enjoyed the summer job, but in her new, full-time job, she was in an administrative role. The work was okay, but she felt underutilized.

During her first year out of university, Thea also spent time helping people in the Downtown Eastside (DTES). This is one of the poorest places in Canada. She worked in soup kitchens and assisted in acquiring supplies for an abused women's society. Her exposure to the life of the downtrodden concerned her. Drawing on her recent studies, she pondered solutions to the misery she was witnessing.

Leandro Berretta was now an item in her life. He often helped her in her work in the DTES. Leandro was frustrated with his job prospects, and he had decided to return to UBC to study computer science, a second degree for him.

Thea was also looking at her options. She wrote the LSAT exam, which qualified students for law school. While she did get accepted into two schools of law, neither of them was located in Vancouver. She and Leandro wanted to stay together in Vancouver at this point.

Back to academia

Thea shared her experience on the DTES with Brian Elliott at UBC. After listening to her passion for finding solutions to the plight of the DTES, he suggested she consider doing a Master of Arts degree to study homelessness.

Thea applied to graduate school and succeeded in starting her program in the fall semester of 2002. Leandro managed to obtain student housing on campus, and in October he asked Thea to live with him. Rent was $800 per month. Fortunately for them, Thea had a job as a teaching assistant that paid $800 per month. The following year, Leandro graduated and then he and Thea were married.

Thea relished her further studies, and her thesis advisor, Brian Elliott, inspired her to produce an insightful examination of the homeless occupation of the vacant Woodward's Department Store, near Vancouver's Downtown Eastside.

In 2004, Thea earned her Master of Arts degree, graduating at the top of her class.

Her first jobs were with a charity and then the Government of Canada. Neither rang any bells for her. She continued sending out resumés to upgrade her opportunities. My sister Kay lived in New Westminster at the time. She told Thea of an opportunity at Douglas College, where there was an opening for a sociology instructor. Thea applied for the position and again asked Brian Elliott for his support by way of a letter of reference. To their mutual surprise, she got the job.

In 2005, she walked into her first staff meeting and was told the meeting was for faculty, not students. At twenty-nine years old, she was the youngest lecturer on staff.

Thea and Leandro were now set. They both had jobs they enjoyed. They had bought a beautiful one-bedroom apartment with a view in trendy Kitsilano. Their goals as a young couple were achieved, for the most part.

Several years later, they discussed the notion of starting a family. They were in their early thirties. In January 2008, baby Chloe arrived.

Another development that year was that Thea entered Simon Fraser University (SFU) for her PhD in sociology. She was the only faculty member in her faculty at Douglas College with a master's degree. All the other faculty were PhDs, and she felt it was important to take this next step.

Thea and Leandro moved next to a two-bedroom Kitsilano condo so Chloe could have her own room and Thea could have a den in which to study.

Thea's academic performance in the past was at the top of her peers, and she believed she would "stomp it" with her PhD. She advanced through her coursework in her typical fashion.

Several unexpected forces were at play. She underestimated the pressures of motherhood. The PhD required far more work than she thought it would, and she also underestimated how much she loved it. When she wasn't caring for her child, she was lecturing at the college. When she wasn't working or child-minding, she was studying.

Something's gotta give

Preparing for her comprehensive exam was chaotic. Changing diapers, cramming for the exam, and teaching during the day were all leading to a recipe for disaster. Had this been just three years earlier, it would have been a cakewalk, with no child to mind and all the time needed to concentrate on course material. This time, however, Thea failed her comprehensive exam. Her circumstances were simply too demanding. She was also carrying her second child at the time.

Additionally, unlike the inspirational Brian Elliott, Thea's dissertation advisor was completely unsympathetic to her situation. She was demanding and mean spirited at a time when the slightest note of encouragement would have helped. Thea was surprised her advisor was one of her obstacles to achieving her goal. She had also underestimated the strong pull of her family life.

Thea made the difficult decision to withdraw from her PhD program in the second trimester of her pregnancy.

Child care

One of the greatest laments of many working Canadians is the lack of affordable child care. Thea was paying $1,500 per month for one day a week of child care. Claire helped her two days a week, and Thea and Leandro did two days a week. This problem takes many employable women out of the job market.

Madison Berretta arrived in January 2011. This required Thea to gear down her teaching to part-time hours. As her income decreased, their cost of living continued to climb. The paraphernalia children require meant additional space was required, so Thea and Leandro were now in a house.

In September 2012, another daughter, Berkeley Berretta, was born. The Berretta family was now 2.1 people larger than the average Canadian family.[2]

Douglas College had employed Thea for eight years. In 2012, she chose to leave her college-teaching career and focus on raising her children. Thea knows many strong, well-educated women who excel at their work and also have children. She knows they also have strong support systems, like nannies. If they had deferred starting their family for ten years, like their friends, it would have placed them in a stronger financial position.

Both Thea and Leandro wanted to be responsible for nurturing their own children. Having a younger family was a choice they also agreed upon. As discussed in earlier pages, choices carry costs.

The pull of Crescent Beach

Throughout Thea's life, the Crescent Beach Swimming Club had always been a positive experience. She had grown up in the summer club system, first as a beginning swimmer. She earned a Kidd medal as one of the six youngest swimmers of the summer. At the age of eight, she had qualified to go to the provincial championships in Trail, where she represented the CBSC and won the bronze medal of her swim event, the fifty-metre butterfly. This singular event had changed Thea. She realized she had potential, and it shaped her confidence to enter her late French immersion schooling, the Point Grey Mini School, and the many other life challenges she faced.

Thea had gone on to take leadership training and become a swim coach to other young CBSC swimmers. Her familiar summer surroundings and acquired friendships formed wonderful memories. She wants her girls to have the same enjoyable, enriching experience of Crescent Beach.

Contemporary schooling in the 2000s

Leandro and Thea were well equipped to know how their children should be schooled. They both realize, as did their parents and grandparents, the value of education to the future well-being of their girls. They want the very best for their family.

In the early 2010s, they began their research into early childhood education. They realized that early learning sets the foundation for the later years. They found data to assess the quality of early development ratings by school districts.[3] They also used the Fraser Institute's school performance ratings to help locate the appropriate school for their children.[4]

Interestingly, the elementary school closest to them rated poorly. It was located next to a low-income housing complex. The school was rated as an urban school, which required it to serve nutritional breakfasts and lunches that might not have been available at home. Thea and Leandro both recognized this school was likely attended by new immigrants to Canada. For them, it was not wanting to disassociate from this cohort so much as it was the desire to enhance their girls' learning experience by choosing a different school.

Using the school performance reports, they were able to determine school academic ratings, and the type of parental support most appropriate for them. Perhaps due to Thea's influence, and also buttressed by the reports, they chose a French immersion elementary school for the girls. Language is important, as it opens doors for people. Of course, one doesn't just show up at the door to enroll. The Berrettas had to apply and commit to being involved in the girls' learning experiences. This type of parental engagement was part of the contemporary schooling process.

Advancing to the next decade, their eldest daughter, Chloe, was set to start her secondary education. Again, the apple does not fall far from the tree. Thea and Leandro helped her apply to several high schools that offered Mini Schools. Her resumé was professionally crafted to maximize her success as a candidate for the limited positions. She was successful in receiving several invitations to Mini Schools. However, she also threw her hat in the ring for a position in the city's best independent all-girls school. It possessed the highest academic standard in the Fraser Institute's performance report. She received a great deal of support from her friends and families who were previous attendees at the school. This was also favourable to her application. She was accepted! This young girl is poised for more academic successes, and so, too, are her sisters, who will follow in her footsteps.

Thea and Leandro continuously strive to set up as many opportunities for their children as possible, and one goal they have for them is a university education. They have planned for this path by saving through a Registered Education Program (RESP), which will help pay for the high cost of education. Over the years, the federal government has occasionally offered a national child benefit program. These payments have always been deposited in the girls' RESPs.

Refugee girls would likely long for this experience of educational self-improvement. It is likely Thea's daughter will not have to experience car bombs exploding next to her school or kidnappings from her school due to religious zealots as some refugee families have experienced in their homelands. Canada's laws protect women's rights and freedoms. Yet this success for the Berretta girls developed over two generations of Canadians. It is a journey of intergenerational scope. Those who follow in these footsteps will find it hard at first, but with commitment and hard work, lives will improve.

Thea hopes her girls attend university, get well-paying jobs to care of themselves, find someone to love, and have happiness in their lives. She hopes to be there to support them in their journey.

WITH THE CHILDREN gradually becoming less dependent on her, Thea has the opportunity to rejoin the job market. In order to find a job that will pay well and give her the summer months off (so she can return to her beloved Crescent Beach with her family), she finds herself back at university, training as a teacher. The BC Ministry of Education requires a specific curriculum that will take Thea about a year to complete.

In the old days, they would have rolled out the carpet and engaged Thea as a teacher, given her credentials. Not so today in the BC's educational system.

Why all the fuss? In order for Thea to achieve a full-time salary, with a package of benefits including a retirement superannuation, she has to fulfill the ministry's teaching requirements.

Living in a huge city like Greater Vancouver takes a great deal of money. Living costs continue to escalate, including the cost of housing, while earnings are not rising at the same pace. Thea's additional earning power will be important to keep the Berretta family finances covered.

Thea is concerned about her girls' future. With Vancouver being so prohibitively expensive, she wonders if the entire family will remain where they live now, or if they will all move somewhere more affordable. She also has concerns about retirement. Will she and Leandro have done enough in their work life to afford their retirement? These are the ponderings of a second-generation Canadian.

CHAPTER 18

CIRCLING BACK TO THE REFUGEES

THEA WAS IN her paternal grandparents' lives for thirty-two years. Her first recollections of Mike and Natalie were a picnic on Vancouver's idyllic Spanish Banks. She recalls a chicken dinner on a red-and-white checkered tablecloth.

Love and caring attention from them pervade her memories. She never saw the negative influence of alcohol or the dysfunctionality in the lives of her grandparents. Mike and Natalie attended her school and sporting events, and they looked after Thea and her siblings when Claire and I needed to be away. They helped with transportation to school and events, they hosted and joined in all family events, and, in general, they were always there for their granddaughter.

She never considered them as refugees, originally. They were just her grandparents. They were typical Canadians who watched NHL hockey on Saturday nights and enjoyed picnics and the holidays. Her evolved life of privilege has desensitized her to her roots. When asked about her roots on her father's side of the family, she will say that her family history is well documented to the point where she is aware that her great-grandparents likely sacrificed a great deal to allow her to live her privileged life. She hopes to be a knowledge keeper for the family history.

She recognizes that immigration is important to Canada, because without it, our population will decline. If this were to occur, the burden of the Canadian social safety net would become too costly to maintain. Immigration is also important for the cultural betterment of the nation. It is through diversity that the nation prospers and enriches itself.

Refugees figure into this diversity. Thea has little if any experience with refugees in Vancouver, likely because Vancouver is too expensive for most and especially for a typical refugee family. Fortunately for the refugees in her extended family, they were accepted into already diverse prairie communities.

As her time with her grandparents was coming to an end, 2008 was a milestone year. Thea had just started her PhD program and she and Leandro began their family. In July, they introduced Mike and Natalie to their great-granddaughter. Thea recalls Natalie holding her little bundle of joy and singing a 1950s song called "A Bushel and a Peck" to the little baby. Thea continues to sing this song to her children. The baton of pure love was passed from one mother to another with this memorable visit.

Like ships passing in the harbour, as the great-granddaughter entered the harbour of life, Mike and Natalie shipped out later that summer.

CHAPTER 19

CONCLUSION: A CALL TO PAY IT FORWARD

THE TRUE AND lasting legacy of the Russian refugees was freedom for their families.

In their new country, they could worship as they wished. They could assemble and associate freely. They could travel where they wanted. They could own land and grow businesses. They were equal among others (no longer were they "non-preferreds"). They had legal rights. They could keep the customs and traditions of their heritage. They possessed the freedom to express their opinions. They could live freely and without fear.

All descendants of the Russian refugees are encouraged to remember the value of freedom. Freedom is not free. One has to stand up for what one believes in. Events or forces that may threaten one's freedom can occur. Civil war, autocracy, and one of the greatest concerns, apathy, can steal freedom away. What must one do to protect freedom? Every Canadian citizen has a responsibility to vote. Canadians need to involve themselves in each election. Participation rather than apathy ensures the will of the people is served.

CONCLUSION: A CALL TO PAY IT FORWARD

It is hard to know what life for the descendants would have been like had the Russian refugees been denied entry, say for insufficient funds. There is precedence for denying entry. Recall that in 1914, Canadian immigration officials denied entry to 340 Sikhs, 24 Muslims, and 12 Hindus on the *Komagata Maru*. They returned to India and faced harsh treatment, and some were even killed upon their return.

Today there are millions of refugees looking for the same opportunity extended to the Russians almost one hundred years ago.

Since 1950, the UNHCR has helped resettle roughly 50 million people to restart their lives. Among them, 200,000 Hungarian refugees who fled to Austria in 1956. Some of those refugees settled in Canada, and specifically in Port Alberni, through these efforts.

At the end of 2019, the UNHCR reports 79.5 million people were forcibly displaced worldwide. Twenty-six million are refugees, half of whom are under eighteen years old. The top hosting countries are Turkey, Colombia, Pakistan, Uganda, and Germany. The top source countries include Syria, Venezuela, Afghanistan, South Sudan, and Myanmar.[1]

All Canadians indirectly help refugees, because the Canadian government continues to play a humanitarian role with organizations like the UNHCR. But given the statistics noted above, each Canadian citizen, including the descendants of the original Russian refugees, could do more. Appendix A offers information about private sponsorship of refugees. Imagine the life of a refugee sponsored today and their Canadian family one hundred years into the future.

A grateful extended family recognizes a generous philanthropist, a sponsor, the Government of Canada, and one Russian refugee, Nikifor, who did the best he could with his opportunity.

PART THREE

CHAPTER 20

TODAY'S REFUGEES

Raison d'être

Like the Andreeffs and the Sidoroffs, today's refugees are searching for a safe haven. They want to live their lives free from tyranny, abuse, discrimination and fear. They want a community where graft, bribery, and blackmail are no longer the currency needed for everyday living.

The price to be paid for asylum

What many refugees must endure are camps and detention centres where communications to the outside world are forbidden, violence occurs among both detainees and attendants, medical facilities and medicines are in poor supply, nutrition is lacking in quantity and quality, detainees' mental health conditions are untreated, sanitation is poor, and accommodations are cramped.

Even before being detained, asylum seekers face frightening obstacles. A recent article illustrates this: "Between 1975 and 1995, almost 800,000 refugees left Vietnam by boat. They faced pirates, overcrowding and storms. According to the United Nations High Commissioner for Refugees, between 200,000 and 400,000 died at sea."[1]

The world has also experienced increasing conflict over time. Sadly, this has increased the numbers of refugees and decreased intake of certain refugees in some countries. For example, the destruction of the World Trade Centre in New York caused countries to be on the watch for more terrorism. The United States began to review applicants from Muslim countries more discerningly. Australians grew anxious about the number of asylum-seeking boat people touching their shores from places like Malaysia and Indonesia. They made the political decision to either send boats back to their country of origin or, failing that, to send all boat people to Manus Island in Papua New Guinea for "processing." Manus Island has a detention centre that the Australian government had arranged to warehouse boat people, paying Papua New Guinea to use this facility. It has also contracted with the island state of Nauru for a second detention facility. These extreme actions were quietly managed over the last twenty years. The horrendous conditions in these facilities were exposed by organizations like Human Rights Watch and Amnesty International.[2]

OVER THE YEARS, refugees have faced numerous versions of screening by the Canadian government. The Bolsheviks forced their hand on the Russian refugees who were living in Harbin, China, a century ago: return to the Soviet Union for repatriation as Soviets or stay in China. China was sending signals that they had to move on or join the Chinese Communist Party. Canada, Australia, and the United States were opening up their land, and they were looking for immigrants. The Russian Red Cross asked the Canadian trade commissioner based in Shanghai in July 1923 to take some of their 16,000 Russian refugees. Communications in those days were, of course, by posted letters. It wasn't until May 6, 1924, that the Canadian government granted visas to twenty-one families (116 refugees). The government relied completely on the representations of the Red Cross and the CPR Colonization Department.

In Part Two, I noted that thousands of Hungarians and Czechs had medical and security checks waived by the government for the sake of their personal safety and the required speed of evacuation.

That was then. Today, asylum seekers to Canada need to have their immigration application accepted; they need either governmental or private sponsorship; they need a medical check-up; they need someone to vouch for their character; and they need to be interviewed by immigration officials. It can take up to two years before all the dots get connected. In fairness, the government's role in their selection process, aside from humanitarian considerations, is to ensure that each candidate will contribute to the country and does not have a dark past that might indicate a risk to a peace-loving nation.

Case studies in private sponsorship

Many refugees come to Canada through private sponsorship. Where letters and teletype communications were used in the past, today's refugees use WiFi, cell phones, and the help of influencers to capture the attention of the Canadian public. (An influencer is a person who uses social media to create a presence. That presence is noticed by large numbers of followers.)

Two refugees who made it to Canada were an Iranian and a Syrian. They managed social media themselves, and their stories created their celebrity.

Amir Taghinia

Born in Iran, Amir dreamed about experiencing the world outside of Iran. He didn't fancy being drafted into the military when he turned eighteen, so he lobbied his parents to help him get his passport.

Few countries will offer a visa to someone with an Iranian passport. Malaysia was an exception. They offered Amir a five-year temporary visa in 2008. He spent his time learning languages, specifically English and Malay, and saving money for his future.

Eventually, his visa expired. An overstay is an offence. He learned that, for a price, certain people could "adjust" his permit for another six months.

Amir's plan was to sell his motor scooter, buy a plane ticket to Indonesia, and find a human smuggler. His destination was Christmas Island, an Australian territory. He planned to seek asylum in

Australia. Australia was a signatory to the 1951 Convention Relating to the Status of Refugees. Under these circumstances, he was hopeful of his chances of acceptance. He landed in Jakarta, made his way to Bogur, and paid $7,000 in US dollars to a human trafficking agent.

After what he described as a twenty-hour ride in a van with other people with the same plan, he arrived on the coast in the dead of night. They were put into a rubber dinghy and transported to a waiting fishing troller. In all, the boat carried eighty-five people.

Says Amir, "I put my chances of drowning on this boat as high as 99 per cent."

Approximately three kilometres off Christmas Island, they were intercepted by an Australian patrol. Perhaps by design, to keep from being turned back, or by coincidence, the boat's water pump failed, and the boat was taking on water. It managed to make it to the island, where the refugees were interned; the boat was taken offshore and scuttled.

Amir spent thirty days incarcerated on Christmas Island. Some people were permitted to go on to Australia, but most of the group was sent to Manus Island.

As detention centres go, Manus was very prison-like.

The camp offered a points system for good behaviour. These points could be used for items in the canteen. Over the course of several years, Amir was able to parlay his points into an Android cell phone with a charger and a phone card. With his English and a phone, he was now able to form a presence with the outside world. He could advocate on Facebook for those languishing in Manus. (This is the very reason phones were banned from the camp. If the authorities found any, they would confiscate them.)

In 2015, Amir had a chance meeting with Chelsea Taylor, a Canadian public health nurse living in Torquay, Australia, who was administering vaccinations at the camp.

He had applied several times, unsuccessfully, for immigration to the US. He then began to focus on Canada. He could complete his application using his phone. He needed to find a Canadian character reference, so he sought out Chelsea Taylor to provide one. She was a key piece of his immigration file. He texted and emailed her to plead his case to her. By coincidence, Chelsea returned home to Canada in 2016. Amir's force of personality motivated Chelsea to beseech her father to help bring Amir to Canada.

On Halloween night in 2017, Amir arrived in Vancouver, the result of a private sponsorship. It has to be noted that Amir had accomplished what few had done before.[3]

Amir's fondest hope is to show Canadians that refugees can be good for Canada.

Hassan Al Kontar

Hassan was born and raised in Suweida, Syria. He became known as the man@theairport and has written a book about his experience which carries the same moniker.[4]

In 2006, he decided to move to the United Arab Emirates (UAE) to work in the insurance business. He is well educated and a cultured man looking for new opportunities.

Time can be an enemy to a foreigner, as was the case when Hassan's passport expired in 2011. With an invalid passport, he couldn't request an extension for his work permit, which also expired. His employer recognized the risk incurred by keeping him, so his employment was terminated. With no income, he struggled to make ends meet. His landlord sued him for his unpaid rent. He became homeless. As if things weren't bad enough, the civil war back home was raging. He managed to elude the authorities for six years, but he was eventually arrested and jailed for some two months.

He relied on his family to get him a new passport. In 2017, the UAE sent him to Malaysia, where he was granted a three-month permit to stay, but again, he overstayed. He had planned to get a flight to Ecuador. He had extended family living there, and Ecuador was a signatory to the 1967 Protocol Relating to the Status of Refugees, meaning he could seek asylum there.

Yet again, he needed help from his family to acquire the airfare. Turkish airlines had a routing that would take him to Ecuador.

However, when he tried to board the flight with his one-way ticket, they refused to let him fly. Desperate to leave Malaysia, he successfully boarded a flight to Cambodia. Upon arrival, his entry to the country was rejected, and he was placed on the next plane back to Malaysia.

He was looking for a simple humanitarian solution where there was none. No country was prepared to offer him residency, and Malaysia had banned him from re-entry for five years for his permit violation. He was a foreigner trapped in the Kuala Lumpur International Airport Terminal 2 airport (KLIA2).

Hassan was a survivor. He knew how to get by. But what he needed most was a country to offer him asylum. He turned his efforts to social media to raise awareness of his plight.

As he puts it, people have good and bad intentions. Some would ask him to endorse their product, and others would offer proposals of marriage. Hassan knew any of these considerations depreciated his real objective of finding a humanitarian solution.

His first ray of light came in April 2018. As Hassan describes it in his book, "Iman, the Syrian woman living in Turkey who sent the message to Khoulod in Ghana, had introduced me and my story to a woman named Vanja at the same time. Vanja was an immigrant from the former Yugoslavia, who'd been living in Canada for years and was involved with a humanitarian group there that sponsored and helped refugees."[5]

Vanja connected with Canadians Laurie Cooper and Stephen Watt, who both sent friend requests on Facebook to Hassan. Both Laurie and Stephen were experts at connecting people in the immigration process. To help Hassan, the BC Muslim Association, guided by Shawkat Hasan, agreed to sponsor him, and Laurie arranged employment for Hassan in Whistler, BC, and advocated for him via the CBC. Andrew Brouwer, who heard the program, stepped forward to offer pro bono representation. Then, in June, Laurie announced that Hassan's file was approved for review. Typically, this can take up to twenty-four months.

Hassan could tell he was onto the real deal here, and all he had to do was wait. Entering into the story in late August was Nuseir (Nas) Yassin, a Harvard-educated social media influencer. He is a Palestinian-Israeli who has millions of followers who watch his daily one-minute videos on the Nas Daily website. Yassin thought Hassan's story needed a wider audience. He couldn't go to Malaysia to meet Hassan, because he carried an Israeli passport, but he was able to send his associate, Agon Hare. They made a video that described Hassan's life in KLIA2 for the past seven months and explained that he was an asylum seeker trapped in the airport.

Within three days, the video was viewed 18 million times. It had certainly achieved the effect of widespread awareness of Hassan's story, but it also raised the ire of Malaysian authorities. Hassan was interrogated by governmental officials, and then he was jailed for the embarrassment he caused for the Malaysian government.

The heat on this case had been turned up to critical levels. The Canadians were pleading for Hassan to keep a low profile. The Malaysians were considering their options, which included sending Hassan to Syria and certain death.

The behind-the-scenes efforts by the Canadians were remarkable. After fifty-eight days of incarceration, Hassan was handed a ticket to fly to his new home, Canada. It can be said that Yassin's video was very disruptive for Hassan's application for immigration, but, on the other hand, it spurred on many people to make the right call. It should be pointed out that appropriate background· checks and medicals were performed as required in all immigration cases.

These are two outlier immigration cases that show the usefulness of private sponsorship. Single individuals can make huge contributions to the lives of others less fortunate.

CHAPTER 21

THE CATALYTIC CONVERTERS OF PRIVATE SPONSORSHIP

PEOPLE WHO OPERATE as catalytic converters take toxins like hatred, tyranny, fear, and discrimination that are endured by refugees and convert them into useful by-products like caring, considerate, and inclusive communities for refugees to live in. There are many who do selfless work for the betterment of their communities. Here are a few of them.

Chelsea Taylor

Chelsea is a nurse by profession. She has worked with the UN agency the International Organization for Migration, which is based in Geneva. She resides in Torquay, Australia. As a Canadian living in Australia, she was called upon to provide vaccinations on Manus Island in 2015. It is there she first met Amir Taghinia. In a visit to Canada, she was telling her parents about the conditions she had witnessed on Manus Island. She also mentioned a force of nature that she had met on the island: Amir. She beseeched her parents to do anything they could to help Amir. Her father, Wayne, rallied supporters, including the United Church of Canada. He made overtures to federal MPs, who carried his letter of support to the Minister of Immigration, Refugees and Citizenship. The Taylors really went to bat for Amir. Their efforts paid off because of one person stepping forward.[1]

Laurie Cooper

The whole world grieved as it witnessed the lifeless body of three-year-old Alan Kurdi washed up on a Grecian beach. A boat carrying a group of refugees had capsized. Laurie Cooper is a Canadian and the mother of grown children. She has motherly instincts for caring for others. She and her group of friends brainstormed for ways to help the most recent refugee crisis. Laurie was tasked with finding out what kind of help was needed. What she found out was that "boots on the ground" were needed as much as cash. Laurie had banked Air Miles points and booked two weeks of holiday. Much to her husband's chagrin, she and a friend decided to go to Lesbos, Greece.

Upon arrival, she noted a broad cross-section of volunteers. She met a woman whom she had called during her fact-finding work. Laurie and her friend were put to work making sandwiches—thousands and thousands of sandwiches. Later, because they had a rental vehicle, she was tasked with transporting the elderly and infirm to the camps. Laurie said that the Syrian refugees were gracious and calm, despite the calamitous circumstances that they had endured.

Laurie made several more trips to Greece and noted that she was meeting well-educated people who were simply displaced by war. She used her connections to arrange seasonal employment in Whistler, BC. Additionally, she secured sponsorship by the BC Muslim Society to bring twelve displaced Syrians to Canada. When asking for money to support refugees, Laurie prefers to ask people if they would like an opportunity to change someone's life.

In 2018, her network of volunteers drew her attention to Hassan Al Kontar. Though she is zealous in assisting refugees, she is also prudent. She and her fellow catalytic converter, Stephen Watt, had talked with Hassan at great length. They wanted to ensure he was genuine, and discovered he was. He had stayed true to his values while trapped in the Malaysian airport.

Something else Hassan remained true toward was a fellow asylum seeker on Nauru Island. Hassan was asked to spread the word about the suffering and inhumane treatment of refugees on Nauru and Manus Islands. Hassan shared this with Laurie. Again, Laurie's caring nature took over. Upon further research, she learned that the US had agreed to take close to one thousand people off the islands. With more than two hundred remaining, Laurie set the wheels in motion to bring the rest of the refugees to Canada. If she is asked how she manages do all this work, Laurie explains, "I just keep falling or failing forward." She believes in action. Even if one doesn't get the desired result, one will learn and grow from the experience. She is a founding member of Canada Caring, an organization devoted to helping refugees.

Bringing the remaining refugees to Canada was a significant undertaking, and it needed the involvement of major players. Mosaic BC is a recognized immigrant settlement organization that has worked in the Vancouver community for over forty-five years. The group is a Sponsorship Agreement Holder (SAH), which means the federal government recognizes its capabilities to properly settle immigrants. In partnership with Mosaic BC, the Refugee Council of Australia, and Amnesty International, #OperationNotForgotten was launched in 2019.[2]

The actual emigration of these refugees was affected by the COVID-19 outbreak.

Russian Refugee Relief Society of America, Inc.

Few details exist about this organization. What can be determined through correspondence and news articles of the time is that, in 1924, it appeared to catch the wave of displaced Russian people emigrating to North America.

Its board consisted of liberal Americans and Russian expatriates. The key players in this story were Captain Robert P. Macgrath, Prince Felix Youssoupoff, and Mr. Serge Ughet.

THE CATALYTIC CONVERTERS OF PRIVATE SPONSORSHIP

The first mention of the organization is in a May 21, 1923, article in the *New York Times* titled "To Aid Russian Refugees." It states that the society had started a campaign to raise $100,000 to relieve immigrants. The purpose of the society was to act as a clearing house for refugees from Russia after they were admitted to America. Mention is also made that the US had a quota system limiting the number of refugees accepted each year.[3]

Captain Macgrath was the society's executive secretary. Macgrath was a veteran of both the Boer War and the First World War. He was wounded in battle, which resulted in his left arm being amputated.[4] In January 1924, the Commissioner for the Russian Red Cross, Prince Alexander Golitzin, wrote a letter to the deputy minister of immigration in Ottawa, pleading for Canada to open its doors to Russian refugees. For Golitzin's part, he said his organization would pledge $100,000 to aid with transportation costs.[5] Later, in April of that year, he met Deputy Minister W.J. Egan and Captain R.P Macgrath in Ottawa, guaranteeing financial support to the amount of $25,000 for the first group of Russian refugees.[6] He also mentioned that their support was time-sensitive because in July of that year, the American quota would reopen to receive Russians in America.[7]

Prince Youssoupoff was a wealthy Russian aristocrat known for his philanthropy. He was a member of the society's finance committee. In February 1924, he leaned on his celebrity status to announce three fundraising balls in New York City for the benefit of the society.[8] In May, he wrote a letter to the editor of the *New York Times* appealing for donations to the society.[9]

Serge Ughet was the financial attaché and the chargé d'affaires in Washington for the Russian imperial and provisional governments. He arrived in the US in 1917 and became very enamoured with America.[10] He was the money man of the society. On June 17, 1924, he gave the Canadian government his assurance that full commitment of financial support outlined by Macgrath back in April was forthcoming and with that, the 116 Russian refugees disembarked from the *Empress of Russia* in Vancouver.

One civilization

Through his celebrity status, Hassan was sought out as a speaker after his arrival in Canada. At one conference, Carey Newman, a Kwagiulth and Coast Salish artist and professor at the University of Victoria, stepped up to the lectern. He invoked the spirit of his ancestors so they could be present to inspire wisdom and bravery. He explained his nation's history so it would not be forgotten.

This opening touched Hassan deeply. He connected these feelings with his memories of his family telling their similar reflections of the past as they sat around the kitchen stove in Suweida.

"Only one, only one. Only one human civilization: east, north, south, west, it doesn't matter; different cultures, we are all human." These were the thoughts of Hassan Al Kontar in 2019 as he sat in this conference setting.[11] Stories like this and those of millions of others share common sentiments: with the help of others, a peaceful life in freedom is possible.

APPENDIX A

HOW TO PRIVATELY SPONSOR A REFUGEE

No one wants to be a refugee.

The story of the Russian refugees described people who were forced out of their native country. They feared persecution if they returned to their country because they were religious, they had owned land and wanted to continue to do so, and they had differing political opinions from the emergent rulers following the Russian Revolution.

The path of a refugee to get accepted into Canada today is much different than theirs was.

There is a distinct difference between an immigrant and a refugee. The immigrant chooses to come and settle permanently from another country for a better life. The refugee, through no choice of their own, is seeking protection outside of their country.

Canada relies on immigration to support population, economic, and cultural growth. The 2020 annual report of the Ministry of Immigration, Refugees and Citizenship Canada states that in 2019, approximately 340,000 newcomers were welcomed to Canada.[1] Among them were roughly 48,000 refugees and protected persons. Within that group, 19,000 were privately sponsored refugees.

In a global refugee settlement effort, Canada leads many counties through its Private Sponsorship of Refugees Program (PSR). The Government of Canada controls the refugee application process but encourages private citizens to manage the settlement process. The government also ensures the refugee screening process is both fair and appropriate for the safety of Canadians.

Canadian citizens can sponsor refugees in three ways: through Sponsorship Agreement Holders (SAH), Groups of Five (G5), or Community Sponsors (CS). Instructional resources for these various methods are available through the Refugee Sponsorship Training Program (www.rstp.ca).

Sponsoring refugees comes down to providing funds, assisting with the paperwork for applicants, and then, upon the refugees' arrival, offering the social, financial, and emotional support to help the refugees integrate into Canadian society.

The process is similar to a house renovation project. You can pay a contractor to do the work in a professional manner or you can choose the do-it-yourself (DIY) option. In the contractor analogy, the Sponsorship Agreement Holder (the equivalent of the contractor) is funded by other agencies and the actual donations to fund the refugee go directly to their sponsorship. This means that all the necessary steps to manage the settlement of the refugee are managed by the SAH.

In the DIY option (G5 and CS), Canadian citizens walk through each step of the settlement process with the refugee, leading them by the hand and helping them get started. The minimum time commitment to support the refugee in Canada is twelve months. This includes helping the refugee with shelter, food, clothing, furniture, incidentals, and language training (if required); orientation for medical, dental, and transportation services; assistance with job searches and provincial assistance programs; and lastly, with introductions to Canadians of similar backgrounds.

The sponsoring of a refugee can be highly rewarding. The methods of sponsorship will depend on each group's capabilities. A sponsored refugee who becomes a permanent resident will live a free life. In time, they will become a contributing member of our Canadian society.

And as a member of our society, they will have that special feeling of gratitude to live in Canada, as described in the story of the Russian refugees. The opportunity to give such freedom to a refugee exists is in every Canadian when they decide to pay it forward and sponsor a refugee.

ALMOST ONE HUNDRED years ago, the Canadian government allowed 116 Russian refugees to enter Canada to farm and help populate the Prairie provinces. They landed in Homeglen, Alberta, a hamlet that no longer exists. Their descendants form at least two more generations of Canadians since the arrival in Homeglen, and they have all moved on throughout Canada. As the milestone of one hundred years since that landing (June 18, 1924) approaches, there will be an opportunity to remember the kindness offered to those refugees by the Russian Refugee Relief Society of America. That organization paid the bulk of the landing money required by the Government of Canada ($17,500 of the required $25,000). Without the landing money, entry to Canada by the Russian refugees may have been denied.

For those of you who have read this book, or who have similar origins as a refugee family member and who want to join Mosaic BC's 2024 centennial project of financially supporting a refugee family, go to the Mosaic BC website (the centennial project's designated Sponsorship Agreement Holder) using the QR code shown below to make your tax deductible contribution to the Homeglen Legacy Fund.

An applicant refugee family of four requires $25,000 to $30,000 of funding. The goal of the centennial project is to raise $30,000. Your generous financial support will provide Mosaic BC with the funds they need to do this humanitarian work. Pay it forward and give a family its freedom.

APPENDIX B

THE CANADIAN NAMING GAME OF THE 1920S

I T CAN BE difficult following the characters in this story due to their changing names. Names of people change over time for a variety of reasons. In the early part of the 1900s, Canadians in general followed British standards. As such, when a teacher heard a foreign name, they were emboldened to change it. Likewise, when an immigration officer received a Russian immigrant into Canada, he didn't ask their preference in terms of name recognition. For example, when the Andrievs landed in Vancouver, their documented name was changed to Andreeff because a religious sect from Georgia called the Doukhobors had arrived earlier in Canada with names that were all registered with the ending "ff."[1] The officer perhaps reasoned that "they all look the same," so he altered the immigrants' name to what he thought it should be like.

Another source of change was the individuals themselves. In school, learning his writing method, Nikifor Andreeff spelt his last name Andruff by collapsing the double "e" into a "u." The Sidoroff family also saw the younger generation opt for a slight change, to Sideroff. Marriage was another source of changing names.

On reflection, it is sad many traditional root names were lost with these arbitrary changes.

Here is a guide to follow most of the characters in the story:

THE CANADIAN NAMING GAME OF THE 1920S

Aganasi Sidoroff, Afric Sidoroff

Akim Andriev, Ike Andreeff

Anesya Andreeff, Jean Andreeff, Jean Koyman

Borise Sidoroff, Syd Sidoroff

Constantine Andreeff, Nick Andreeff, Nick Andruff

Constantine Mishukoff, Cons Mishiekof

Darya Andreeff, Doreen Andreeff, Doreen Calvert, Doreen Riedijk

Elena Andriev, Elena Andreeff

Father Artemy Solovieff

Feodosia Andreeff, Fannie Andreeff, Fannie Schischikowsky

Fiena Andreeff, Fi Andreeff, Fi McIntyre, Fi McIntyre-Olsen

Gregory Andriev, Gregori Andreeff, Gregory Andreeff

Ilarion Sidoroff, Lorne Sidoroff

Ivan Andriev, John Andreeff

Klavdia Andreeff, Gladys Andreeff, Gladys Lillejord

Larivon Andriev, Laurence Andreeff, Lorne Andreeff, Lawrence Andreeff

Laurens Koyman

Lucaria Andreiv, Lucaria Sidoroff

Marusa Andreeff, Mary Andreeff

Natalie Sodorova, Natasha Sidoroff, Dolly Sidoroff, Natalie Andreeff, Natalie Andruff

Nikifor Andriev, Mikifor Andreeff, Michael Andreeff, Mike Andruff

Palagaya Kosheiff, Polly Andreeff

Palagaya Sidoroff, Polly Sidoroff, Polly Elder

Paraskavaya Reznick, Pearl Reznick, Pearl Sidoroff

Philip Andriev, Phillip Gregory Andreeff

Procopius Sidorov, Prokofi Sidoroff, Peter Sidoroff

Taisia Sidoroff, Jessie Sidoroff, Jessie Mennie

Timofei Sidoroff, Thomas Sidoroff, Tom Sideroff

Valentina Andriev, Viola Andreeff, Vi Kalugin

Vasili Andriev, William Andreeff, Bill Andreeff

Vera Sideroff, Vicki Lomax

Vicari Sidoroff, Vic Sidoroff, Vic Sideroff

Zinayeda Andreeff, Zina Andreeff, Zena Clark, Zena Waterman

ACKNOWLEDGEMENTS

THE MANY PEOPLE who have helped in this story must be acknowledged. As happens in a work of this nature, some may be overlooked, but they are not forgotten; it is only that my memory is not perfect in recalling past events. Here are those I wish to mention: Polly Elder, Doreen Riedijk, Darlene Parker, Ray Parks, Terry Bettenson, Vicki Lomax, Vic Sideroff, Tom Sideroff, Kay Johnson, Laurie Buck, Fanny Schischikowsky, Colleen Reid, Shane Koyman, Madeline Watchorn, Susan McIntyre, Bill Potter, Claudine Nelson of the Alberta Genealogical Society, Dr. John Edworthy, Dr. Bill Lang, Derek Mullan, LLB, Courtney O'Hara Library and Archives Canada, Connie Andreeff, Karen Wasylciw, Greg Nesteroff *Castlegar News*, Iris Challoner of Mosaic BC, Sharon Butler of Mosaic BC, Karlee Kapler of the *Fairview Post*, Jan Peterson, Lynn Slobogian, Charlie Gailloux, Bill Majercsik, Stephen Watt, Amir Taghinia, Wayne Taylor, Laurie Cooper, Lorisa Schouela, Lama Alrakad, Andrew Brouwer, Hasan Al Kontar, Lynn Duncan, and a special thanks to my editor, Karla Decker, who was very supportive and helpful in the last edits of my story.

NOTES

CHAPTER 1

1. Polly Elder, *All This Shall Pass*, p. 75.

2. Correspondence of J.S. Dennis to Percy Reid June 2, 1924, advising of a change of departure date and ship. Library and Archives Canada, Heritage-Immigration Program, Headquarters central registry files C7372 Image 1482. The *Declaration of Passenger to Canada* forms shows the booking agent stationed at Kobe, a port south of Yokohama, but Yokohama is written on the top of each declaration. Also, date of sailing was June 4, 1924. It is possible they got on the boat in Yokohama and then stopped at Kobe for sailing on June 5.

3. Elder, *All This Shall Pass*, p. 72.

4. Ibid. p. 75.

5. Handwritten notes of Mike Andruff, Sr., "During the Russo-Japanese War in 1904–05," describing stories his father, Phillip, had shared with him, undated, p. 2.

6. Wikipedia: "Pyotr Stolypin" https://en.wikipedia.org/wiki/Pyotr_Stolypin

7. Fiena McIntyre-Olsen, Susan McIntryre, ed. *Our History, Our Heritage: Andriev Family Stories*, p. 33.

8. WW1 Casualty and Death Tables, "The Great War and the Shaping of the 20th Century." PBS/WGHBH. https://www.youtube.com/watch?v=hYQtsQL6uzA&ab_channel=the66percent

9. McIntyre, *Our History*, p. 3.

10. Elder, *All This Shall Pass*, p. 39.

11. David Scheffel, "Old Believers in Canada," *The Encyclopedia of Canada's Peoples*. Posted December 12, 2012. https://oldbelievers.wordpress.com/2012/12/14/russian-old-believers-in-canada/

12. Correspondence from Russian Red Cross, Harbin, to J.W. Ross, Shanghai, July 1923, Library and Archives Canada, Heritage-Immigration Program, Headquarters central registry files C7372 Images 1333 and 1334.

13. Correspondence between R.P. MacGrath, A. Golitsin, and J.W. Egan, January 31, 1924, Library and Archives Canada, Heritage-Immigration Program, Headquarters central registry files C7372 Image 1401.

14. Ibid, p. 3.

15. Correspondence from J.S. Dennis to J.W. Egan, April 29, 1924, Ibid, Image 1448.

16. Correspondence from Egan to MacGrath, February 7, 1924, Ibid, Image 1405.

17. Correspondence Dennis to Egan, April 8, 1924, Ibid, Image 1428.

18. Correspondence Dennis to Black, July 11, 1923, Ibid, Image 1340.

19. See attachment to 15 above, NB: First page of list is missing in the archives.

20. Correspondence Black to British consul general, Harbin, May 6, 1924, Library and Archives Canada, Heritage-Immigration Program, Headquarters central registry files C7372 Image 1456.

21. Maria von Rosenbach, *Family Kaleidoscope, From Russia to Canada*, p. 146

22. Correspondence Jolliffe to J.S. Reid June 5, 1924, Library and Archives Canada, Heritage-Immigration Program, Headquarters central registry files C7372 Images 1482.

23. Telegram Egan to Reid, June 15, 1924, Ibid, Image 1491.

24. Telegram, Dennis to Egan, June 17, 1924, Ibid, Image 1498.

25. Memo Blair, June 17, 1924, Ibid, Image 1497.

26. Correspondence, Egan to Reid, June 18, 1924, Ibid, Image 1505.

CHAPTER 2

1. Maria von Rosenbach, *Family Kaleidoscope, From Russia to Canada*, p. 146.

2. David Scheffel, *Russian Old Believers and Canada: A Historical Sketch*, p. 4.
3. Rosenbach, p. 147.
4. Ibid, p. 149.
5. Telegram J.S. Dennis to J.W. Egan, June 17, 1924, Public Archives Canada, Immigration Program, Headquarters central registry files: C7372 Image 1498.
6. Polly Elder, *All This Shall Pass*, p. 102.
7. Correspondence of Dennis to Egan, July 21, 1924, PAC C7372 Image 1511.
8. Rosenbach, p. 151.
9. Ibid, p. 152.
10. Ibid, p. 151.
11. Ibid, p. 148.
12. Correspondence, Dennis to Egan, June 26, 1924, Public Archives Canada, Immigration Program, Headquarters central registry files: C7372 Image 1514.
13. Elder, p. 84.
14. Elder, *Sidoroff Family Tree Book*, p. 14.
15. Fiena McIntyre and Susan McIntyre, ed., *Our History, Our Heritage: Andriev Family Stories*, pp. 10 and 14. *Peshki*, the game, was played with special cut pieces of willow. Pieces were colored white and black, like checkers. The method may be described as a combination of playing checkers and pick-up sticks.
16. Correspondence, Orest Dournovo to Blair, June 18, 1925, Public Archives Canada, Immigration Program, Headquarters central registry files: C7372 Image 1880.
17. Province of Alberta, *A Booklet of Information on Progress, the Resources and Opportunities of the Province of Alberta*, p. 18.
18. Rosenbach, p. 149.
19. Correspondence, P.L. Naismith, Calgary, to J.S. Dennis, Montreal, February 25, 1926, Glenbow Alberta Archives CPR Papers, Box 84, File 209.
20. Rosenbach, p. 155.

NOTES

21. Correspondence, Skinner to Commissioner of Immigration, Ottawa, September 19, 1925, Public Archives Canada, Immigration Program, Headquarters central registry files: C7372 Image 1966.

22. Correspondence, J.S. Dennis to W.J. Egan, March 26, 1926. Ibid, Images 2067 and 2068.

23. Correspondence, N. Van der Vliet, Calgary, to Dennis, Montreal, January 12, 1926, Glenbow Alberta Archives CPR Russian Colonization Papers, Box 84, File 679.

24. Correspondence, N. Van der Vliet, to Dennis, March 27, 1926. Ibid.

25. Elder, *Sidoroff Family Tree Book*, p. 4.

26. Ibid, p.157.

27. Correspondence (in Russian) Sidorov to Pical, Montreal, December 26, 1926. Glenbow CPR Colonization Papers, Box 84 File 680.

28. Correspondence (in Russian) Pical to Sidoroff, Homeglen, January 10, 1927. Ibid.

29. Scheffel, "Russian Old Believers in Canada," *Encyclopedia of Canada's Peoples*, pp 10-11.

30. Scheffel, Ibid, "Migration and Settlement."

31. Correspondence, Dennis to Egan, Ottawa, April 29, 1924, Public Archives Canada, Immigration Program, Headquarters central registry files: C7372 Images 1448.

32. Ibid.

33. David Hall, "Sir Clifford Sifton," January 22, 2008, *The Canadian Encyclopedia*, Historica Canada.

34. Land Grants of Western Canada, 1870-1930, Library and Archives Canada. https://www.bac-lac.gc.ca/eng/discover/land/land-grants-western-canada-1870-1930/Pages/land-grants-western-canada.aspx

35. Province of Alberta, *A Booklet of Information on Progress, the Resources and Opportunities of the Province of Alberta*, p. 18.

36. Library and Archives of Canada, Homestead Grant Registers, R190-75-1-E. https://www.bac-lac.gc.ca/eng/discover/land/land-grants-western-canada-1870-1930/Pages/land-grants-western-canada.aspx

37. Government of Canada, "Duncan's First Nation Inquiry–1928 Surrender Claim, Indian Commission," September 1999, p. 60.

38. Hall, "Sir Clifford Sifton."

39. Truth and Reconciliation Commission of Canada, *Honouring the Truth, Reconciling for the Future: Summary of the Final Report of the Truth and Reconciliation Commission of Canada*, 2015, p. 1.

40. Ibid, p. 211.

41. McIntyre, *Our History, Our Heritage: Andriev Family Stories*, p. 3.

42. Correspondence, Dournovo to Blair, April 1, 1933, Public Archives Canada, Immigration Program, Headquarters central registry files: C7373 Image 397.

43. Elder, p. 162.

44. The Russian Refugee Relief Society of America Inc. was a little-known philanthropic organization. Prominent on the Executive and Finance Committee of the organization was Prince Felix Youssoupoff (this spelling was taken from the Society's letterhead). Not considered a businessman, Prince Felix saw his capital dissipate quickly, most of all during the 1929 stock market crash.

CHAPTER 3

1. *The Geographical Journal*, Vol. 158, No. 3, November 1992, p. 286.

2. Correspondence, Sideroff to the author, April 2020.

3. Fairview Town Council, *Heart of Gold: Fairview 1928–1978*, p. 21.

4. Provincial Archives of Alberta Accession 1974.0048, Film: GL-590, File Number: 41372, Application for Patent.

5. McIntyre, *Our History, Our Heritage*, p. 11.

6. Ibid, p. 21.

7. Ibid, p. 42.

8. Ibid, p. 6.

9. Elder, *Sideroff Family Tree*, p. 211.

10. McIntyre, *Our History, Our Heritage*, p. 35.

11. Email, Elder to author November 24, 2020.

NOTES

12. McIntyre, *Our History*, p. 35.
13. Wikipedia, "Basic reproduction number," https://en.wikipedia.org/wiki/Basic_reproduction_number
14. McIntyre, *Our History*, p. 27.
15. Reg Whitaker, *Canadian Immigration Policy since Confederation*, p. 13.
16. Elder, *All This Shall Pass*, comment attributed to George Lebedkin, p. 109.
17. Library and Archives Canada, Ocean Arrivals 1919–1924, Vol. t-14945, p. 47.
18. Canada.ca, "History of citizenship legislation, *Canadian Citizenship Act*, January 1, 1947."
19. Library and Archives Canada, Naturalization Records 1915-1952, Canadian Gazette 1935, p. 2149.
20. Provincial Archives of Alberta Accession 1974.0048, Film: GL-590, File Number: 41372, Province of Alberta correspondence to Phillip Gregory Andreeff, noting Certificate 95Y83.
21. Fairview Town Council, *Heart of Gold*, p. 23.
22. Endnote 4 refers to a 1934 record of 80 acres of cropped land. This calculation assumes an average of 15 acres were cleared each year. Therefore, in 1936 it is likely 110 acres were cleared.
23. See Endnote 4.
24. McIntyre, *Our History*, p. 39.
25. Email, Elder to author, March 15, 2020.
26. Ibid, March 19, 2020.
27. Email, McIntyre to author, March 10, 2020.
28. Elder, p. 193.
29. Robert N. Pripps, *The Big Book of Massey Tractors*, p. 72.
30. Google search: eugenics defined.
31. Wikipedia: "WW2 casualties."
32. Certificate of Marriage, Province of Alberta, September 18, 1942, In Andruff personal files.

33. McIntyre, *Our History*, p. 24.
34. *Canadian Food Studies*, Vol. 5 No. 3, September 2018, p. 101.
35. Reg Whitaker, *Canadian Immigration Policy*, p. 15.
36. This was a story that Natalie shared with her family in discussing Mike and Natalie's early days together.
37. Igor Gouzenko, *This Was My Choice*.
38. "The Gouzenko Transcripts," Deneau Publishers & Co. 1946, p. 30.
39. Gouzenko, *This Was My Choice* p. 268.
40. Ibid, p. 117.
41. Ibid, pp. 197-98.
42. John Porter, *The Vertical Mosaic*, p. 1.
43. Ibid. p. 51.
44. Wikipedia: "1946 Vancouver Island earthquake."
45. The personal notes of Mike Andruff, Sr. chronicling his life from 1921 to 2005, p. 1.
46. Wikipedia: "Port Alberni Mill."
47. Library and Archives Canada, 1949 Federal General Election, Voters' List 1949, 58749, p. 1.
48. Wikipedia: "Leduc No. 1."
49. Fairview, *Heart of Gold*, p. 45.
50. Ibid, p. 44.
51. Correspondence, Sideroff to author, March 2020.
52. The author's notes of an April 23, 2020, phone conversation with Vic Sidoroff.
53. "1952-1967 Reducing Poverty, Human Resources Development Canada," online record sourced April 2, 2021.
54. *Fairview Post*, Obits, "P. Andruff, Gage Farmer, Dies," October 1953.
55. Alberta Genealogical Society, Andreeff Probate ref. 20-035, Last Will and Testament, Form 7, The Inventory and Valuation.

NOTES

56. Elder, p. 168.
57. *Fairview Post*, Wedding Announcements, "Popular Couple Wed," October 1954.
58. Telephone interview with Vicki Lomax (Vera Sidoroff), April 28, 2020.
59. Email, Johnson to author, December 30, 2020.
60. Telephone interview with Vic Sideroff, April 23, 2020.
61. Telephone interview with Kay Johnson, May 25, 2020.
62. Telephone interview with Fannie Schischikowsky, May 2, 2020.
63. *Fairview Post*, "Accident Mars Old Timers Fair, Father and Son Trampled By Horses," August 11, 1955.
64. Correspondence, Tom Sideroff to author, March 2020.
65. Correspondence, Vicki Lomax to author, April 23, 2020.
66. Wikipedia: "Alberta Medical Care and Nursing."
67. Case No. 12019 Michael Andruff, Plaintiff vs. The Waterhole Oldtimers' Association, Defendant, Statement of Claim, p. 4.
68. Telephone interview with Terry Bettenson, January 23, 2020

CHAPTER 4

1. Hupacasath First Nations Website (hupacasath.ca), "History, Hupacasath People"; Jan Peterson, *The Albernis: 1860-1922*, p. 1.
2. Government of British Columbia, Government of Canada, "The Report of the British Columbia Task Force, The First Nations of British Columbia," "Historical Background," p. 4, June 28, 1991,
3. Ibid, p. 5.
4. Dennis F. K. Madill, *British Columbia Indian Treaties in Historical Perspective*.
5. Government of British Columbia, Government of Canada, "The Report of the British Columbia Task Force, The First Nations of British Columbia, Historical Background," p. 21.
6. Jan Peterson, *The Albernis: 1860-1922*, p. 27.
7. Ibid, p. 63.

8. Ibid, p. 218.

9. Ibid, p. 221.

10. Ibid, p. 240.

11. Correspondence, Mike Andruff, Sr., personal files, undated, unaddressed, circa fall 1956.

12. Correspondence A.F. Taylor to A.V. Parminter, August 8, 1957. Residential School Archives Project, TheChildrenRemembered.ca

13. Laurie Buck, *The Alberni Years*, personal notes, p. 4.

14. Ibid, direct quote, p. 9.

15. Correspondence, N.C. Willson to Mike Andruff, Sr., April 24, 1958.

16. Case No. 12019 Michael Andruff, Plaintiff vs. The Waterhole Oldtimers' Association, Defendant, Statement of Claim, p. 4.

17. Ibid, Reasons For Judgement of the Honourable Justice Primrose, September 30, 1959, p. 9.

18. Telephone interview with Ray Parks, August 12, 2021

19. Statistics Canada, Historical Stats of Canada, Average weekly wages and salaries, by major groups of manufacturing, 1939–1975; Review of the Port Alberni Forest Industry, Macauley & Associates, April 30, 2007, p. 2.

20. Reg Whitaker, *Canadian Immigration Policy*, p. 18.

21. Wikipedia: "Camelot," accessed September 2020.

22. Rod Mickleburgh, *On the Line: A History of the British Columbia Labour Movement*, pp. 122, 128.

23. "1952–1967 Reducing Poverty, Human Resources Development Canada," online record sourced April 2, 2021.

CHAPTER 5

1. Reg Whitaker, *Canadian Immigration Policy since Confederation*, p. 19.

2. Document, Student's Report Card, B.C. Vocational School. Nanaimo, Term: February 19, 1968.

3. Wikipedia: "New Westminster," accessed September 12, 2020.

4. Wikipedia: "Apollo 11," accessed September 12, 2020.

NOTES

5. Land Titles and Survey Authority of British Columbia, New Westminster Land Titles Office, Agreement for Sale, Document number E67404 Dated August 19, 1969.

6. Website: https://rockstarinnercircle.com/real-estate-investing-articles/agreement-for-sale-strong-real-estate-investment-strategy/ September 12, 2020.

7. Personal notes of Mike Andruff, Sr., a timeline perspective, p. 2.

8. Land Titles and Survey Authority of British Columbia, New Westminster Land Titles Office, Application for Registration of Fee-simple, Document number G1840, Dated October 22, 1971.

9. *Castlegar News*, November 21, 1982, p. A3.

10. Mike Andruff Sr., personal notes, May 9, 2000, address to the 2000 Family Reunion, p. 4.

11. Ibid; Whitaker, p. 21.

12. Nick Andruff, *Now What?*, p. 122.

13. Diane Strandberg, *Castlegar News*, "Antiques lost in fire," August 4, 1982.

CHAPTER 6

1. Ronald L. Cosper, "Alcoholism," *The Canadian Encyclopedia*, online, February 6, 2006, under section "Drinking in Canada."

2. The author's notes of a phone conversation with Vicki Lomax (Vera Sidoroff). Vicki recalled from her Hines Creek days; she had always known Natalie as a drinker. She partied all the time. Notation from April 28, 2020, interview.

3. Email, Elder to author, March 19, 2020.

CHAPTER 7

1. Telephone interview with Kay Johnson, May 25, 2020.

2. Jan Peterson, *Twin Cities: Alberni–Port Alberni*, p. 263.

3. Ibid, p. 264.

4. British Columbia Public Schools, Primary Division Report Card, Michael Andruff, Year of Primary Division 1958–59, School District 70 (Alberni), Remarks from personal file.

5. Province of British Columbia, "Ninety-sixth Annual Report, Public Schools, Superintendent of Education, 1966/67," p. 24.

6. Telephone interview with Bill (William) Majercsik, author's notebook, on October 13, 2021.

7. *Twin City Times*, Port Alberni, "Scouting News." March 1, 1961.

8. *West Coast Advocate,* Port Alberni, "Christmas Tree Farm Handed to Alberni's Scouts," February 2, 1961.

9. Telephone interview with Charles Gailloux, December 1, 2020.

10. Ibid.

11. Peterson, p. 309.

12. University of Victoria Libraries Collection, Internet Archives, *Daily Colonist* Newspaper Collection, March 29, 1964.

13. *Times Colonist*, "Vacation Means Competition," April 5, 1966, from Claire Andruff personal file.

14. Peterson, p. 300.

15. 2nd Annual Hockey Jamboree Program, Port Alberni Civic Arena, 1965, p. 6, from Mike Andruff Sr.'s collection of hockey articles pertaining to author.

16. *The Alberni Valley Times*, "Local Boys on Cougar Try-Out List, "September 27, 1967.

17. Peterson, p. 283.

18. Ibid, p. 329.

19. John Ivison, *Vancouver Sun*, National Post Section, p. NP4, .December 16, 2020.

CHAPTER 8

1. *Nanaimo Free Press*, undated, (circa 1967), "Volleyball Tournament Champions."

2. *Nanaimo Free Press*, undated (circa 1968), "Vancouver Island Midget Hockey Champions."

3. *The Columbian*, circa 1968, "Royals–Victoria open Friday."

4. HockeyDb.com, January 2021, Robert Love.

NOTES

5. *The Columbian*, circa 1968, "Cougars take 10-5 Win."
6. *The Columbian*, circa 1969, "Draw at UBC, Royals Battle With Rockets."
7. Paul Laurendeau and Celine Cooper, *Official Languages Act, The Canadian Encyclopedia,* online, accessed May 17, 2019.

CHAPTER 9

1. Don Brewster, personal file, Invoice of caterer, Aida Wallbanks, 8 September, 1971.
2. *Ubyssey*, Commerce undergrads elected, February 12, 1974, p. 8.
3. Richard Blackwell, *Globe and Mail*, "Remember When: What we have learned from the 1980's and that 21% interest rate," May 13, 2015, p. 5.
4. The author's personal Canada trip journal, 1974.
5. Ibid, May 16, 1974 entry.
6. Planned Parenthood, *The Birth Control Pill: A History*, p. 6.
7. Grace Kena et al, "The Condition of Education 2014."
8. US Census Bureau, "Statistical Abstract of the United States, 2010: The National Data Book."
9. Bureau of Labour Statistics, "Women in the Labour Force: A databook."
10. Claire Andruff's personal Europe trip journal, 1975.
11. Ibid, May 6, 1975.

CHAPTER 10

1. Richard Blackwell, *Globe and Mail*, "Remember When: What we have learned from the 1980's and that 21% interest rate", May 13, 2015. p. 1.
2. Ibid, p. 5.
3. Matthew Andruff, Poetry, Grade 8, Block A, 1993, p. 6.
4. Alyse Kotyk, "Tensions over time: A primer on the Canada-US softwood lumber dispute," *Globe and Mail,* May 9, 2017.
5. Wikipedia: "Carmanah Walbran Provincial Park," last edit December 19, 2020.

6. Rowan Haigh and Ian Marcus, "The Organochloride Issue and the Pulp & Paper Industry after the British Columbia 1992 Effluent Regulation."

CHAPTER 11

1. Telephone interview with unnamed neighbour, author's notebook, October 13, 2021, with added reminiscences from Claire Andruff on her friendship with our neighbour, who passed away in 2017.

2. Claire Andruff's personal Europe trip journal, May 12, 1975.

3. Angus Reid Institute, "Crisis of Faith? Even practising Catholics say Church has done a poor job handling sexual abuse issue," May 28, 2019.

CHAPTER 12

1. Rob Carrick, "A house three times your income? Think again," *Globe and Mail,* November 5, 2015.

2. Telephone interview with Ray Parks, author's notebook, February 15, 2021.

3. Jan Raska Ph.D, "1968 Pier 21 and the Prague Spring Refugees," (updated August 21, 2020), Canadian Museum of Immigration at Pier 21. And conversations with Ray Parks.

4. Wikipedia: "Funeral of Diana, Princess of Wales," accessed February 1, 2021.

CHAPTER 13

1. Postcard from Claire Andruff to author from Versailles, October 13, 2001.

2. Email from Thea Andruff to author, "I AM ON VACATION," October 15, 2001.

CHAPTER 14

1. Statistic Canada, Census Program, "Does education pay? A comparison of earnings by level of education in Canada and its provinces and territories," November 29, 2017.

2. Bryony Lau, "Canada resettles more refugees than anyone," *National Post,* Vancouver, December 26, 2020, p. NP1.

3. Douglas Todd, "A Call for Public Review of Foreign Student Policy," *Vancouver Sun,* January 23, 2021, p. B3.

NOTES

4. Canadian Taxpayers Federation, debtclock.ca, Debt Clock interactive worksheet, February 8, 2021.

5. Wade Davis, "The Unravelling of America," *Rolling Stone* (online), August 8, 2020.

6. Jonathan Manthorpe, "The Dangerous Drift to Unchallenged Leadership," *Vancouver Sun*, January 18, 2021, p. B2.

CHAPTER 15

1. Wikipedia: "Generation X," accessed April 16, 2021.

2. Wikipedia: "Varicella vaccine," accessed April 16, 2021

3. Correspondence from Alexandra Loyd to Thea Andruff, May 16, 1986.

4. General Gordon Elementary School Certificates for Honor Roll 1988, Honour Roll 1989, and Citizenship 1989, A. W. Paterson, Principal.

5. N.L. Drugge to Mr. and Mrs. Andruff, Honour Roll Correspondence, 1989 December 15, 1990 April 20, 16 January 1991, and R. Calder to Parent/Guardian Honour Roll Correspondence, 8 April 1992.

CHAPTER 17

1. Wikipedia: "Golden Key International Society," accessed May 4, 2021.

2. 2016 Census: "The Canadian families of today and yesteryear," Statistics Canada, Catalogue number: 11-629-x Issue number: 20170006, August 2, 2017.

3. EDI BC 2019 Provincial Report, "Human Early Learning Partnership," University of British Columbia, Wave 7, accessed May 4, 2021.

4. Fraser Institute, "School Performance," accessed May 4, 2021.

CHAPTER 18

1. The UN Refugee Agency, "Figures at a Glance," www.unhcr.org, accessed April 7, 2021.

CHAPTER 20

1. Shawn Conner, "New Play gives voice to refugee experience," *Vancouver Sun*, October 28, 2021, p. C5.

2. Michael Garcia Bochenek, "Australia: Appalling Abuse, Neglect of Refugees on Nauru," Human Rights Watch Report, August 2, 2016.
3. Interview with Amir Taghinia, author's notebook, November 2, 2021.
4. Hassan Al Kontar, *man@the_airport, How Social Media Saved My Life*.
5. Ibid. p. 113

CHAPTER 21

1. Telephone interview with Wayne Taylor, November 8, 2021.
2. Zoom interview with Laurie Cooper, October 31, 2021.
3. *New York Times*, "To Aid Russian Refugees," May 21, 1923
4. R.P. Macgrath, "War Veteran," *New York Times*, August 1, 1937
5. Correspondence MacGrath and Golitzin to Egan January 31, 1924, Library and Archives Canada, Heritage-Immigration Program, Headquarters central registry files C7372 Image 1401.
6. Correspondence Dennis to Egan, April 29, 1924. Ibid, Image 1448.
7. Correspondence Macgrath and Burgess to Egan, February 15, 1924. Ibid, Image 1415.
8. "Three Russian Balls, Series Arranged by Prince and Princess Youssoupoff–Other Charity Affairs," *New York Times*, February 10, 1924.
9. Prince F. Youssoupoff, "Plan of Russian Refugee Relief, letter to the editor printed May 1, 1924, April 23, 1924.
10. Serge Ughet, 78, "Czarist Official," *New York Times*, May 10, 1963.
11. *man@The_airport*, p. 8.

APPENDIX A

1. Mendocino, M. *2020 Annual Report to Parliament on Immigration*.

APPENDIX B

1. Polly Elder, *All This Shall Pass*, p. iii.

BIBLIOGRAPHY

Al Kontar, Hassan. *man@the_airport: How Social Media Saved My Life*. New Westminster, BC. Tidewater Press, 2021.

Andruff, Nick. *Now What?* Canada: Nico Publishing, 2004.

Angus Reid Institute. "Crisis of Faith? Even practising Catholics say Church has done a poor job handling sexual abuse issue." Vancouver, May 2019.

Bochenek, Michael Garcia. "Australia: Appalling Abuse, Neglect of Refugees on Nauru." Human Rights Watch. August 2, 2016.

Bothwell, Robert. Granastein, J.L. "The Gouzenko Transcripts": The Evidence Presented to the Kellock-Taschereau Royal Commission of 1946. Toronto. Deneau Publishers & Company, 1946.

Bureau of Labour Statistics. "Women in the Labour Force: A databook." Washington, DC, 2014.

Crescent Beach Swimming Club. *100 Summers: The Crescent Beach Swimming Club, 1918—2018*. Self-published. 2018.

Elder, Polly. *All This Shall Pass*. Duncan, BC: Self-published, 1995.

Elder, Polly. *Sidoroff Family Tree Book*. "The Heritage Tape." Duncan, BC: Self-published, 1988–89.

Fairview Town Council Jubilee Project. *Heart of Gold: Fairview 1928–1978*. Edmonton, 1978.

Fraser Institute. "School Performance." Online, May 4, 2021.

Gordon, Hugh, Philip Halkett, George Macauley, and Howard Saunders. "Review of the Port Alberni Forest Industry." Province of British Columbia, Ministry of Forests and Range Operations Division. Victoria: April 30, 2007.

Gouzenko, Igor. *This Was My Choice*. Toronto: J.M. Dent & Sons. Toronto, 1948.

Government of British Columbia, Government of Canada. "The Report of the British Columbia Task Force. The First Nations of British Columbia." Victoria, June 28, 1991.

Government of Canada. "Duncan's First Nations Inquiry—1928 Surrender Claim." Ottawa, September 1999.

Haigh, Rowan, Ian Marcus. "The Organochloride Issue and the Pulp and Paper Industry after the 1992 Effluent Regulation, Technical Report." Fisheries and Oceans Canada, UBC: Vancouver. April 1995.

Hall, David. "Sir Clifford Sifton." *The Canadian Encyclopedia*. Toronto, Historica Canada. January 22, 2008.

Hamley, Will. "The farming frontier in northern Alberta." *The Geographical Journal*. Vol. 158, No.3. UK. Willie & Blackwell. November 1992.

Kena, Grace, et al. "The Condition of Education 2014" (NCES 2011-14-083). Washington, DC. US Department of Education, 2014.

Madill, Dennis F.K. "British Columbia Indian Treaties in Historical Perspective." Ottawa: Research Branch, Corporate Policy Department of Indian and Northern Affairs, 1981.

McIntyre, Fiena, Susan McIntyre, ed. *"Our History, Our Heritage: Andriev Family Stories."* Souvenir booklet of the Andruff family reunion, July 1, 2000. Osoyoos, BC: Self-published, 2000.

Mendicino, Marco E.L., Hon. "2020 Annual Report to Parliament on Immigration." Immigration, Refugees and Citizenship Canada publications. Ottawa, 2020.

Mickleburgh, Rod. *On The Line: A History of the British Columbia Labour Movement*. Pender Harbour, BC: Harbour Publishing, 2018.

Peterson, Jan. *The Albernis: 1860—1922*. Lantzville, BC: Oolichan Books, 1992.

———. *Twin Cities: Alberni--Port Alberni*. Lantzville, BC: Oolichan Books, 1994.

Planned Parenthood Federation of America. "The Birth Control Pill: A History." Fact sheet. New York: June 2015 (last update).

BIBLIOGRAPHY

Porter, John. *The Vertical Mosaic.* Toronto: University of Toronto Press, 1965.

Pripps, Robert N. *The Big Book of Massey Tractors: A Complete History of Tractors.* Massachusetts: Voyageur Press. 2001.

Province of Alberta. *A Booklet of Information on Progress, the Resources and Opportunities of the Province of Alberta.* Alberta, 1927.

Qualman, Darrin, A. Haroon Akram-Lodhi, Annette Aurelie Desmarais, and Sharada Srinivasan. "Forever young? The crisis of generational renewal on Canada's farms." Manitoba. *Canadian Food Studies*, Vol. 5, September 2018.

Scheffel, David Z. "Russian Old Believers and Canada: A Historical Sketch" *Journal of Canadian Ethnic Studies*, Vol. 21, No.1, pp. 1-18. Calgary, AB, 1989.

———. "Russian Old Believers in Canada," *Encyclopedia of Canada's People.* Posted December 12, 2012. https://oldbelievers.wordpress.com/2012/12/14/russian-old-believers-in-canada/

Statistics Canada. "Does education pay? A comparison of earnings by level of education in Canada and its provinces and territories." Ottawa. Census Program, November 29, 2017.

Truth and Reconciliation Commission of Canada. *Honouring the Truth, Reconciling for the Future, Summary of the Final Report of the Truth and Reconciliation Commission of Canada.* Toronto: James Lorimer & Company, 2015.

University of British Columbia. "EDI BC 2019 Provincial Report." May 4, 2021. Human Early Learning Partnership. 2016–2019 Wave 7.

US Census Bureau. "Statistical Abstract of the United States. 2010. The National Data Book," 129th edition. Washington, DC, 2009.

Von Rosenbach, Maria. *Family Kaleidoscope, from Russia to Canada.* Vancouver, BC: Self-published, 1976.

Whitaker, Reg. *Canadian Immigration Policy since Confederation.* Ottawa. Canadian Historical Association, 1991.

INDEX

ACKA Enterprises Ltd., 93, 95-104, 113, 148, 153, 174, 176
Al Kontar, Hassan, 221, 225, 228
Alberni. *See* Port Alberni
Amnesty International, 218, 226
Amur Valley, Siberia, 13, 16, 32
Andreeff, Anesya, xi, 39, 59, 66, 233
Andreeff, Bill. *See* Andriev, Vasili
Andreeff, Constantine, 30, 52, 55-56, 59, 62, 65, 79, 81, 83, 87, 90, 93, 103, 116, 233
Andreeff, Darya, xi, 52-53, 67, 99, 108, 233
Andreeff, Doreen. *See* Andreeff, Darya
Andreeff, Elena. *See* Andriev, Elena
Andreeff, Fannie. *See* Andreeff, Feodosia
Andreeff, Feodosia, xi, 43, 48, 63, 66, 70, 233
Andreeff, Fi. *See* Andreeff, Fiena
Andreeff, Fiena, xi, 47, 66-67, 233
Andreeff, Gladys. *See* Andreeff, Klavdia
Andreeff, Gregori. *See* Andriev, Gregory
Andreeff, Gregory. *See* Andriev, Gregori
Andreeff, Ike. *See* Andriev, Akim
Andreeff, Jean. *See* Andreeff, Anesya
Andreeff, John. *See* Andriev, Ivan
Andreeff, Klavdia, 32, 233
Andreeff, Laurence. *See* Andriev, Larivon
Andreeff, Lawrence. *See* Andriev, Larivon
Andreeff, Lorne. *See* Andriev, Larivon
Andreeff, Marusa, 29, 233
Andreeff, Mary. *See* Andreeff, Marusa
Andreeff, Michael. *See* Andriev, Nikifor
Andreeff, Mikifor. *See* Andriev, Nikifor
Andreeff, Natalie. *See* Sodorova, Natalie
Andreeff, Nick. *See* Andreeff, Constantine
Andreeff, Phillip Gregory. *See* Andriev, Philip
Andreeff, Polly. *See* Kosheiff, Palagay
Andreeff, Viola. *See* Andriev, Valentina
Andreeff, William. *See* Andriev, Vasili
Andreeff, Zina. *See* Andreeff, Zinayeda
Andreeff, Zinayeda, xi, 27, 30, 52, 62, 233
Andreiv, Lucaria, 11, 15, 27, 30, 36, 43-44, 47, 49, 158, 233
Andriev, Akim, xi, 11, 27, 30, 40, 46, 49, 233

INDEX

Andriev, Elena, xi, 11, 14, 27, 30, 39, 41–43, 50, 52–53, 57, 66–67, 79, 87, 97, 104, 116, 133, 156, 233
Andriev, Gregori, 11, 13–14, 16–18, 21, 23, 26, 28–29, 31, 42, 46, 55, 67, 233
Andriev, Ivan, 11, 13, 233
Andriev, Larivon, 13–14, 28–29, 32–34, 36, 233
Andriev, Nikifor, xi, 5, 36, 43, 61, 66, 69, 74–78, 89–91, 116, 117, 142, 156, 213
    Andruff Iron Works, 63–64
    anglicization of name, 27, 40–41, 45, 232, 233
    arrival in Canada, 11, 15, 23–24, 27
    assisted-living facility, 117–19
    becoming a grandparent, 106, 111, 118, 177, 183, 210–11
    children, 55, 67, 84, 128, 132, 140
    citizenship, 50–51
    death, 119, 123–25
    injury, 68–73, 79, 82
    lawsuit, 79–80, 84–86, 133
    marriage, 53–55, 57, 109, 111
    retirement, 113–15
    School, 30, 33, 45–46, 144
    Second World War, 54
    work, 46, 51–55, 58–59, 62, 81, 87, 92–107, 110, 112, 127, 133, 134
Andriev, Philip, xi, 11, 13–15, 24, 26–28, 34, 36, 39–40, 42–44, 46, 49–55, 57–59, 63, 65–67, 77–78, 81, 99, 104, 116, 233
Andriev, Valentina, 11, 28, 30, 50–51, 55, 65, 78–79, 233
Andriev, Vasili, 11, 13, 46, 233
Andruff family reunions, 112, 116–17
Andruff, Claire. *See* Brewster, Claire
Andruff, Elena. *See* Andriev, Elena
Andruff, Gregory (Greg), 108, 161, 172, 177, 179, 182

Andruff, Kathleen (Kay), xi, 62, 67–69, 81–82, 86, 89, 91, 125–26, 132–33
Andruff, Laurie, xi, 55, 67–68, 81–84, 89, 92, 95–99, 101–2, 104, 106–8, 110–11, 113–14, 119, 126, 135, 146, 148, 156, 182
Andruff, Matthew (Matt), 107, 161, 163, 172, 177, 179, 182–83
Andruff, Michael Jr. ("Muka-shoe"), x, 5
    childhood, 55, 64, 125–27, 142
    father's death, 123–25
    grandchildren, 118, 159, 183, 204–7
    hockey, 138–40, 144–46, 152
    marriage, 99, 147, 150–51, 189
    school, 128–34, 136–38, 147, 149–51, 155
    travel, 155–56, 179, 182–83
    work, 110, 114, 155, 160, 162–64, 175–76
Andruff, Mike. *See* Andriev, Nikifor
Andruff, Natalie. *See* Sodorova, Natalie
Andruff, Nick. *See* Andreeff, Constantine
Andruff, Philip. *See* Andriev, Philip
Andruff, Thea, 6, 200
    birth, 106, 157, 191, 211
    childhood, 107, 161, 190–92
    children, 118, 183, 205–8
    marriage, 204
    school, 181–82, 193–97, 202–4
    swimming, 177, 206–7
    travel, 174, 181, 198–99
    work, 179, 201–2, 204–6, 209
Arbutus Club, 167, 177, 195, 202

Berretta, Leandro, 201, 203, 206–9
Bishop, Fred, 93, 141, 150
Boat people, 185, 218
Bolshevik Revolution. *See* Bolsheviks *and* Russian Revolution
Bolsheviks, 13–15, 17, 20, 25, 37–38, 218

"Bolshoi Dome," 26, 28–29, 31
Brewster, Claire, 92, 107, 110, 115, 119, 139–40, 146–47, 154, 157–59, 161, 166–76, 233
    children, 106, 108, 163, 182, 190–95
    grandchildren, 184, 205
    marriage, 99, 150–51, 189
    school, 132, 137–38, 149–52, 155–56, 187, 202
    travel, 179, 181–83, 210
Brewster, Don, 141, 150, 157–58, 161, 169, 189, 202
Brewster, Joanne, 150, 157–58, 161, 169, 189, 198, 202
Brewster, Ken, 174, 197

Calgary, AB, 22, 28–30, 41
Calvert, Doreen. *See* Andreeff, Darya
Calvert, Lawrence (Tuffy), xi, 79, 93, 99
Canada Caring, 3, 226
Canadian Citizenship Act, 50
Canadian immigration policy, 12, 16–18, 24, 32, 49, 95, 112, 127, 213
Canadian Pacific Railway (CPR), 11, 18–22, 24–25, 28–33, 36, 58, 70, 101, 157, 218
Castlegar, BC, 100–2, 104, 106, 108, 112, 153–54, 156
Cempirek, Vaslav, 178
Chinese Immigration Act, 16
Clark, Zena. *See* Andreeff, Zinayeda
Cooper, Laurie, 3, 222, 225
Cresent Beach Swimming Club (CBSC), 172–73, 206
Czechoslovakia, 168, 185

Dalian, China, 12, 19, 20, 22
Dennis, J.S., 19, 22, 26–27, 30
Dmohovsky, Vladimir, 19–21, 25–27, 29
Doreen, 91

Douglas, James, 75, 77
Dournovo, Orest, 12, 14, 19–22, 24–27, 29–30

Edmonton, 41, 57, 65, 70, 72, 85, 113, 133
Egan, W.J., 18, 19, 21–22, 27, 32, 227
Elder, Polly. *See* Sidoroff, Palagaya
Elliott, Brian, 202–5
Expo 86, 111, 179, 193

Fairview, AB, 34–35, 41–42, 54, 65, 68, 70–71, 115
First Nations. *See* Indigenous Peoples
First World War, 13, 15, 65, 78, 227

Gage, Alberta, 36, 41, 46, 56, 65, 92, 101, 104, 156, 196
Gailloux, Charlie, 132, 136
Gouzenko, Igor, 17, 60–61, 65
Government of Canada, the, 4, 18, 20, 148, 204, 213, 230–31

Harbin, China, 12, 14, 16–20, 22–24, 29, 32, 46, 218
Hare, Agon, 233
Healy, Sandra, 194, 196
Hines Creek, 42, 46, 54, 57, 62–64, 71–73, 79
Hockey Night in Canada, 89, 113, 192
Holy Trinity Cemetery, 65, 104, 119, 156
Homeglen Legacy Fund, 7, 231
Homeglen, AB, 7, 12, 24–25, 28, 30–34, 36, 40, 43, 46, 51, 54, 81, 87, 113, 231
Hudson Bay Company, 33, 75
Hungary, 131, 177, 185

Independent Order of Foresters, 83
Indigenous Peoples, 6, 33, 35, 75–76, 78, 163–64

INDEX

Alberni Indian Residential School, 91
Beaver Indian Reserve No. 152, 34
Department of Indian Affairs, 35
Hupačasath Nation, 74–75
Musqueam Nation, 160
Qayqayt First Nation, 96
Royal Proclamation of 1763, 75
Squamish Nation, 160
Treaty 8, 33, 35
Truth and Reconciliation Commission of Canada, 35
Tseshaht Nation, 74–75
Tsleil-Waututh Nation, 160

Kalugin, Sam, 55, 78, 87, 93, 233
Kalugin, Vi. *See* Andriev, Valentina
Kennedy, John F., 89, 95–96, 131, 179
Kerrisdale, 99, 107, 109, 112–13, 151, 155, 160, 168–169, 172, 174, 176, 191, 193
Kosheiff, Palagay, 29, 32, 68, 233
Koyman, Jean. *See* Andreeff, Anesya
Koyman, Laurens, xi, 66, 115, 233

Lenin, Vladimir, 37–38, 60
Lillejord, Gladys. *See* Andreeff, Klavdia
Lomax, Vicki. *See* Sideroff, Vera,
Loyd, Alexandra, 193

MacMillan Bloedel (MB), 62, 81, 87, 94, 134, 140–41, 143, 163, 174
MacMillan, H.R., 62, 157
Manchuria, China, 17
Manus Island, Papua New Guinea, 218, 220, 224, 226
McGrath, R.P., 18–19
McIntyre-Olsen, Fi. *See* Andreeff, Fiena
McIntyre, Fi. *See* Andreeff, Fiena
McIntyre, Kenneth (Ken), xi, 66, 79
McIntyre, Susan, 116

Mennie, Jessie. *See* Sidoroff, Taisia
Miles, Lon, 132, 140
Mishiekof, Cons. *See* Mishukoff, Constantine
Mishukoff, Constantine, 28
Mosaic BC, 7, 226, 231, 237

Nanaimo, BC, 94–95, 143–45, 147, 158
Nasedkin, Zoya, 62, 233
New Westminster, BC, 5, 95–97, 99, 102, 145–48, 204
Newman, Carey, 228
Newspapers, 51, 52, 64, 70–71, 136–37, 140, 152, 237

OBS. *See* Old Brothers
Old Believers. *See* Old Brothers
Old Brothers, 5, 17, 25–26, 28–29, 31–33, 46, 49, 53, 64–65, 171
Others, The, 25–26, 28–29, 61, 93, 141

Parks, Ray Archibald, 87, 132, 177
Parks, Trudy, 177
Pical, Boris, 32
Port Alberni, 5, 62–63, 65, 73–75, 81–83, 85, 87–91, 108, 113, 125, 127–28, 131, 134, 136–41, 143, 147, 150, 157–58, 172, 174–77, 185–87, 213
   amalgamation with Alberni, 93–94
   history, 77–78
Primrose, Neil, 85–86
Private Sponsorship of Refugees Program (PSR), 2, 230

Red Cross, 18, 169, 218
Refugee Council of Australia, 226
Reznick, Paraskavaya (Pearl), 45, 233
Reznick, Pearl. *See* Reznick, Paraskavaya
Riedijk, Doreen. *See* Andreeff, Darya
Riedijk, Pieter H., xi, 108

Rosenbach, Maria. *See* von Rosenbach, Maria
Ross, Clark, 62, 233
Royalty
    Diana, Princess of Wales, 111, 178-79, 193
    Prince Alexander V. Golitzin, 18, 227
    Prince Charles, 111, 193
    Prince Felix Youssoupoff, 37-38, 226-27
    Queen Victoria, 44
    Tsar Nicholas II, 13, 37
Russia. *See* Union of Soviet Socialist Republics (USSR)
Russian Orthodox Church, 46-48, 57, 134
Russian Red Cross, 17-18, 218, 227
Russian Refugee Relief Society of America Inc. (RRRSA), 18-20, 22-23, 30, 37-38, 226
Russian Revolution, 14, 37, 229

Schischikowsky, Fannie. *See* Andreeff, Feodosia
Schischikowsky, Louis, xi, 62-63, 79
Schools
    A.W. Neill Junior High School, 82, 137
    Alberni Elementary School, 81, 128, 177
    BC Institute of Technology (BCIT), 98
    John Barsby Junior Secondary School, 144
    Lonesome Pine School, 27, 30, 33, 61
    New Westminster Secondary School (NWSS), 99, 146
    Point Grey Mini School, 194, 206
    Ranger School, 43, 196

University of British Columbia (UBC), 99, 105, 117, 147, 149-50, 153, 155, 161, 182, 201-3
Second World War, 54, 61, 127, 157
Ships
    Empress of Asia, 20
    Empress of Russia, 12, 21, 65, 227
    Harbin Maru, 12
    Komagata Maru, 4, 16, 213
Siberia, 13, 28, 31
Sideroff, Tom. *See* Sidoroff, Timofei
Sideroff, Vera, 67-69, 71, 236
Sideroff, Vic. *See* Sidoroff, Vicari
Sidoroff, Afric. *See* Sidoroff, Aganasi
Sidoroff, Aganasi, 233
Sidoroff, Borise, 27, 236
Sidoroff, Dolly. *See* Sodorova, Natalie
Sidoroff, Fred, 54, 108
Sidoroff, Ilarion, 31-32, 233
Sidoroff, Jessie. *See* Sidoroff, Taisia
Sidoroff, Lorne. *See* Sidoroff, Ilarion
Sidoroff, Lucaria. *See* Andreiv, Lucaria
Sidoroff, Natasha. *See* Sodorova, Natalie
Sidoroff, Palagaya, 35-36, 47, 108, 233
Sidoroff, Pearl. *See* Reznick, Paraskavaya
Sidoroff, Peter. *See* Sidorov, Procopius
Sidoroff, Polly. *See* Sidoroff, Palagaya
Sidoroff, Prokofi. *See* Sidorov, Procopius
Sidoroff, Syd. *See* Sidoroff, Borise
Sidoroff, Taisia, 30, 233
Sidoroff, Thomas. *See* Sidoroff, Timofei
Sidoroff, Timofei, 48, 64, 71, 233
Sidoroff, Vic. *See* Sidoroff, Vicari
Sidoroff, Vicari, 64, 69, 235
Sidorov, Afanasi, 13
Sidorov, Luka, Sidoroff, Luka, 12-13, 18, 23, 26, 31, 55
Sidorov, Procopius, 13-15, 28, 31, 233

INDEX

Sifton, Clifford, 33, 35, 49
Sinclair Mills, 58–59, 61
Sinclair, Ian ("Sinky"), 126–27, 196,
Sodorova, Natalie, xi, 47, 89, 53, 74,
   78–79, 92–93, 123, 125–26, 133,
   135, 146, 182, 233
   alcohol use disorder, 5, 80–82,
      107–11
   assisted-living facility, 117–19
   becoming a grandparent, 106, 111,
      118, 177, 183, 210–11
   children, 64, 67
   citizenship, 54,
   death, 119
   foster child, 91
   health, 114–19
   husband's accident, 68–72
   married life, 61–63
   retirement, 112–13
   work, 79, 95–103, 105, 107, 109–
      110, 112–13
Solovieff, Artemy, 46, 65, 236
Soviet Union. *See* Union of Soviet
   Socialist Republics (USSR)
Sponsorship Agreement Holder (SAH),
   7, 226, 230–31
Stalin, Joseph, 65
Stamp, Edward, 77
Stolypin, Pyotr, 13

Taghinia, Amir, 219, 224
Taylor, Chelsea, 220, 224
Taylor, Robert, 53,
Trotsky, Leon, 37

Trutch, Joseph, 76
Turner, John, 152

Ughet, Serge, 22, 30, 226–27
Union of Soviet Socialist Republics
   (USSR), 23, 38, 59, 65, 112, 125, 218
United Nations High Commissioner
   for Refugees (UNHCR), 1, 200,
   213, 217

Van Horne, Cornelius, 29, 157
Vancouver, BC, 4, 5, 11–12, 19, 21–23,
   28–29, 50, 77, 96, 99, 105–9,
   111–13, 140, 143, 145, 148–50,
   158–59, 169, 176, 182–83, 191,
   193–94, 198, 202–4, 209–11, 221,
   226–27, 232
Vancouver Island, 5, 62, 74–75, 78, 81,
   102, 107, 117, 132
Victoria, BC, 21, 52, 75, 77, 91–92, 96,
   98, 107, 136, 140, 145, 157, 177,
   228
von Rosenbach, Maria, 22, 25, 26–27, 29

Waterhole Oldtimers' Association,
   79–80, 82, 85
Waterhole Oldtimers' fairgrounds, 68
Waterman, Zena. *See* Andreeff,
   Zinayeda,
Wetaskiwin, AB, 12, 22, 69
Willson, N.C., 79–80, 85

Yassin, Nuseir (Nas), 223

MICHAEL ANDRUFF is the author of ten self-published travel books. He is a first-generation Canadian and was in a unique position to observe his refugee father over the course of his lifetime, which provided the material for his memoir, *The Russian Refugees*. The solitude brought on by the COVID-19 pandemic and the notion of writing a family history revealed to him the importance of the private sponsorship of refugees in Canada. After a long career in business, he is now happily retired and lives in Vancouver, BC, with his wife, Claire.

For more information on the Homeglen Legacy Fund, visit mosaicbc.org/about/donate/homeglen-legacy-fund or scan the QR code below.